The Source

OF

HUMAN GOOD

By HENRY N. WIEMAN

Southern Illinois University Press

Carbondale and Edwardsville

Feffer & Simons, Inc.

London and Amsterdam

TABLE OF CONTENTS

PART I. GENERAL NATURE OF VALUE

PART II. SPECIFIC KINDS OF VALUE

TECHNICAL POSTSCRIPT

INDEX

PART I

General Nature of Value

CHAPTER I

The Way Good Increases

THERE are as many ways to lay hold of value as there are ways to take hold of a cat. You can seize the legs, the tail, or the nape of the neck; all are equally part of the cat. If you grab the tail or the legs, you have not missed the cat; you truly have it. But the consequences are often disastrous and at best uncertain, since it is not a very useful way to take hold of a cat. You learn quickly—in fact, only too quickly—that you had better take hold of the nape of the cat's neck if you want to do anything with it.

So it is with value. Any theory of value is true if it identifies value with some one or more of the elements which we find are always present whenever we choose between alternatives. Any theory that does this is true, at least if special epistemological and metaphysical speculations are not brought into question. They are different ways of taking hold of the same reality; but, though equally true, they are not equally useful. It is not enough to take hold. We want an interpretation of value that will not only identify value but will also enable us to do something with it.

DIFFERENT INTERPRETATIONS OF VALUE

There are as many elements in the situation determining choice as there are parts of a cat. To all these elements men have turned in seeking to take hold of value. The naïve person seizes upon the simplest and most obviously identifying element when he says that value resides in the thing that lures him. We all speak of "good" apples and "bad" apples, of "good" men and "bad" men, as though the value were in the thing that attracts us. Even the most sophisticated person, in his unreflective moments, will feel and act as though the value could be identified with the object valued.

But we soon discover something peculiar about value. The object can apparently remain unchanged and yet the value of it depart completely. The doughnut which was a glory to my youth becomes an evil thing in my dyspeptic age. Value may induce a fleeting glow in some object, only to pass at the flicker of an eyelash. The smiling presence may suddenly become a horror. Laying hold of value by seizing objects proves to be as unreliable, as deceptive, and as useless a procedure as taking a cat by the tail.

How can value come and go and change into its opposite when the thing that is so diversely valued remains unchanged in every way whereby we identify it as the same? Such reflections cause many a man to turn to another simple element in experience. Perhaps value does not reside in the object at all; perhaps it more characteristically dwells in the mind of the individual, in his likes, his interests, his desires and purposes. Perhaps value is not an object; perhaps it is a state of mind.

Another group of men, more deeply impressed and profoundly disturbed by the transient and perishing character of value, are driven to locate it in some rarified or remote aspect of experience or even in a transcendental realm. They seek to demonstrate that what we call "value" does not inhabit the mind except as a transitory visitor. Value, they say, is initially in the mind of God and only imperfectly and derivatively in the mind of man. Others feel compelled to insist that value is an eternal essence that appears occasionally to rest upon the material and spatial things of time, only to fade again into its eternity. Still others come to call value an indefinable quality, whether eternal or not. And still others hold that value is a transcendental, concrete whole, nontemporal, nonmaterial, nonhistorical, but, nevertheless, a complete and total unity which casts the light

[4]

of value upon existing things in this world when conditions
are specifically favorable.

One final group, as dissatisfied with these transcendental
notions as with the simple ideas equating value with object
or a state of mind, sees value as a relation between the desiring mind and the thing desired. Still others, of like tem-
per, identify value with a total complex situation so ordered
as to carry and manifest what we call "value."

All the different theories of value can be classified according to the element of human existence to which they turn
in answering the question, "Where and what is value?"
whether it be in the mind of man, in the mind of God, in
abstract eternity or in concrete eternity, in the simple context of mind and object or in the complex context called the
"situation."

Each of these six answers receives support from a group
of philosophers. The first two are subjective theories, locat-
ing value in the mind, the first in the mind of man, the other
in the mind of God. The third and fourth answers are the
transcendental theories: value is an eternal abstract essence
or quality, or it is a concrete but transcendental reality. The
fifth and sixth answers can be called the "contextual interpretation" of value, for they identify value with the context in which seeking and evading and choosing occur.
Value is a simple relation between desiring mind and thing
desired; or it is a total complex situation, including whatever must be taken into consideration by practical operations which determine choice so that predictable outcomes
can be known and approved. The context thus understood
does not include the whole universe, since most of the universe can be ignored in making choices yielding outcomes
which can be predicted and approved. In fact, one never
could make such choices if he tried to deal with the whole
universe. One of the chief goals of science is to limit the situation to those particular elements with which one can op-

erate in determining choices which yield predictable outcomes. In dealing with most values, one cannot do this
after the manner of the natural sciences, but one must do it
in another way, as we shall try to show.

The sixth interpretation, in which value is identified with
the total complex context, is the one that we shall develop
in the pages that follow. As we have said, we take it not
because it alone is true. We take the complex contextual interpretation for the same reason that we take a cat by the
nape of the neck. Both in practical action and in intellectual
inquiry, we can do more with value when we take it this
way. The "context" is circumscribed to include just those
things with which we must operate whenever we choose
and act and reflect in a way to determine a future that can
be more or less continuously approved. Hence it is deliberately designed from the beginning for utility. But this use-
fulness must be demonstrated. That is largely what this
book tries to do.

NATURALISM

This reply to the question "What is value?" is the answer
of the newer naturalism, a movement or development in
contemporary thought akin to, but to be sharply distinguished from, the older naturalisms, which tended toward
reductive materialism. It asserts that there is nothing in
reality accessible to the human mind more basic than
events and their qualities and relations. ("Relations" is another word for "structure.") No knowable cause or ex-
planation for anything that happens can reach deeper than
events and their structure and qualities. This view claims
to be able to take account of all the intricacies and subtleties
—all the height, breadth, and depth of human existence—
omitting, explaining away, flattening out, or truncating
nothing. We shall have no recourse to any "transcendental

[6]

grounds, orders, causes or purposes"[1] beyond events, their qualities, and relations. Naturalism bases this claim on thorough analysis of the method by which any knowledge whatsoever can be obtained. We shall interpret value, in the following pages, entirely in terms of events, their qualities and relations (structure). The richest and highest values sought and found by religion and morals are interpreted as structured events and their possibilities.

In selecting this naturalistic version of reality, we have had to choose between two great traditions which Western civilization has inherited. Each presents its own interpretation of what is supremely important for all human living. One is Jewish Christian, the other Greek Christian. The Jewish tradition declares that the sovereign good works creatively in history. While this ruling creativity is said to have form, the importance of it lies in its creative potentialities and not in its form. The Greek tradition, on the other hand, declares that the sovereign good is essentially a system of Forms or a Supreme Form. The one tradition gives supreme authority to the creative event, the other to the Form. Our interpretation follows the Jewish tradition in giving priority to the creative event.

But there is one respect, being naturalists, in which we depart from both traditions: we ignore the transcendental affirmation in the Jewish Christian tradition of a creative God who not only works in history but resides beyond history. The only creative God we recognize is the creative event itself. So also we ignore the transcendental affirmation in the Greek Christian tradition of the reality of Forms of value, uncreated and eternal, having causal efficacy to constrain the shape of things without themselves being events

---

[1] See *Naturalism and the Human Spirit*, ed. Yervant Krikorian, especially the chapter on "Categories of Naturalism," by William Dennes; see also D. C. Williams, "Naturalism and the Nature of Things," *Philosophical Review*, LIII (1944), 417–43.

at all. The only forms of value we recognize are produced by the creative event. Even possibilities, so far as relevant to actual events, are created. The form of the creative event itself at our higher levels of existence is determined by the creative process at more elementary levels. In our view the higher levels of existence spring from, rest upon, and are undergirded by the lower.

God as events

Thus the active God derived from the Jewish tradition and the Forms derived from the Greek tradition are both brought down into the world of time, space, and matter and are there identified as events displaying a definite structure with possibilities. When we insist that nothing has causal efficacy except material events, by "material" we mean not merely pellets of inanimate matter but also events that include the biological, social, and historical forms of existence. These, however, never cease to be material. Nothing has value except material events, thus understood, and their possibilities.

These claims rest upon an analysis of our experience, revealing that no transcendental reality could ever *do* anything. It could not make the slightest difference in our lives except in the form of some happening, some event. In other words, nothing can happen if it does not happen. But when the transcendental becomes an event, it is no longer transcendental. We cannot know anything, and nothing can make the slightest difference in our lives unless it be an event or some possibility carried by an event. Transcendental realities literally have nothing to do after we have discovered that all value, all meaning, and all causal efficacy are to be found in the world of events and their possibilities. Therefore, the transcendental must be ignored, except as an imaginative construction of the human mind. Since we never shall know everything, the transcendental might be retained as a mythical way of representing what is yet to be discovered. But that device has proved so confusing and misleading that we think it is better dropped. Since this is our position, an alternative title for this book might read: "What Is Value? Naturalism Answers."

With this approach we shall look at several common ways of seeking the increase of human good. One of the most common of all is to seek it by multiplying goods. Some deny that goods are truly contributory to value unless they satisfy; hence for them satisfaction rather than goods must be increased. Or, again, others think that the increase of human power of control is the key to the problem. These and other practical ways of taking hold of value must be examined before we attempt to develop more fully the idea of value which we find to lead to the most effective practical action and the most fruitful intellectual inquiries into the problem of human good and how it can be increased.

THE VALUE OF GOODS

Goods under most circumstances are good; but they are not always good. More and better food, improved sanitation, medical care, housing, increase of knowledge, and technical skill are goods. But when Hitler provides more and better food and medical care and encourages increase of technical skill solely to get a larger and more deadly army, these goods are not good. Even goods which we might list as always and everywhere good, such as abolition of slavery; laws forbidding exploitation of children; legislation to secure rights of workers; free public schools; humane treatment of criminals; cultural opportunities for the common man; political power exercised to provide personal liberty and social justice; wider distribution among individuals of aesthetic, spiritual, and moral endowments, cannot, taken by themselves, in every instance of their occurrence be called good. Hence any assertion of their goodness requires qualification. If one uses one's imagination or searches history, one can find conditions under which one of these or any combination of them might occur in such a way as to yield more evil than some other alternative.

Since these goods can and do occur in situations in which they are not good, we know that they do not carry in themselves, intrinsically and essentially, the nature of goodness. Something over and above their bare existence must pertain to them to make them truly good.

Since these goods are in so many cases good, this might seem to be an academic question. In our age, however, one good turned evil, one mistake, can have such far-reaching results that this has become an urgent, practical question. It must be answered if we are to avoid disaster.

When the only damage that we could do to the great organism of human welfare was to cause a slight bruise, we did not need to know the source of health and vitality or the exact medicaments for cure. But when our power becomes so great that we perform capital surgical operations upon the historical and social order of human existence, we must know what makes for life and what makes for death. If we do not, we shall surely destroy ourselves. If we perform the operation for the sake of goods that are not always and everywhere and necessarily good, we shall produce devastation when we think that we are serving the abundant life. The hit-or-miss method of choosing the better by promoting goods that have ordinarily yielded benefit will not work any longer. When we have such power, such scope, and such precision in determining what the future will be, we must know exactly what we are doing for good or for ill.

One objection often is raised to this inquiry concerning what is good necessarily and always. It is the claim that what is good for one person is not good for another. What is good for one age or culture must be radically changed to fit the need of another period. We must not impose our own provincial appraisals upon other peoples and eras. We must be tolerant and broad minded and let each individual in each time and place judge for himself what is good and what is evil for him. Then only, say these objectors, can we avoid tyranny and injustice.

Analysis of the actual facts will reveal that this alleged tolerance and provision for justice in allowing each individual to decide what is good and what is evil for him is, in truth, diabolical. One age cannot be separated from another, nor can one people or culture. The hope of man lies in cumulative development through history; and human good can be increased only by progressive accumulation of good through a sequence of generations. If one age must tear down what previous ages have built, to achieve the good peculiar to itself, and if the present must rear a good for itself that becomes an evil for a later period, then the past can no longer provide building-stones for the present, and history becomes an evil and not a resource.

No time or people can cut free of the times preceding or of the times oncoming. What we choose as our good to a great extent determines the good and ill of other times and peoples, and their judgment is fateful in taking from us or in giving to us the sources of human welfare. We cannot extricate ourselves from the consequence of choice made by times and peoples however remote, since they are connected in sequence with others up to our own. Since what any age or culture chooses or seeks as good and evil for itself becomes inevitably destructive or constructive of the good and evil of others, it is imperative to discover and make clear that principle which distinguishes good and evil for each and for all in every age and situation. If we cannot do this, each age will destroy what the other builds and seeks.

It is true that each person, each time and place, has a unique goodness never again to be duplicated. But there must be some general principle of goodness whereby we can choose and rear the unique good of each so that it will be constructive and not destructive of the unique good of other

[11]

persons, times, and places. As the web of life weaves all times and places and persons into an ever more closely woven network of interdetermination, this general principle for distinguishing the constructive from the destructive becomes progressively urgent. The life and death of increasing millions hangs on our discovery of a universal principle that can guide us in choosing good that is common to all.

SATISFACTION AS THE GUIDING PRINCIPLE
OF CHOICE

The simplest statement of the guiding principle of choice is satisfaction. More and better food, improved sanitation, medical care, and housing are good because they satisfy desire. Abolition of slavery, free public schools, and laws forbidding exploitation of children are good because they enable more people to get what they want.

This beautifully simple statement may be true; unfortunately, it is also useless. We cannot use it to guide our choices to outcomes which will be enduringly and deeply satisfying even for ourselves. Much less can we use it to seek and find goods that will be mutually supporting and not mutually destructive between different individuals, peoples, and times.

One cannot follow predicted satisfaction of interest as a guide because interests undergo an unpredictable transformation when one meets the conditions and follows the procedures necessary to seek their fulfilment. Noting a few of these conditions and procedures will render obvious the futility of all endeavor that seeks value by way of outcomes which predictably satisfy the interests that one happens to have at the beginning of the endeavor.

To satisfy interest one must learn to want what other people will permit one to have. Others are seeking and struggling, in some cases with great power. If one cannot somehow find a satisfaction that will be co-operative and mutually enriching with theirs, one will never find satisfaction in a world in which mighty powers struggle each for its own good. Nor can abundant satisfaction ever be achieved unless one learns to seek and want what can be enriched by the progressive accumulation of many past ages, since nothing is more puny and subject to frustration than the human being unsustained by the heritage of the past and the creative synthesis of the efforts of innumerable people now living. The abundance of rich and varied satisfaction for man can be achieved in no other way. Only as the individual seeks and finds a good that is created progressively by past ages and many diverse contributors can he escape bitter and increasing dissatisfaction.

Obviously, no individual can seek and find what the ages have produced and what the many today co-operatively can sustain if he simply follows the guidance of what he happens to want at the beginning of his quest. His wants and his satisfaction cannot be his guide. His guide must be what will transform his wants and satisfactions so that they will fit the specifications and demands of what history and society can co-operatively and progressively rear to greater abundance.

Satisfaction of human want may be true enough as a statement specifying the nature of value, but it is worthless as a guiding principle. We cannot use it to find our way to the greater good; we cannot even use it to escape the most destructive evils. Rather, when we take the satisfaction of our present untransformed wants as our guide, we move into the jaws of evil and away from good in terms of satisfaction itself.

QUALITY AS THE GUIDING PRINCIPLE

There is another answer to the question "What is good?" Good is a quality. Some say it is a pleasant quality; others assert that it is an indefinable and unanalyzable quality

[13]

which cannot be characterized as pleasant or unpleasant but which we intuitively apprehend as the quality of goodness. Although these are diametrically opposed interpretations of the nature of goodness, their differences need not concern us in this discussion.

Doubtless the assertion that good is a quality is perfectly true. Also, at the bottom level of analysis, beyond which we can proceed no further, the quality which is good may be indefinable, even though at other levels it can be defined as pleasant quality. But regardless of the truth of these controversies, this interpretation of value is useless as a guiding principle for human conduct and choice. The dispute over whether value is a quality or not, whether it is definable or not, is academic and irrelevant to any important problem concerning the conduct of human living.

Quality, like satisfaction, is useless as a guiding principle, for the very simple reason that the qualities in events as they emerge are often radically different from the quality which they acquire as they loom behind us in the perspective of a vast system of interconnectedness which we call "meaning." As the years pass, the event first encountered with misery or sweetness takes on many other qualities through its connection with other happenings. The event embarrassing today may be comic tomorrow. What now seems to be a mountain peak of life's fulfilment may sink to the level of daily routine when the wisdom of a lifetime has appraised it. The face of a friend, haunting the borders of conscious awareness, may take on, with passing years, qualities we never could have foreseen at the first meeting.

Perhaps the good is that quality which events acquire as the centuries pass, and we see how these occurrences bear upon the enrichment of human existence or discern in our own life the unfolding of a meaning which connects in critical juncture those happenings of twenty years ago with many other events. Perhaps our lives today have a depth

[14]

THE WAY GOOD INCREASES

and richness of quality which they never could have had without the hushed echo and faint refrain of those happenings of long ago; perhaps the good of life is precisely this coherence of quality and meaning. But this fulness of rich meaning can emerge only with the passage of time. The quality on the face of the passing event cannot tell us what its contribution will be when it has found its place in the story that unfolds with the years.

HUMAN CONTROL AS THE
GUIDING PRINCIPLE

There is a third familiar answer to the question "What is good?" Although this answer claims to be very practical and useful, the claim is deceptive. We often hear that the only sure road to the greater good is the road of human control. Once we have the techniques and the power to direct the course of events so that they will issue in foreseen consequences of greatest value as appraised beforehand by our most competent experts, or even our wisest men, we shall be on the highway to human fulfilment. So the conclusion is reached: Good is human control. Greater good is more human control, not only over subhuman processes of nature but also over the social process and the course of history. The shift from drift to mastery of events under the control of human purpose is the transition from impoverishment to abundance of value.

Here again we have a principle which may be true in the sense that increase of human good brings with it an increase in man's power to direct the course of events. But this principle becomes worthless when used as a guide to greater good because the proposition just stated cannot be reversed. Good includes human control, but human control is not necessarily good. It is not true that increase in man's power to direct the course of events will automatically issue in the increase of human good. Not even when the future outcome

[15]

has been appraised as the best possible by our wisest men does increase of human power to control the course of history necessarily yield any increase in value. This can be demonstrated without departing from the principles upheld by the very men who defend this way as the best road to human fulfilment.

Perhaps John Dewey is the most famous advocate of human control as the guiding principle to the greater good. Dewey himself has many times asserted that any transformation of man's estate in the direction of greater good will transform the human mind itself with its evaluations and appreciative consciousness. If that is true, a notable consequence follows. The human mind, before the sequence of events whereby it will be transformed so as to appreciate the new creation, cannot appraise the value of that innovating outcome which will render its evaluations different from what they are now.

If Dewey means that the outcome of control may be fuller release and more potent working of a transformative process, which we must not try to control in the sense of determining what it shall produce but only serve by holding all our values subject to the transformation which it will work upon us, then Dewey's assertion is true. But most of the time he seems to be saying that we can foresee the consequences of value, can appraise them as the best possible prior to our attainment of them, and can then direct the course of events to their attainment. Demonstration of the error of this claim will appear frequently in what follows.

QUALITATIVE MEANING AS THE
GUIDING PRINCIPLE

We have rejected four interpretations of the nature of value: value as goods, value as satisfaction, value as quality, and value as human control. We have rejected them not because they are false but because they are useless as guiding principles for human conduct and choice. We have rejected each without using any other criterion of value save what that particular theory itself asserted value to be.

The course which we shall follow in constructing an interpretation of value will be radically different from any of these. We shall try to demonstrate that there is a creative process working in our midst which transforms the human mind and the world relative to the human mind. We shall then show how transformation by this process is always in the direction of greater good. The human good thus created includes goods, satisfaction of human wants, richness of quality, and power of man to control the course of events. But the greater good cannot be attained by seeking directly to increase goods or satisfactions or quality or power. These can be increased only by promoting that kind of transformation creative of the greater content of good when created good is interpreted as qualitative meaning. Throughout the writing that follows we shall take as our guide the creative event, which produces qualitative meaning.

Qualitative meaning, as we shall consider it, is *created good*. But there is a prior kind of good here called *creative*, which alone is the source of life's abundance. Only as we learn to deal intelligently and devotedly with creative good can we handle the practical problem of good and evil. Hence creative good is the goal of our inquiry; but to find it we must follow the trail of qualitative meaning.

"Qualitative meaning" is not a term that is intelligible on its face, but it can be simply explained. As the human organism reacts, it distinguishes and relates events. When it so distinguishes and relates events that what is happening now enables it to recall or otherwise know the sequence of events leading up to the present and also enables it to anticipate future possibilities, we say that these present happenings are "signs." They are signs because they are so related to an order of past events and future possibilities that we

[17]

THE SOURCE OF HUMAN GOOD

can know the order of those past events and future possibilities with some degree of probability when the sign-events
happen. These signs have meaning; the meaning is this order
of past events and future possibilities which the present happening represents to us. For example, I hear footsteps. They
are a sequence of events distinguished by certain qualities
which we call "distinct sounds." If these events were not
signs, I would not call them "footsteps." They would be
simply a sequence of events distinguished by qualities. But
they are sign-events. They are signs because they signify
that someone is approaching.

After twenty years I hear those same footsteps. Now the
breadth and depth of meaning conveyed to me by that series
of events is far greater. Surges of feeling arise which those
steps could not arouse twenty years ago. I greet the person
who is approaching even before I can see him. I feel a complexity of qualities pertaining to that person by way of
these faintly discernible sounds called "footsteps." These
events are no longer merely distinguished by certain sounds.
They are connected with innumerable events—tragic and
comic, bitter and sweet—that have happened through the
years. Something of the quality of many events occurring
in the past is packed bodily into the present when I hear
those footsteps. I even feel by anticipation something of the
quality of emerging future events, when foreseen possibilities have been actualized by association with the person
now approaching.

What we have just described is qualitative meaning.
Qualitative meaning is that connection between events
whereby present happenings enable me to feel not only the
quality intrinsic to the events now occurring but also the
qualities of many other events that are related to them.
Qualitative meaning is that connection between events
whereby the present happening conveys to me the qualities
of other happenings and some qualities pertaining to what

[18]

will happen in the future, as the future is interpreted by the past.

Qualitative meaning is intrinsically good. Good increases as qualitative meaning increases. But why is qualitative meaning good? We shall answer that question in many ways as we proceed. Different questioners will demand different answers according to the theory of value held by each. We shall try to satisfy every one, in each case defining value in his own terms.

One group will not be able to see any value in qualitative meaning unless it satisfies human want. To him we reply without equivocation: Qualitative meaning is good, is positive, intrinsic value, because it satisfies human want. That is to say, it is one ingredient in every instance of satisfaction.

But we have just been asserting that satisfaction is no guide to the greater good. Now we are identifying qualitative meaning with the good of life because it satisfies human want. There is no contradiction in this. The striving to satisfy human want will lead to frustration and defeat unless one follows the right guide. What satisfies will not serve as such a guide unless one carefully discriminates from among all the different elements contributing to satisfaction that one thread running through all satisfaction of human want which does, in fact, lead on progressively to ever larger fulfilment of want when such progression is at all possible under existing conditions. Satisfaction as a gross fact is not the criterion of value that we shall use; it is not the guiding thread we seek. But since many can see no sense in the word "value" or "good" except in terms of satisfying human want, we are quite willing and able to demonstrate our interpretation of value in their terms.

Not satisfaction of human want and not even qualitative meaning itself is the guiding thread we seek, although the thread we seek must lead to abundant satisfaction and qualitative meaning. The guiding thread—the thread that guides infallibly because it does not break and fail in the midst of great disasters, frustrations, and destructive conflicts—is not qualitative meaning, but it is what produces qualitative meaning. Therefore, we can find it best by tracing qualitative meaning to its source. This source, this genesis of qualitative meaning, we shall call the "creative event." We shall analyze and describe it at length in chapter iii. This creative event always yields the best possible in each situation, no matter how frustrative and perplexing the situation in other respects may be, provided that we make this creative event our primary concern, and succeed in setting up the conditions it demands in order to occur.

The creative event, we shall find, weaves a web of meaning between individuals and groups and between the organism and its environment. Out of disruptions and conflicts which would otherwise be destructive, it creates vivifying contrasts of quality if it is able to operate at all. Thus it can utilize frustration and disaster to create and weave into the web of life's meaning vivid and diversified qualities, thus adding immensely to the richness of its variety and the depth of its significant connections. This happy outcome ensues if the participant individuals provide the conditions under which the creative event can occur. One of the most important of these conditions is the self-giving of the individual himself to such transformation. In weaving the web of richer meaning, the creative event transforms the individual person so that he is more of a person. In the beginning it creates the human person out of the living organism of the infant. Likewise, it creates and progressively transforms human community and the course of history.

Man can do much to provide the conditions releasing the full creative power of this event, including the self-giving of his own person to be transformed by it and to serve it above all. Also he can remove many obstructive conditions hindering its efficacy. But he cannot himself do the work of the creative event.

With this preliminary glance at the source of human good, we turn to a further examination of qualitative meaning. We do this in order to get a better view of the creative event itself, to which we shall come in the third chapter. After exploring qualitative meaning we shall follow it upstream until we find its source. This source and not qualitative meaning itself must be our first consideration in every situation if we are to attain life's fulfilment.

Qualitative meaning is any structure of interrelated events, together with their possibilities, when these events have appreciable qualities and when the structure as a whole can be represented by signs. Signs are those events belonging to the structure which serve to represent the structure as a whole. The possibilities pertaining to such a structure make up that part of the structure not now embodied in actual events. With this understanding of qualitative meaning, let us look at some of the different ways in which it may be appraised as good.

It is good to feel the quality of events by way of signs, hence by way of qualitative meaning, because in this way one can increase enormously the scope and diversity of events felt, without exhausting the energy of the organism or exposing it to danger or destruction. Many events and possibilities are highly enjoyable when kept in proper relation to other events and possibilities and at proper distance from the organism. In retrospect or prospect and at spatial distances, they may contribute richly to the appreciable fulness of life but might be highly destructive of life or of the capacity for appreciation if they were brought into direct contact with the organism. By way of signs these events that might be harmful may be brought into those relations and maintained in those relations wherein they promote the widest and freest ranges of appreciation. Signs and meaning have this value both because they conserve the energy of the organism and also because they enable it to use its energy in the most strategic manner. The energy required to interpret a sign is often negligible. A spoken word, a flash of light, the sound of thunder, are signs enabling one to feel the quality of events which would be exhaustive or destructive beyond endurance if the organism were exposed to the direct impact of some of the events signified.

It is good to feel the quality of events by way of signs, because in this way one can feel through the sensitivities of other people. One can see through a million eyes, hear through a thousand ears, both of the dead and of the living. Through the signs by which men communicate their feelings to one another, there is established an infinitely complex and far-reaching network of telepathic feelers, which reach from the tips of my nerves far out into the complexities of society. They bring to me the secrets of many hearts.

It is good to feel the quality of events by way of signs, because in this way one can feel the qualities of past events. These telepathic feelers reach far back beyond the bounds of recorded history. They bring even more abundantly the feel of events that have been recorded. They save to me my childhood and the lives of my parents and grandparents, in some measure. The great struggle of man is to overcome the perishing of time and conserve the qualities of past events by which alone the present can have depth and richness of meaning. Whenever a mature person dies, a wealth of precious quality and meaning, slowly acquired through the years, is lost. "I wonder if anyone remembers what I remember?"—a depth of memory, an echo lingering through the years until I die, then hushed forever. Much is remembered only by you and passes into oblivion when you cease to exist; but some is saved. Art is the great savior of the qualities of past events, not merely "works of art" but all those signs by which "our echoes roll from soul to soul and grow, forever and forever." All signs which communicate from person to person and from group to group, with minimum loss, the qualities of events that each has known are examples of art. Through these signs the qualities of the past roll up like a snowball. Much is lost; yet, as men learn to use signs that communicate qualitative meaning and learn to interpret such signs, as they acquire the health, the nervous energy, the leisure and the education, and the other instruments and conditions necessary, they can save more, very much more, than is now saved. The supreme periods of human culture have been those times when men have saved most from the past and so have brought the present to its highest fulfilment; for there is no other possible way to enrich the present except by conserving and recovering the qualities and meanings of past events.

It is good to feel the quality of events by way of signs, because in this way the universe comes qualitatively alive. Dead matter takes on color and sound and all the emotional tones that go to make what we call the "life of conscious awareness." As more events become signs, as these signs take on richer content of qualitative meaning, as these meanings form a network of interconnective events comprehending all that is happening in the world, this universe becomes spiritual. It becomes more deeply and pervasively meaningful. It becomes the house of the human spirit, responsive to human need, expressive throughout of hope and fear, joy and sorrow, triumph and failure, defiance and despair, love and fellowship. Events cease to be material things merely and become a language, a prophecy, and a song.

Creative good is the guide we must follow if we are to find the way to life's supreme fulfilment in qualitative meaning.

DEMONIC GOOD

Nevertheless, qualitative meaning, for all its goodness, can become demonic and therefore is not to be trusted as a

[23]

guide to the greater good. In fact, the very goodness of qualitative meaning can carry men down to impoverishment and destruction. Qualitative meaning becomes unreliable the moment it usurps the greater good of which it is merely the product and for which it must function as a servant. It has a way of pretending to a completeness of meaning and value actually offered and given only by a reality with a goodness incomparable to its own. All qualitative meaning lies open to this perversion, and every good is in danger of becoming thus demonic. The greater the good, the greater the danger of this perversion. The gravest peril that men have to face resides in the way qualitative meaning, created good, can arouse an absoluteness and supremacy of loyalty which only its source, creative good, the generating event, really commands.

What renders a perilous situation even more perilous is the way, diversely and subtly manifested, in which good turned demonic conceals its treacherous claim and character by assuming and feigning the guise of its master. The terror and treachery of demonic good resides in the hidden deceptions that graven images always perpetrate on men— they claim and appear to be otherwise than what they actually are. They tell a man that he is invulnerable precisely at the moment of his greatest vulnerability. For this reason, qualitative meaning cannot serve as a reliable guide for human choice. We must search for a reality in terms of which we can recognize demonic good as demonic and discover its sole corrective.

The modern world displays many instances of good turned demonic. For example, the sense of nationality, one of our most precious inheritances, endowing the several peoples of the world with vital identity and vivifying contrasts, has overplayed itself into the distortion that is nationalism. Similarly, an awakened sense of sexuality, another of the great goods of life, has grown excessive and irresponsible, threatening to cut itself off from the bonds, conditions, and regulations that render its expression subservient to creative transformation. Industrial production, enormously magnified in our time, may become obsessive in like manner. Community, for which the atomized individual of today so deeply hungers, when attained in bonds of love and dear delight, becomes a poison if it commands devotion against the creative source and transformer of it. Every value pursued in modern life can become demonic—beauty, truth, morality alike—if and when it excludes the demands of creative good in the name of the false finality of what has been created. In so far as goods become demonic, they impoverish and destroy, rather than conserve and increase, the good of human life, for they oppose their creator. For this reason, men cannot safely endure happiness too long or too great unless that happiness be rooted in creativity itself.

All this carries a terrible warning to the modern world, for the danger today is greater than ever before because of our increased power to control the conditions and outcomes of life within certain areas and intervals. The moment of our greatest triumph can become the moment of our greatest defeat. When we have solved the problem of controlling the atomic bomb, if we ever do; when we have corrected the evils of nationalism, industrialism, and class conflict, we shall encounter the greatest possibility for evil in human history, even though it will also be the greatest possibility for good. For the very goodness of the good may become a mocking idol, fooling men into a deceptive happiness, as if they were so good as to be able to obstruct the source of their goodness. When men allow the calm of high happiness to dome their lives entire, the good of life sinks slowly but surely and imperceptibly into atrophy.

All this carries a challenge as well as a warning. Man never extricates himself from the evil that comes from demonry. But the evil can be fought in one's own person, in society, in history. Thereby it may be progressively conquered to a degree not yet known. The danger is dark, but hope also may be high if we face squarely this demon, analyze his nature, and minutely examine the conditions generating his existence. Perhaps never in the long story of man did this evil so darkly threaten and hope so brightly beckon as today. Before we seek out the guide and savior that can deliver us, we must look deeply into the novering night that shrouds this demon. Until we understand the nature of this evil and our own predicament, we cannot seek or find that salvation offered by the creative event when it is lifted to dominance in human concern.

CHAPTER II

The Human Predicament

THREE features intrinsic to man's way of apprehending value render life perilous, with the rising power of technology. This peril can be escaped by redirecting human endeavor from service of good already created to service of the generating source of all good. To accomplish this reversal in the direction of human devotion, we must have a reinterpretation of human good and how it originates. Catastrophe waits on exercise of the power of modern technology if this reversal is not accomplished, because our sense of values is wholly inadequate and unreliable to serve as a guide in use of such power. So long as power was weak, this unreliability of the human value-sense did not invite disaster. Now it does. To see the treachery inherent in man's appreciative consciousness when it directs the tremendous power of modern technology, we must examine the three characteristics which make his apprehension of value unreliable.

FAULTS OF THE HUMAN VALUE-SENSE

The first of these characteristics is the limited range of human appreciation. The values which man can appreciate are microscopic compared to the depth and fulness of value involved in every important human undertaking. To label unappreciated values "potential" removes the danger and difficulty of this human predicament not at all.

There is a second crippling fault in the human sense for value. Whatever apprehension of good and evil man attains is always distorted, when not perverted, by the domination of self-concern. Even when my action seems not to be self-centered because it is directed to certain interests of

[27]

other people, nevertheless it is self-centered in the sense that these interests of others have some special bearing upon my own fulfilment, and exclude from my consideration other interests not so apparently relevant to this prime concern of mine.

A third feature of man's way of discerning good and evil is equally dangerous to our existence when technology magnifies the power of human control over the course of events. It is resistance to change in the structure of appreciative consciousness. Man distinguishes good and evil according to certain forms which have been called the Gestalt of his conscious awareness. One might say they are the apertures through which the mind senses the good and evil of events and possibilities. They are slits variously structured for different minds. For each man they are shaped by his intimate group, by his ruling interest, and by his past experiences. These forms, structures, apertures, always become more or less fixated and will not undergo the transformations required to detect values peculiar to other groups, other cultures, and other interests and situations different from his own past experience.

Here again we have a characteristic of the human way of apprehending value not seriously dangerous throughout most of man's history except in rather unusual circumstances. Man did not and could not deal very potently with situations involving basic values for other intimate groups, cultures, and interests alien to his own. Above all, the world did not undergo radical and swift transformation as a rule. So the narrow slits of conscious awareness, determined by past experience and marking out the distinctions between good and evil for human discernment, were fairly reliable.

Today modern technology has changed all that. Newly generated distinctions of good and evil peculiar to the new situation often carry the issues of life and death, because the power we wield today involves us with groups and cultures alien to our own, accelerates change, and deepens the level at which it occurs. But it is not possible to transform the structure of consciousness so as to catch these newly emergent distinctions at the level and with the scope necessary to direct aright our power of control. The tender growth of emergent good derived from other groups and created anew as life goes on is the only ground of hope we have in a close-knit and changing world. But we kill the undetected growth of new values because the structure of our awareness excludes them from our apprehension.

How, then, can we be saved? Only, we repeat, by seeking another guide to direct our use of power very different from the human way of apprehending value. We cannot change the structure of the human value-sense in a way to make it fit to direct our power grown mighty with technology. The three limitations noted are intrinsic to the human consciousness. Scope of appreciation can be widened, to be sure; distortion and perversion by self-concern can be mitigated; established forms of appreciation can be rendered somewhat more transformable. But these improvements are negligible for the problem under consideration, namely, finding a directive which will so guide our use of power that it will not destroy the good we have and cut off hope of any increase but will rather serve to order the world so that good will grow and previously undetected values will break into consciousness. When we continue to use our power in service of the good we discern with the faulty sense of value peculiar to our minds, darkness swiftly gathers. The more strenuously we act and the more earnestly we serve under such guidance, the more swiftly comes the night. This is the fate of man when technology gives him power.

RELIGIOUS OBSTRUCTION

This fate can be escaped. But when we turn to follow the way of salvation, we find a barrier set up by the great redemptive religions—and pre-eminently by Christianity. Here is the most tragic irony of all: The great religions, seeking to save, have developed an ideology peculiarly fitted to the need of man in the days of his weakness. But this very same ideology, now in the days of his power, blocks the way of salvation. If we look down the path of escape, we can see how one of the major teachings of Christianity bars the way.

The way of escape, we remember, is to use the power of technology not to serve the good as discerned through the structure of appreciative awareness but to serve the creative source of all good. The creative event magnifies the good of the world, both the good appreciated and the good beyond the reach of appreciation, called "potential" if you wish. It expands the range of appreciation to the limit of human capacity when conditions are provided to release its efficacy. It corrects self-concern to the bounds of our willingness to meet its demands, and it transforms the established structure of conscious appreciation so that we can apprehend newly emergent values in a changing world. Above all, by serving the creative source we serve the good of all, as we cannot do when we serve only the created good which is accessible to our appreciation through the narrow and distorted slits of conscious awareness.

This is the way we must go when the power of technology is put into our hand, but it is not the way men generally have gone. Doubtless, a few saints and sages and fellowships of faith have lived under dominant devotion to creative good rather than allow created good to direct their lives. But today science and technology at our command must be put to the service of creative good. No longer is it sufficient for individuals in personal commitment to do this. The powerful shapers of social structure and human history must be put to this service.

Here is our problem, perhaps the most pressing of our

time. Science must be directed to searching out the conditions demanded by the source of human good so that this creative power may produce the values of life for all; and technology must be applied to setting up those conditions which science discovers to be required. If science and technology are not used in this way, they will destroy us because they will then be put into the service of those diverse and conflicting values which the restricted, self-centered, and group-centered consciousness of man can apprehend. But the creative source of human good is not now interpreted in such a way that science and technology can be applied to its service. The great religions portray it as being the shaper of events, or the overruler of them, or somehow generating them, but not itself a structure of events. Yet science cannot find the demands of an alleged reality which is not an order of events, nor can technology serve it, because these mighty instruments can work only in the world of events. Therefore, unless we can find the source of human good in the form of an order of events, we are doomed, if our analysis of the human predicament is correct.

This is not the problem of "reconciling science and religion" as ordinarily understood, namely, removing contradiction between their respective affirmations. That problem is twaddle compared to this. We are here discussing, not logical inconsistency, but life and death.

The problem before us can be put in another way. Science and technology are today the shapers of history and must be either the great constructors or the great destroyers. To be constructors they must primarily search and serve the demands of creative good and only secondarily the created goods that issue from this source, for reasons already stated. They cannot do this if the source of human good is beyond the reach of reason and beyond the bounds of time, hence inaccessible to rational-empirical inquiry. This is so because science and technology are guided by rational-empirical inquiry and cannot be conducted in any other way. Yet Christian leaders are saying that the divine source transcends reason and cannot be observed. If they are right, then our fate is determined. But perhaps they are not right. At any rate, let us not give up so easily. Let us examine the claim that this reality transcends reason; and let us see if we cannot find its presence in an order of events that can be searched by methods of observation. If we succeed, science and technology can become the great constructors, not because they of themselves can increase the good of life, but because they then can remove obstacles and provide conditions releasing the creative power which does conserve and magnify the good of life. If we fail, science and technology will become the devastators of civilization. Nothing less than this is our predicament.

By "transcending reason," the religious leaders do not mean merely transcending what we have to date discovered. If that were all they claimed, their point would apply to everything we know—this table, for example, or yonder spoon. Of course, there is always mystery if, by mystery, no more is meant than the unexplored and the uncomprehended. Nobody is denying that. But "transcending reason," in the special sense under consideration, means more than this common fact pertaining to everything whatsoever in existence. It means transcending those rational criteria by which anything is distinguished from anything else.

It is true that our religious leaders all insist that Christianity must be rational. That is, they urge Christianity to use reason to the last limit of reason's reach. But, they add, reason does not reach far enough. Hence, when man trusts in reason as though it reached to the last penetration of distinguishing apprehension, he falls into serious trouble, such as we are experiencing today. Our religious leaders are asserting that Christian faith must direct man's commitment to something beyond the reach of Reason, not merely beyond its present grasp.[1]

THE REACH OF REASON

We must examine reason to see what this claim of transcendence means. The structure of reason can be studied in abstraction, apart from any concrete realities discriminated. The outstanding example of this is pure mathematics and logic. But the proper use and value of it, apart from aesthetic contemplation and mental gymnastics, is to distinguish any concrete reality from any other. Only with these criteria would it be possible for the utmost perfection and completion of reasoning to distinguish true from false, good from bad, right from wrong, God from man, creator from creature, and so on through every realm of reality.

In what sense can religious faith or any other outreach of man transcend reason? Only by transcending the distinc-

[1] Perhaps the outstanding representative of this interpretation of Christianity is Paul Tillich, who has formulated the position with more philosophical thoroughness than any other. Reinhold Niebuhr, George Thomas, Theodore Greene, Pitt Van Duesen, Edwin Aubrey, and many others, as well as more extreme leaders like Barth and Brunner, go along with Tillich on this issue, although they differ in many other respects. Also many in literary and learned circles outside the ranks of professional religious leaders follow Tillich in this particular. Paul Tillich makes plain that what commands "ultimate concern"—the unconditional commitment of faith —is Being as Such, beyond the reach of all inquiry. Anything accessible to human inquiry can only be some restricted form of Being. It cannot be Being as Such. This Being as Such corresponds to Kant's noumenal realm. Knowledge cannot attain to it, although faith must assert it. Perhaps no wording of this position would satisfy all the holders of it. Perhaps no one of them would accept any wording save his own. But the central point we are making is common to them all: Human inquiry cannot get knowledge of any specific character which will identify with assurance the essential nature of the ultimate referent of our faith and our ultimate concern. Any specific character or form, such as Christ, may serve as a symbol, pointing human faith and concern, human awareness and acknowledgment, to this X. But the character of the symbol must not be identified with what is symbolized. Such an interpretation of the outreach of faith is peculiarly appealing to an age passionately seeking a faith but disillusioned and skeptical of every formulation heretofore accepted and followed. We are here declaring that this position, held by so many today, is fatal to man in the days of his power.

tions whereby any reality whatsoever can be distinguished from any other. Then sin would be merged and mixed indistinguishably with what is not sin, creator confounded with creature, right and wrong lost in a blur of paradox, love and hate distinguishable only by arbitrary dictate. In such an eventuality, appeal to revelation as going beyond reason would not help at all because revelation transcending reason would itself not be distinguishable from its opposite and the content of revelation would be a murk of indistinguishable parts.

Religious leaders who talk of transcending reason certainly do not intend all this. But this is the implication of what they are saying, once their concepts are clarified and their intellectual integrity preserved.

The desperate need of our time is for a faith that can direct man's commitment to the creative source of all human good as it works in the temporal world, open to rational-empirical search and to service by modern technology. This urgency of circumstance makes clarification and criticism necessary. When the atomic bomb engenders action cutting deep into the tissues of human existence, the cutting will kill or cure according as we know where the vital organs are and how they work. The vital organ in this case is the creative event which gives us our humanity, with all its potentialities of supreme fulfilment. This must be guarded, and only a faith that understands can serve this source of life intelligently with such a knife in hand. A faith that glories in transcending reason in such a time as this is a deadly danger.

There is another kind of transcendence, even worse, which our religious leaders are attributing to the source of human good. It is transcendence of the whole realm of temporal existence. It is transcendence of time. The evil of this is not that it makes men indifferent and inactive in the concerns of this world, for men with such a faith are often excessively active; the evil is that it makes them unwilling even to try to find the ultimate creative source of human good in the temporal process because they deny that it is there—only its temporal manifestations are there. It is as though a man performing a surgical operation were to deny that the vital organs are in the body at all. Only their temporal manifestations are there, he says, but, since they themselves are not there, no cutting of the knife can seriously hurt them. Such a man should never be allowed to perform a capital operation. But we have come to the time when men of faith are driven to perform such an operation. They must work with modern technology releasing atomic energy. They have no choice but to do this; for the course of events will not be turned back and permits of no drifting. Therefore, religious faith so interpreted as to render it rationally incompetent must be driven out.

Our religious leaders exhort us to "accept" and "come to terms with" the findings of science and philosophy. But that is not enough. Indeed, it is fatal. Faith must itself do the seeking and finding. Merely to accept and come to terms with searchings and researches not driven by faith itself is to accept and come to terms with findings that conceal the reality we seek. Secular science and philosophy, no matter how highly endowed, cannot find what they do not seek; and they cannot seek what only faith can seek, if they have not the faith. Therefore, faith is betrayed when it merely accepts and comes to terms with the findings of secular search but cannot itself conduct rational and empirical inquiry into the deepest sources of human good. Obviously, it cannot conduct such inquiry when it believes this source to be beyond the reach of human inquiry and not in the temporal world at all.

Here we come to the tragedy apparent in all this work of our present religious leaders. What they intend to do is exactly opposite to what they actually accomplish. Their intent in appealing to the eternal, the superhistorical, the transcendental, the unconditioned, or however they designate it, is the noblest. Their intent is to deliver man from the relative goods of history and save him from giving supreme devotion to what becomes demonic when commanding such complete self-giving. We are deeply indebted to them for making us acutely aware of this deadly evil forever hanging over the life of man. But what they actually do, in their attempt to avoid it, is to involve us more helplessly in this fate.

Analysis of the concept of the eternal makes this apparent. The eternal, superhistorical, transcendental, nontemporal, cannot receive anything from man because such receiving would involve some sort of change and hence time and history. Therefore, man cannot serve the eternal or honor it or do anything for it. All the sorrow and loss and struggle and fulfilment of history come to nothing at all if the eternal is the reality allegedly served by it or for which it is done. This follows necessarily from the fact that the eternal cannot change and hence can receive nothing and acquire nothing from what happens in time. Thus, to set up any eternal, superhistorical, time-transcending reality as the ground and goal of our existence, the meaning and purpose of all we do, the recipient and fulfiller of our sacrifice, is to throw us back helplessly into the temporal process, for there alone can any difference be made. It throws us back *helplessly* because, having put all our faith and hope upon the eternal, we are incapacitated for seeking out and finding in the temporal world that creative event which does, in fact, find progressive fulfilment in and through our lives when we meet the conditions demanded.

This is the tragedy unveiling itself in the work of our religious leaders and the community of those they reach. Thinking to serve the eternal when, in fact, they can only serve something going on in time, they are blinded to the way of salvation laid open in the temporal process. Seduced by the Greek idol of eternity, they cannot find the living God in time as revealed in Christ and the Hebrew prophets.

Increasing precision is always required as man's power increases. Lack of precision becomes fatal when mighty instruments of power are put into the hand of man. We have such instruments today in the form of modern technology, and especially atomic energy. With these instruments we are cutting deep into the vital tissues of our common life. We must know, with a precision never before demanded, what is actually the creative source of human good, how it works, and what conditions must be maintained to enable it to continue working.

FAITH AND TECHNOLOGY

The bomb that fell on Hiroshimo cut history in two like a knife. Before and after are two different worlds. That cut is more abrupt, decisive, and revolutionary than the cut made by the star over Bethlehem. It may not be more creative of human good than the star, but it is more swiftly transformative of human existence than anything else that has ever happened. The economic and political order fitted to the age before that parachute fell becomes suicidal in the age coming after. The same breach extends into education and religion.

Men having interests in the economic and political order will vehemently deny that such a change is required of them. Men with vested interests in religion may admit that the change is demanded in the economic and political realms but will repudiate any such claim for their own special area. They will have many arguments to prove that their faith is more deeply laid, more enduring, more immune from change than affairs economic and political. Their faith may very well reach for deeper levels of existence and may seek access to a more important reality than any other human con-

[37]

cern. But their faith is no more exempt from change in respect to the intellectual forms by which it must be lived than any other. These forms must undergo reformation as radical as any if faith meets constructively the new order of life which has been literally hurled at modern man by this coercive event.

Someone will begin at once to point to the well-known fact that cultural and social changes are never sudden. When truly significant, they require centuries for realization. Of course, this is true. The change we are now considering is the cultural shift gradually produced by modern technology. Extensive use of machinery began about 1850 and will continue for a long time to come. The release of atomic energy is merely the climax of much that has gone before. But the use of atomic bombs in war dramatizes the transition that has been occurring and may well usher in its final and consummative phase. After the age of technological consummation has been completed, the time of increasing technology may give place to a different kind of cultural achievement. Meanwhile, the bomb that fell over Hiroshima has psychological consequences that greatly accelerate the reordering and reinterpreting of human life demanded by technology grown mighty.

This bomb has become a symbol giving to all human life a new meaning with portent of dread and splendor. Not the physical impact of the bomb or the economic changes it may induce but the sudden presentation of alternative destinies for the human race divides history into the age before and the age after the release of atomic energy. It calls for a radical redirection of man's controlling devotion. Not the greatest good he can appreciate but the process which creates him and all the good of life is what he must serve. Not the goal but the source, not the highest but the deepest, not the total unity but the creator of unity, not the universe as known to him but the generator and recreator of

[38]

every universe he can ever know, must be his guide and master when he reaches the peak of power.

The creative source of value must come first in man's devotion, while the specific values apprehended through the narrow slit of human awareness must come second, if we are to find the way of our deliverance and the way of human fulfilment. This reversal in the direction of human devotion is not new. It is, we believe, the very substance of the original Christian faith. What is new is the need to reinterpret the creative source of human good in such wise as to render it accessible to the service of the mighty tools of science and technology.

We must try to demonstrate the original Christian nature of this reversal in the direction of human devotion. Otherwise, it will seem alien to the best in our tradition. In fact, it is not alien but essential and intrinsic to that best. If this is true, we should be able to see the truth of it by simply looking objectively at the events which originated the Christian faith. No subtle logical devices or rationalizing systems should be required. Let us, then, look at these originative events of our traditional religion, endeavoring to see them as naïvely and objectively as possible. The creative source of human good operating in time and plainly accessible to rational-empirical inquiry, yet commanding this reversal in the direction of human devotion, should stand there in clear silhouette.

THE ORIGINATING EVENTS OF OUR FAITH

Jesus engaged in intercommunication with a little group of disciples with such depth and potency that the organization of their several personalities was broken down and they were remade. They became new men, and the thought and feeling of each got across to the others. It was not merely the thought and feeling of Jesus that got across. That was not the most important thing. The important thing was that the thought and feeling of the least and lowliest got across to the others and the others to him. Not something handed down to them from Jesus but something rising up out of their midst in creative power was the important thing. It was not something Jesus did. It was something that happened when he was present like a catalytic agent. It was as if he was a neutron that started a chain reaction of creative transformation. Something about this man Jesus broke the atomic exclusiveness of those individuals so that they were deeply and freely receptive and responsive each to the other. He split the atom of human egoism, not by psychological tricks, not by intelligent understanding, but simply by being the kind of person he was, combined with the social, psychological, and historical situation of the time and the heritage of Hebrew prophecy. Thus there arose in this group of disciples a miraculous mutual awareness and responsiveness toward the needs and interests of one another.

But this was not all; something else followed from it. The thought and feeling, let us say the meanings, thus derived by each from the other, were integrated with what each had previously acquired. Thus each was transformed, lifted to a higher level of human fulfilment. Each became more of a mind and a person, with more capacity to understand, to appreciate, to act with power and insight; for this is the way human personality is generated and magnified and life rendered more nobly human.

A third consequence followed necessarily from these first two. The appreciable world expanded round about these men, thus interacting in this fellowship. Since they could now see through the eyes of others, feel through their sensitivities, and discern the secrets of many hearts, the world was more rich and ample with meaning and quality. Also— and this might be called a fourth consequence—there was more depth and breadth of community between them as individuals with one another and between them and all other men. This followed from their enlarged capacity to get the perspectives of one another and the perspectives of all whom they might encounter. Of course, this apprehension of the other's perspective is never perfect and complete. But the disciples found themselves living in a community of men vastly deeper and wider than any before accessible to them.

Thus occurred in the fellowship about Jesus a complex, creative event, transforming the disciples as individuals, their relations with one another and with all men, and transforming also the appreciable world in which they lived.

Let us not be misunderstood. The creative transformative power was not in the man Jesus, although it could not have occurred apart from him. Rather he was in it. It required many other things besides his own solitary self. It required the Hebrew heritage, the disciples with their peculiar capacity for this kind of responsiveness, and doubtless much else of which we have little knowledge. The creative power lay in the interaction taking place between these individuals. It transformed their minds, their personalities, their appreciable world, and their community with one another and with all men. In subsequent chapters we shall try to demonstrate that this creative power is the source of all good in human existence. What happened in the group about Jesus was the lifting of this creative event to dominate their lives. What happened after the death of Jesus was the release of this creative power from constraints and limitations previously confining it; also the formation of a fellowship with an organization, ritual, symbols, and documents by which this dominance of the creative event over human concern might be perpetuated through history. Of course, there was little if any intellectual understanding of it; but intellectual understanding was not required to live under its control in the culture then and there prevailing, for men did not have our technology.

[41]

The creative event is always working in human life, but ordinarily it is ignored and excluded from human concern and the intent of devotion. Other interests usurp its place in the life of man. Salvation is found only when it is lifted from this ignored and excluded level relative to human concern and is made the dominant directive of human endeavor. What happened in the group about Jesus was this lifting of the creative event from the subterranean depths to the level of domination. We repeat: this did not mean any intellectual understanding of it by the disciples. Rather it occurred because Jesus and other factors present were of such sort as to release the power of this event to such a measure that it achieved domination over these lives.

This lifting to domination could not, however, by itself alone, accomplish the salvation of man. It had to be perpetuated in history. Otherwise, it could not reach you and me. It could not reach the atomic age, when salvation and destruction were to become more decisively than ever before the alternative destinies of man.

This domination is not perpetuated in the sense that any group of people lives continuously under the supreme control of this creative interchange, but it is rather perpetuated by ritual, myth, and Bible, so used and interpreted that people can always recover a sense of the supreme importance of the source of all good to be found in creative interaction. Hence the ritual and myth, the symbols and the Bible, become the "means of grace." The church is the historic continuity of these means by which men may recover a renewed access to that way of life in which creative interchange dominates the life of man as it did in the fellowship of Jesus. The perpetuating symbolism and ritual may become a hollow shell, transmitting nothing of importance; but, even so, the vital significance and function of it can be restored. On that account it continues to be, even when hollow and formal, the most precious heritage of man, for it is

perpetuating
Symbolism + ritual

the means by which the creative event can again be lifted to dominate human devotion and command the complete self-giving of man to its saving and transformative power.

But we must continue the Christian story. We have told of the life of Jesus. The death of Jesus is equally important. Indeed, it is indispensable to our salvation. So long as Jesus lived, the creative event was bound to limits and confined by obstructions which would have prevented it from bringing salvation to man if Jesus had not been crucified. To see this clearly, let us transpose the situation to our own time and see it by way of an analogy.

The fourfold creative event which we have described as dominating the fellowship of Jesus is present in our own lives also. But it can work with us only so long as it measures up to the standards of American culture. Just so long as it creates good that is felt to be good by Americans, we may follow it and yield to its transforming power; but we will not allow it to transform us and our world in such a way as to include the needs and interests of Communists.

Now that is the way it was with the disciples before the Resurrection, when this creativity could work with them mightily but only within the confines of the hope of Israel and the perspective of their inherited culture. Jesus might be the Messiah, but, if so, he must do what the prophets said the Messiah was sent to do, namely, give to all the world the immeasurable blessings of the Hebrew heritage—even as Japan today sought to bless the world by giving all men the good of Japanese culture descended from heaven. Americans have the same noble impulse with regard to American democracy. In like manner, before the Resurrection, the disciples of Jesus were unable to undergo the transformations of creative interchange beyond the bounds of their cultural heritage.

What happened at the Resurrection was the breaking of these bounds, whence issued the "power of the Resurrec-

[43]

tion," about three days after the Crucifixion. When Jesus was crucified, his followers saw that he could never carry to fulfilment the mission of the Jewish people as they conceived it; hence there was no good in him of the sort that had led them to follow him. They had thought that he would save the world by making supreme over human existence the good as seen in the perspective of Jewish culture. Now they saw that he never could do anything of the sort. He was not the messiah they had expected, and, so far as they could see, he was no messiah at all. The depth of devotion and the glory of the vision they had possessed made their disillusionment all the more bitter and devastating. They had given up everything for him, and now he was shown to have no good in him of the sort they could understand or appreciate. They reached that depth of despair which comes when all that seems to give hope to human existence is seen to be an illusion. This was the immediate consequence of the Crucifixion.

After about the third day, however, when the numbness of the shock had worn away, something happened. The life-transforming creativity previously known only in fellowship with Jesus began again to work in the fellowship of the disciples. It was risen from the dead. Since they had never experienced it except in association with Jesus, it seemed to them that the man Jesus himself was actually present, walking and talking with them. Some thought they saw him and touched him in physical presence. But what rose from the dead was not the man Jesus; it was creative power. It was the living God that works in time. It was the Second Person of the Trinity. It was Christ the God, not Jesus the man.

OUR NEED OF SALVATION

If this account and analysis of what originated the Christian faith has in it any truth, it shows the reversal which human devotion must undergo if we are to be saved. What blocks the saving power of the creative event is the projection of human purpose as sovereign over it. While this blockage of creativity by human purpose could, in times past, hold man to a meager and dying level of existence, it could not bring on great destruction because man did not have sufficient power to be so destructive. Only now in the age of man's power does the domination of human purpose over the creative event bring us to the edge of the abyss.

How and why this false order of domination can be so destructive should be apparent enough. Suppose we imagine the very wisest and noblest and most righteous men given supreme authority. Suppose philosophers, in Plato's style, were kings. Suppose all men recognized them to be the noblest and best, as, in truth, they were. Thus they themselves could know themselves to be so and would thereby derive the confidence required for such high office. But the human mind cannot possibly fathom the vital needs and interests of others without the kind of interchange which we have called the "creative event." Therefore, if this creativity were subjected to the domination of the projected purpose of these good men, they would, inevitably, with their righteousness suppress and kill the good of the vast majority of other men—all this with the best intention in the world. But if these other men had some control over the power of modern technology, they would rebel against this deadly righteousness. Furthermore, these righteous men, being cut off from the source of creative intelligence, would rapidly decline in their power. So, even if they were given supreme power in the beginning, they could not monopolize it continuously. Hence would arise opposed and conflicting groups. If they all, or any two opposing groups, had access to atomic energy, the dominant authority of human righteousness over the creative event might lead to the destruction of man.

Nothing is so deadly as the noblest and most righteous human purpose when it is made dominant over the creative event. The order of domination must be reversed in the age of atomic power. Creative interchange must dominate, whereby the needs and interests of others get across to me, transform my own mind, my own desires and felt needs, so as to include theirs and thereby vastly magnify the appreciable world for each and the depth of community among all. There is no other way of salvation; and the greater the power of man, the more imperative becomes the demand of the living Christ to take sovereignty over human purpose. The living Christ is the domination of the creative event as revealed in Christ two thousand years ago and perpetuated through history in the way already noted.

FAITH AND KNOWLEDGE

The demand for precision and fulness of knowledge about what commands religious commitment does not exclude faith. To think that it does is to misunderstand the nature of faith. The notion is prevalent that faith can survive only when knowledge is inadequate. This would be true if faith were a belief sustained by less evidence than is required to lift the belief to the status of knowledge. But such is not the case. Faith is not essentially belief at all, although faith generally has a belief. Religious faith is basically an act—the act of giving one's self into the keeping of what commands faith, to be transformed by it, and to serve it above all. More specifically, it is the act of deciding to live in the way required by the source of human good, to maintain association with a fellowship practicing that commitment, to follow the rituals designed to renew and deepen this commitment, to search one's self for hidden disloyalties to this devotion, to confess and repudiate these disloyalties. All habits, interests, and structures of personality are thus condemned when they hinder the living

[46]

of the life demanded. This complex act is faith; the beliefs are merely incidental to it.

The decision to live in the new way—the first part of the total act of faith—cannot occur unless two preceding conditions have been fulfilled. The individual must have had fellowship with people living in this faith, and he must have encountered difficulties sufficiently serious to make him want to live in commitment to what creates all good rather than in commitment to his own independent purpose. More accurately, religious faith of the sort here considered is a shift from a life finding basic security in created goods over to a life finding basic security in the creative source of all good. Living in this new way, one must be ready to relinquish any created good when it hinders the work of the creative source and to receive newly emergent good when the creative source so demands.

Since faith is an act, it is neither a belief going beyond the evidence nor knowledge. It may be guided by beliefs which are not knowledge or it may be guided by no belief at all. In this latter case the guide is tradition and the ways of a fellowship. But, still again, faith may be guided by the most thoroughly tested and accurate knowledge. Since the essence of faith is not the belief but the self-giving, the belief may be supported with evidence to the point where it becomes knowledge, or it may be credulity without evidence, with all gradations in between. Or, still again, the belief may be lacking altogether when ritual, habit, and tradition of a special fellowship take the place of belief in guiding the act of faith.

Never does human knowledge plumb the full depths of the reality commanding religious commitment of faith. When we say that it must be brought within the reach of human inquiry and precise knowledge, we are not in any way contravening that assertion. Even when the beliefs directing religious commitment become knowledge of the most precise and thoroughly tested sort, still the knowledge never exhausts the reality commanding the faith. This reality works in the fellowship more deeply and potently than knowledge can reach, and this deep working at the roots of personality where growth is nourished is what engenders full commitment of religious faith. This holds true even when knowledge concerning this creative source of life becomes indispensable and well established. Knowledge is needed today not primarily to engender faith but to guide faith in the service of creative good when science and technology are the tools we must use in rendering this service. Also, it should be added, if these tools are not used to serve this creative source but are directed by our own wants and purposes, our purposes so empowered will determine the conditions of human life so completely as to shut out the deep working of the creative event at those profound levels where it transforms the personality and awakens the full commitment of faith. Thus, even in the interest of noncognitive faith, we must have knowledge of this creative reality or opportunity to gain knowledge of it, in order to guide us in our use of the instruments of power. Only so can we guard from desecration those deeps where human life and its source meet in communion beyond the reach of knowledge.

FAITH AND DESPAIR

Other elements in our tradition, more or less mythically expressed, illumine the human predicament as it is here interpreted. These elements are not only religious but also moral and philosophical. For example, there is a tradition concerning the meaning of history. According to this doctrine, the chief lesson to learn from history by those able to understand is despair. All human outreach after the good, so these traditions declare, ends in defeat. Numbers of people throughout considerable stretches of time may seem to prosper; but, sooner or later, the surge of circumstance hurls

[48]

them back into futility or frustration, and the magnitude of their fall often seems to be measured by the greatness of the illusory good they have attained.

This fate of man in history, so the doctrine runs, is the judgment of God—the judgment imposed because man uses his power and prosperity to serve the good as discerned by his own appreciative consciousness rather than the good as determined by the creative power of God. The more power and wealth he attains, the more perverse, or at any rate the more potent, does he become in this misdirection of human endeavor.

This judgment of God and the despair it brings are not merely condemnation; they really open the way of salvation and fulfilment; for despair concerning the reliability of his own appraisal of value may lead man to commit himself to the healing and guiding grace of God.

There is no virtue in despair for its own sake; for it may be one of the worst of all evils. But when it turns man to trust the grace of God alone and not his own reason or sense of value or other human power, it opens the way to life's fulfilment. As a gateway into this transformed way of living, where security is found in the power and goodness of God, despair is the highest wisdom.

If it be true that the structure of man's appreciative consciousness is microscopic in range, distorted in form, and resistant to change, as we have tried to show, this ancient religious teaching is correct, even though it is often cloudy and unintelligible in the manner of its expression. The "grace of God" would then be creative transformation become dominant in the life of man. Despair would apply not to man's capacity to undergo transformation on meeting the required conditions but to the ability of his reason, his empirical findings, his appreciative awareness, or any other such capacity of the human mind to attain the greater good except as it is used to search and serve the demands of the creative event. Every human capacity has its noble and indispensable task to fulfil, namely, to search out the nature of this creativity and to meet the conditions it may demand. But the actual directing toward the good and the actual achievement of it can be exercised not by any ability of man but only by the creative event when accepted as sovereign over life. When thus operative in its sovereignty, it is called the "grace of God" in the particular religious tradition noted; it is also called "the risen and the living Christ."

There is likewise an ancient moral teaching closely akin to this religious doctrine. Man must despair of achieving righteousness is this moral claim; yet he must not cease to strive. To retire from the battle because he is doomed always to do evil when he tries to do good or to conceal his tragic state by asserting falsely his power to do good—these are the two basic moral errors. These errors may arise through misinterpreting the nature of the good so that man can achieve what is mistakenly represented to be the goal of moral endeavor, or they may arise through misinterpreting man's own power. All this is not to be understood as meaning that moral striving can accomplish nothing of value. The evil done by righteous striving is not so great as that done by the unrighteous, although this may happen at times. "Righteous" here means utmost striving to do the right while despairing of success. Man's highest moral attainment is thus to combine moral despair with moral striving, according to the tradition we are examining.

If man's destiny is to be transformed into something different from what he is, if his high mission is to be the carrier of creativity to a new level of existence beyond anything now in the world, then this kind of moral sense is exactly what would be expected of him. If he cannot achieve what he ought to achieve except by undergoing transformation from larva to butterfly, then so long as he is larva, his conscience should drive him toward attainments impossible for

[50]

him in his larval state. But such striving and such conscience are unendurable, and no man can tolerate them unless he goes beyond the naked moral demand and seeks,
through confession, repentance, and self-giving (religious
faith), a power other than human which lifts and transforms him most effectively precisely in this moment of
deepest despair and most earnest effort. With such a faith
the despair is not misery but carries a sweetness and a
peace with renewed effort.

The teachings of Jesus concerning a righteousness which
no man can reach and his beatitudes bestowed on the poor
in spirit, the mourners, the meek, and persons who hunger
and thirst after righteousness make sense if our analysis of
the human predicament is correct. Also it renders intelligible his persistent teaching about high attainment through
self-sacrifice and his own triumph over history by undergoing destruction. But the authority of Jesus is not sufficient to support the interpretation that we are defending,
nor is any other authority, bearing whatsoever sanctity.
Nothing but persistent and rigorous inquiry and the evidence thus found can support any teaching. Yet if this interpretation of man's predicament is true, it would seem
reasonable to think that many have found the truth of it in
ages past, or at least have lived unwittingly according to
its demands. Most of all should this be true of those whom
the world declares to be supreme exemplifications of our
humanity. Except in this sense, then, we shall dispense
with authority, whether in Jesus or in any other, and continue our inquiry.

One thought must give us pause as we undertake this further search: Perhaps the truth we seek with the minds we
have is as unattainable as the righteousness; perhaps only
the mind of the butterfly can know what we strive to know,
and we are only larvae. But as the moral man who strives in
despair may, by the grace of creative transformation, attain

a righteousness he could not possibly reach without this divine help, so it may be in this striving after truth. If we strive in despair of attaining this truth with our minds as now constructed, they may be reconstructed by a creativity not our own. At any rate, this striving is our fate, whatever may be the outcome. Also this attainment through despair is a philosophical tradition in our inheritance. Socrates was not the first or the last to combine search for truth with despair of finding it—except his mind be transformed; this may continue until human existence undergoes creative change.

It is our faith that man must be transcended in this way or be destroyed; it is our faith that these alternative destinies await him—transformation or destruction. We hope for the transformation, but destruction will descend if we follow the guidance of our own value-sense in disregard of the creative event. Meanwhile, we strive for a righteousness and a truth we cannot attain. Perhaps it is a time for most earnest striving, for we may be nearer to the great transformation than we think.

THE GREAT TRANSITION

We are passing over one of the great divides of history; possibly it is the last high pass over the top mountain range before we enter the valley of abundance—the valley sought by man in all his wanderings since first he was man. Perhaps beyond the high pass, flinty and cold and narrow, is a region where men may live richly under the rule of a re-directed devotion for a thousand years and more. But can we pass over? We see the tracks of other cultures and civilizations on the steep ascent up which we go—they go up with firmness, but they come down tottering. Shall we come down tottering, or shall we not come down at all, dying in the high pass?

That question will be answered not by the statesmen, not

by the industrialists, not by the scientists and military men; for it can be answered only by religious leaders. There is a creativity in our midst, and if it be released to work as it will, we shall go over the high divide into the valley beyond. But it must be proclaimed and interpreted in terms that science can search and technology can serve.

The masses of men keep coming on; they have already reached the entrance of that narrow defile where death and life await them. Never before in all his long pilgrimage has man so fatefully met these two companions. After that meeting, either death or life will be master of man.

CHAPTER III

Creative Good

CREATIVE good is distinguished from two kinds of created good, one of which is instrumental and the other intrinsic. Instrumental and intrinsic created good are alike in the sense that both are made up of events meaningfully connected; but in the instrumental kind the quality of the events is either negligible or irrelevant to their positive value. Eating tasteless or nauseating food might have the instrumental value of providing me with energy for participation later in events yielding intrinsic value. If the food is tasteless, the quality is negligible; if nauseating, there is quality, but the quality is irrelevant to the instrumental value. The eating of such food might, however, take on intrinsic value through other meaningful connections then and there experienced—the friendliness of associates, memories recalled, and happy anticipations. All these qualities flood in upon me from near and far and are experienced in the very act of eating with these people at this time and place. In such an event the eating ceases to be instrumental by taking on rich quality through meaningful connection with many other happenings. The same system of events may be in one reference an instrumental, and in another reference an intrinsic, good.

The shift from instrumental to intrinsic value, through acquisition of qualitative meaning, is a common occurrence in human life. For example, when I chop wood to sustain that other structure of happenings called "the life of my family in our home," the values of the activity may be purely instrumental if *the qualities pertaining to life in my*

[54]

home cannot freely enter conscious awareness as I chop. However, if bonds of meaning are developed between my chopping of the wood and the life of my home, so that the lives of the children and the affection of the wife are vivified in conscious awareness by the very act itself, then the activity ceases to be merely instrumental. Then chopping the wood has taken on those qualities pertaining to the total structure of events called "the life of my home." It is an intrinsic good, no matter how fatiguing it may be.

Therefore, intrinsic value may be defined as a structure of events endowing each happening as it occurs with qualities derived from other events in the structure. On the other hand, instrumental value is a structure of events whereby each happening as it occurs does not acquire qualities from other events in the structure, or, if it does, these qualities are irrelevant to the value of the structure in the reference under consideration.

When there is a break between two or more systems of events such that the qualities of the one system cannot get across to the other, the only meaningful connection between the two must be nonqualitative and instrumental. It is nonqualitative either because the qualities of these connecting events are negligible or because they are irrelevant to the good that is served.

Life can break apart into separate systems of qualitative meaning, when each system is an intrinsic good and when the disjunctions between them are bridged by instrumental good. Any meaningful connection between events which does not carry the qualities from one part of life over to the other parts is, on that account, instrumental in respect to this connective function. It is possible that life might break up into smaller and smaller units of intrinsic good, each unit being separated further and further from the others by longer and longer stretches of instrumental value, relatively barren of qualitative meaning. These instrumental stretches might include events that had intense quality in themselves as bare and isolated events. But value as here interpreted is not merely events having intense quality, even when the quality is pleasant; it is events having rich quality derived from other events through meaningful connection with them. Of course, the quality peculiar to the event now happening may make its own contribution; but it is qualitative meaning, not merely events having quality, which is the good distinctive of human existence. Such good is our concern here.

When good increases, a process of reorganization is going on, generating new meanings, integrating them with the old, endowing each event as it occurs with a wider range of reference, molding the life of a man into a more deeply unified totality of meaning. The wide diversities, varieties, and contrasts of all the parts of a man's life are being progressively transformed into a more richly inclusive whole. The several parts of life are connected in mutual support, vivifying and enhancing one another in the creation of a more inclusive unity of events and possibilities. This process of reorganization is what we shall call the "creative event." It is creative good, standing in contrast to both kinds of created good we have been considering. By means of this creative good, systems of meaning having intrinsic value, previously disconnected so that the qualities of the one could not get across to the other, are so unified that each is enriched by qualities derived from the other. Meaningfully connected events, once instrumental, now become component parts of a total meaning having intrinsic value.

In contrast to the disintegration of life previously sketched, the opposite occurs when creative good is dominant. Under the control of this creativity the life of an individual might, in theory at least, be progressively organized so that the qualities of each part could be experienced while the individual was engaged in some minor role, like walking to town. If this were the case, one's whole life could be qualitatively tasted by way of meaning when one was engaged in any part.

This creative good has kinship with instrumental value, but it is very different from the kind of instrumental value we have described as one kind of created good. It has kinship because it produces more intrinsic created good, and in many cases its own qualities are negligible or are not discriminated and appreciated. Yet it is not instrumental because it transforms the mind and purpose so radically that what it produces is never what the initiating mind intended. Therefore, the initiating mind cannot use it as a means for achieving any anticipated consequence of value that can be foreseen in its specific character. The creative event cannot be used to shape the world closer to the heart's desire because it transforms the heart's desire so that one wants something very different from what one desired in the beginning.

The creative event also has kinship with intrinsic value and yet is very different. It has kinship because in some instances the qualities of the creative event have maximum abundance. The creative event in the life of the artist is sometimes an ecstasy. So also the emergence of new transformative ideas in the mind of the creative thinker, the moment of vision for the prophet, the "rebirth" of the religious convert, or the communion of friends may stand forth as a peak of qualitative meaning. However, in the ordinary run of life, for the most part, the creative event reorganizes the mind and transforms its appreciable world without the qualities of the creative event being themselves discriminated and distinguished from the newly emergent meaning. Rather it is the newly created good that is qualitatively appreciated and not the creative event producing it.

The creative event is so basic to all our further interpre-

[57]

tation of value that we must examine it with care. It is made up of four subevents; and the four working together and not any one of them working apart from the other constitute the creative event. Each may occur without the others and often does, but in that case it is not creative. We have to describe them separately, but distinctions made for the purpose of analysis must not obscure the unitary, fourfold combination necessary to the creativity.

The four subevents are: emerging awareness of qualitative meaning derived from other persons through communication; integrating these new meanings with others previously acquired; expanding the richness of quality in the appreciable world by enlarging its meaning; deepening the community among those who participate in this total creative event of intercommunication. We shall examine each of these subevents in detail.

THE FIRST SUBEVENT

Let us remember that qualitative meaning consists of actual events so related that each acquires qualities from the others. Every living organism so reacts as to break the passage of existence into units or intervals called "events" and to relate these to one another in the manner here called "qualitative meaning." So long as this is done by the organism without the aid of linguistic communication, the range and richness of qualitative meaning is very limited. Not until the single organism is able to acquire the qualitative meanings developed by other organisms and add them to its own can the world of meaning and quality expand to any great compass. Therefore the first subevent in the total creative event producing value distinctively human is this emerging awareness in the individual of qualitative meaning communicated to it from some other organism.

Interaction between the organism and its surroundings, by which new qualitative meaning is created without com-

[58]

munication or prior to communication, is certainly creative. If we were studying the creative event as it occurs at all levels of existence, this creativity at the subcommunicative level would be included. But we have chosen to give attention to what creates value at the human level. What creates value at the biological level is basic to human existence, but it is not distinctively human. We shall give some attention to it, but only for the purpose of seeing more clearly the character of the creative event as it works through intercommunication in human society and history. It is here, where one organism can acquire the meanings gathered by a million others, that the miracle happens and creativity breaks free from obstacles which elsewhere imprison its power. Only at this level can the creative event rear a world of quality and meaning expanding beyond any known limit, sometimes by geometrical progression.

THE SECOND SUBEVENT

The individual becomes more of a personality when these meanings derived from others are integrated with what he already has. His thoughts and feelings are enriched and deepened. This integrating does not occur in every case of communicated meaning, since there is much noncreative communication in our modern world by way of radio, television, movies, newspapers, and casual interchange between individuals. The mere passage through the mind of innumerable meanings is not the creative event. These newly communicated meanings must be integrated with meanings previously acquired or natively developed if the creative event is to occur. This integrating is largely subconscious, unplanned and uncontrolled by the individual, save only as he may provide conditions favorable to its occurrence. This integrating is, then, the second subevent in the four, which together make the total event creative of all human value.

It is in this second subevent that man seems most helpless to do what must be done. The supreme achievements of this internally creative integration seem to occur in solitude, sometimes quite prolonged. When many meanings have been acquired through communication and through much action on the material world, there must be time for these to be assimilated. If one does not for a time draw apart and cease to act on the material world and communicate with others, the constant stream of new meanings will prevent the deeper integration. A period of loneliness and quiet provides for incubation and creative transformation by novel unification. If new meanings are coming in all the time, the integration is hindered by the new ingressions. The creative integration may be greatly aided by worship when worship allows a supreme good to draw into a unity of commitment to itself all the diverse values that have been received from many sources.

Jesus in the wilderness of "temptation" and in Gethsemane, Buddha alone under the Bo tree, Paul in the desert on the way to Damascus, Augustine at the time of his conversion—all these exemplify creative integration in solitude. Many of the great innovating ideas in literature, philosophy, and science have come to men in their loneliness. Also it seems that the individuals through whom the creative event has done most to transform and enrich the world with meaning have been more lonely than other men and have spent more time in lonely struggles. Yet with equal emphasis it must be said that they have had profound communication with others, if not face to face, then through writing and meditation on written words.

But mere solitude is not enough. Nothing can be more deadening and dangerous to the human spirit than solitude. If the mind degenerates into a state of torpor, as it generally does when isolated from communication with others, solitude is not creative. If the mind wanders in vagrant fancy, one idea following another by accidental association, there is no creativity. Or if one engages in minute and intensive analysis of a particular problem or is harassed with many worries, fears, and hopes, solitude may yield nothing. What is required of one in solitude that it may be fruitful? We do not know. We only know that one who is continuously in association with others is not likely to be the medium through whom great creative transformations occur. They who struggle in loneliness to overcome conditions that seem to block the good of human existence are the ones through whom this second stage in the creative event can be fulfilled. Whitehead has said that religion is what a man does with his solitude, and this is profoundly true, even though it be but part of the truth, since much more than solitude is needed. But one of the major unsolved problems of our existence is to learn how to make solitude creative instead of degenerative, as it most commonly is.

The creative event, in all four of its stages, is going on all the time in human existence. When we speak of prolonged solitude, on the one hand, and intensive and profound communication, on the other, as being prerequisite to creative transformation, we refer only to the more striking examples of it. In obscure and lowly form it is occurring continuously in human life, even when decline and disintegration also occur. The latter might be more rapid than the creative process until human life itself disappeared. Nevertheless, the creative event must continue so long as human life goes on because it is necessary to the human level of existence.

THE THIRD SUBEVENT

The expanding and enriching of the appreciable world by a new structure of interrelatedness pertaining to events necessarily follow from the first two subevents. It is the consequence of both the first two, not of either one by itself. If there has been intercommunication of meanings and if they have been creatively integrated, the individual sees what he could not see before; he feels what he could not feel. Events as they happen to him are now so connected with other events that his appreciable world has an amplitude unimaginable before. There is a range and variety of events, a richness of quality, and a reach of ideal possibility which were not there prior to this transformation.

This creative increase in qualitative meaning may not be dramatic and sudden; it may be imperceptible, except as one compares the world accessible to the man of thirty with what he could see and feel and do when he was one year old. However, one must remember that mere expanse in range and complexity of events is not an increase in qualitative meaning. Mere expanse may be achieved by multiplying and lengthening instrumental connections so that life becomes a burden and a weariness. When this happens, it is due to conditions which prevent the creative event from producing increase in intrinsic value. These conditions may be physiological, psychological, social, or historical and most probably are a combination of all of them.

Also it should be noted that this expanded world of qualitative meaning does not continue as a steady vision. The appreciable world in which each man lives from day to day expands and contracts through great variations. Yet the expanded world, once acquired, is not entirely lost, unless some degeneration sets in. It is not always immediately accessible, certainly not in the torpor of sleep and under many other conditions; yet one can at times recover what has been achieved if he retains his vitality and conditions are not too unfavorable. It is at least a memory and a conceivable hope, as it was not prior to the creative transformation.

One important thing to note is that this expanding of the appreciable world may make a man more unhappy and more lonely than he was before; for now he knows that there is a

[62]

greatness of good which might be the possession of man but is not actually achieved. One is reminded of the man who preached through all his life: "God is my Father and all you are my brothers," declaring continuously the blessedness of all-encompassing love and yet living in a world so barren of love that he must have been heart-breakingly lonely through all the days of his life. This lone-liness comes to agonized expression in the story of the temptation, Gethsemane, and the cry on the Cross.

Such a profound sense of loneliness is difficult for any man to bear, and yet it is the hope of the world because the man who feels it is aware of a greatness of love that might be but is not. Such loneliness indicates a vast emptiness which love between men might fill. This loneliness might become so deep and so intense that a man could not endure it unless he were permitted to die upon a cross for love; he might then fill an emptiness no actual love can fill by a sacrificial ex-pression of love. This seeking for a love that is never ful-filled might become so deep and so intense that a man would spend all his life preaching the principles of a kingdom of love that would sound like the beatitudes of madness in a world like this. They could be made intelligible only by attributing them to an illusion that the world was shortly to come to an end and would be transformed miraculously into such a kingdom. Perhaps such loneliness, born of such craving for love between men, would drive a man to that desperate madness in which he dreamed that by dying on a cross he could somehow bring this kingdom of love into existence.

This expanding of the appreciable world, accomplished by the third subevent, is not, then, in its entirety the actual achievement of an increase of value in this world, although it will include that. But it is also, perhaps even more, an expansion of the individual's capacity to appreciate and his apprehension of a good that might be, but is not, fulfilled.

It is the awakening of a hunger and a longing which, in one aspect at least, is a craving for more love between men than ever can be in the compass of his life.

THE FOURTH SUBEVENT

Widening and deepening community between those who participate in the total creative event is the final stage in creative good. The new structure of interrelatedness pertaining to events, resulting from communication and integration of meanings, transforms not only the mind of the individual and his appreciable world but also his relations with those who have participated with him in this occurrence. Since the meanings communicated to him from them have now become integrated into his own mentality, he feels something of what they feel, sees something of what they see, thinks some of their thought. He may disapprove, deny, and repudiate much that has been communicated to him from them, but this is a form of understanding and community. Perceptions and thoughts that are denied are as much a part of one's mentality as those affirmed. They may contribute as much to the scope and richness of one's mind, to one's appreciable world, and to the depth of one's community with others as perspectives which we affirm and with which we agree.

This community includes both intellectual understanding of one another and the feeling of one another's feelings, the ability to correct and criticize one another understandingly and constructively. It includes the ability and the will to co-operate in such manner as to conserve the good of life achieved to date and to provide conditions for its increase.

Paradoxical as it may sound, this increased community between persons may bring with it a sense of alienation and wistful hunger and even anguish, because one is now aware of misunderstandings in the other. He apprehends in the mind of the other, as he could not before, bitterness, fear, hate, scorn, pride, self-concern, indifference, and unresponsiveness when great need and great issues call. Likewise, the other may apprehend in him in somewhat different areas these ailments of the human spirit. Increase in genuine community, which is not mere increase in back-slapping geniality, will include all this discernment of illness and evil in one another. Increase in community is not necessarily pleasant; the good produced by the creative event brings increase in suffering as well as increase in joy; community brings a burden as well as a release. Those who cannot endure suffering cannot endure the increase of human good. Refusal to take suffering is perhaps the chief obstacle to increase in the good of human existence.[1]

These are the four subevents which together compose the creative event. They are locked together in such an intimate manner as to make a single, total event continuously recurrent in human existence. The creative event is one that brings forth in the human mind, in society and history, and in the appreciable world a new structure of interrelatedness, whereby events are discriminated and related in a manner not before possible. It is a structure whereby some events derive from other events, through meaningful connection with them, an abundance of quality that events could not have had without this new creation.

If by "new creation" one simply means something new in the world, a new event that never occurred before, then, of course, every event is creative. But that is not what is here meant. We are limiting our study chiefly to creative event as it occurs in communication between human individuals, and not even all communication displays it. It is true that there is a creative process that has worked through many centuries to bring forth the kind of organism that can participate in the creative event of human communication.

[1] How suffering is related to positive value will be considered in the next chapter.

The subhuman organism and the human organism at the submental level can have creative interaction with environment. This creative interaction which underlies the creativity of linguistic communication is (1) emerging awareness of a new structure of interrelatedness pertaining to events through a new way of interacting between the organism and its material situation; (2) integrating of this newly emergent structure with ways of distinguishing and relating events that had previously been acquired by the organism, thus achieving a more complex system of habits; and (3) consequent expanding and enrichment of the world of events having quality relative to the discriminating feeling-reactions of the organisms.

The thin layer of structure characterizing events knowable to the human mind by way of linguistic specification is very thin indeed compared to that massive, infinitely complex structure of events, rich with quality, discriminated by the noncognitive feeling-reactions of associated organisms human and nonhuman. This infinitely complex structure of events composing this vast society of interacting organisms and their sustaining or destructive environment is like an ocean on which floats the thin layer of oil representing the structures man can know through intellectual formulation. These structures knowable to the human mind can have depth and richness of quality only if they continue conjunct and integral with this deep complex structure of quality built up through countless ages before even the human mind appeared and now accessible to the feeling-reactions of the human organism. But when the human mind in its pride tries to rear its knowable structures as supreme goals of human endeavor, impoverishment, destruction, conflict, and frustration begin because these structures are then cut off from the rich matrix of quality found in organic, nonintellectual reactions.

Any meaning loses depth and richness of quality derived

from this unknown depth of structured events with quality determined by noncognitive feeling-reactions of the organism, when it is treated as an end instead of as a servant to creativity and all that creativity may produce below the level of human cognition. Man can use his knowledge and the truth he seeks to know to serve this creativity. Also he can so live as to keep his achieved meanings closely bound to the rich matrix of qualified events that cannot be known in their specific detail. When he does live thus, he experiences an uncomprehended depth and richness which give content to the abstractions of rationally comprehended structures. When he does not, life loses quality and value.

While we shall be concerned almost exclusively throughout this writing with specifically definable meanings and the creative intercommunication that generates them, because these are the fields of our intelligent endeavor, the importance of the deeper matrix of value must not be forgotten. We live in and by and for it. The creativity of intercommunication works to render this deeper matrix more vivid and appreciable to conscious awareness by way of specifiable structures known to the mind, here called "qualitative meaning." But all this is perverted when these structures of intelligent meaning are treated as though they had value apart from, or sovereign over, the deeper levels of value which are too complex and rich with quality for the human mind to comprehend. For the sake of simplicity of treatment and utility in action, we shall seem to exclude these deeper levels; but we must not ignore them.

We shall exclude from the creative event as here treated not only all the creativity that underlies and provides substructure for communication between human persons but also every event in human experience which does not bring with it a new structure of interrelatedness connecting it with other events in such a way that the human mind and

[67]

its appreciable world are transformed. Most events occurring in human existence are not appreciably creative in this sense. There may well be some minimum level of creativity going on all the time in human existence to compensate for the wastage and loss of qualitative meaning, which is also continuous. But even this continuity of creativity is one chain of events only and does not include innumerable others, some of the others being obstructive and destructive to all good, with no intrinsic good in them that can be called either "creative" or "created." Therefore, the creative event as here treated includes only those events which bring a new structure whereby the human mind distinguishes and relates events in such a way that there is more richness of quality in happenings as they occur and greater range and variety of appreciated possibility. This alone is the fourfold event described as emerging awareness of communicated meanings, the integrating of these meanings to create a new mentality in the individual, a new structure of qualitative meaning in the world, and a deeper and wider community among men.

It should be noted that the creative event, together with every one of the subevents, is an *-ing*. The subevents are emergings, integratings, expandings, deepenings, that is, they are not accomplished facts. After the event is accomplished, it is no longer creative. Hence the creative subevents (as well as the total creative event) are events in process. They are happenings in transit, not finished products, although they yield a finished product. The finished product of these four *-ings*, and hence the product of the total creative event, is always a new structure, whereby some events are more widely and richly related in meaningful connections.

This, then, is creative good. Created intrinsic good, on the other hand, is the appreciable world made richer with quality and meaning by this creative event. It is culture.

Instrumental good, which is also created, is a structure pertaining to events wherein the qualities of the events are not relevant to the value of the structure. It is civilization or technology, in contrast to culture. This threefold distinction of values into creative, created intrinsic, and created instrumental has practical importance, we believe, because the three kinds of value require different kinds of action if human good is to be promoted.

THE HUMAN PROBLEM

The human problem is to shape human conduct and all other conditions so that the creative event can be released to produce maximum good. While this event is continuously occurring in human life, more often despite the efforts of men than because of them, it is not always equally potent and effective. The richness and scope of meaning that it creates, moment by moment, may vary from a minimum to a maximum. What it creates may be small compared to what is destroyed by the impact of uncreative existence. Nevertheless, the whole struggle of human life, the basic problem of industry and government, of education and religion, of sex and personal conduct, of family and neighborhood organization, is to provide and to maintain those conditions wherein the creative event can produce the maximum of qualitative meaning with minimum destruction of previously developed structures which enrich the world.

Much in human life hampers the full release and creative power of this event. When men deceive or fear or distrust one another, when they inflict injustice or smart beneath it, they refuse to communicate meanings that are rich, deep, and precious to them. The worldly-wise wear a poker face, hide behind a mask of bravado or indifference lest others discover the absurd and despicable pretensions they know within themselves. They hold back, lest servants disobey master, lest heroes be dragged from their pedestals. Fear, hate, and suspicion; deceit, concealment, and exploitation; misunderstanding, indifference, and sloth; vindictive cruelty, lust, and sadistic desire; complacency, arrogance, and the insatiable need to feed the ego—all these block and frustrate the creative event. The list runs on without end. Thus the great problem is how to provide conditions more favorable for this creative event so that it can bring forth structures which will endow events with more richness of quality and scope of meaning.

CREATIVE EVENT BIOLOGICALLY INTERPRETED

We have been discussing the creative event solely in human terms; but creativity of a sort operates at subhuman levels, as well as in history. As the sensitivity of an organism increases, as its possible responses become more diverse, as the nervous network by which these responses can be associated with one another becomes more intricate, the organism can distinguish more events in the passage of existence and more interconnections between them. This is the creative process on the biological level.

Far down the animal scale we can trace the first discrimination of events and the first transformation of these events into signs communicating the quality of past happenings. The lower animals come back to the familiar place where they had shelter, food, and drink; they come back to their young and to their mate. The dog greets his master with apparent joy, as though the sight and smell of this familiar figure awakened some of the qualities of past events.

In the human organism sensitivity of discrimination, diversity of response, and complexity of association are vastly expanded. Consequently, for the human organism, far more of the world is discriminated into distinguishable events, and far more of these events are transformed into signs. They communicate more abundantly the qualities of past events and predict more widely and freely the possibilities of the future.

The human organism distinguishes more events in the passage of existence than the dog, and the dog more than the amoeba. Yet even the minutest cell is an organism which breaks up the passage of existence into events. It does this, first, simply by being an organism with its own span of temporal and spatial existence. Thus it forms one single event marked off from all else by the organic character of its own growth and death. But it does more than exist: It draws away from one kind of stimulus; it may grope toward another. Its several reactions are unitary events, distinguished from one another. Furthermore, these reactions distinguish and relate units of passage in what is outside the organism. So, with the organism at its center, a world begins to emerge. It is a world (not merely the passage of existence) by virtue of a multiplicity of events distinguished and related by noncognitive, but discriminating, reactions of the organism. These events might be classified thus: those made, first, by the mere existence of the organism in question; second, by the distinguishable reactions of the organism; and, third, by the distinctions and relations made by these reactions in the passage of existence outside the organism. This world may be very tiny, dim, and vague; but it is the beginning of a world in the sense that events of some sort are distinguished and related to one another. By the time man comes into existence, this world of events having quality is infinite in its complexity and richness and, when we live rightly, reaches our conscious awareness like a deep swell of an ocean beneath the thin layer of our rationally specified structures.

Whether or not the world in its totality was ever nothing more than such a minute and vague beginning of distinguishable and related events, centered in a microscopic organism, we cannot say. We do not know, on the other hand, that vast and complicated organisms may not exist even now in forms quite unimaginable to us. Possibly such organisms react in such a manner as to have a world vaster than our human cosmos because they distinguish and relate events on a scale and with a richness of quality utterly beyond our powers, as our powers in this respect exceed the minute cell. Relative to them we would be minute cells. We may not think there are giants in the earth, or gods, but we mention this speculation to guard against the dogmatism which utterly closes the imagination to unexplored possibilities.

Nor would we dispute whether or not there is some kind of metaphysical reality wholly independent of the reactions of the organism and wholly independent of events. All that is here asserted is that, in terms of human action, the only world we have anything to do with, the only world that contributes to good and evil in any sense that bears upon what we do about it, is the world of events. The existence and reactions of organisms, and these only, can break the continuity of the passage of existence into events. When and if there was ever a time that simple and minute cells of life alone existed in organic form, the only possible events and hence the only possible world were nothing else than the units of reality, discriminated and related by the existence and by the reactions of these organisms. As organisms become more sensitive and more diversely responsive, with more capacity for feeling, the world becomes more ample, more rich with quality, and more meaningful. The creation of such organisms is the creation of the world. This is the work of the creative event at the biological level.

By no means are all biological changes in the direction of greater sensitivity and diversified responsiveness. The protective devices—such as heavy shell, great speed, tusks and claws, and other specializations—which have enabled many organisms to survive have also limited the diversification of their responses and the fineness of their sensitivity. Though these organisms have improved as mechanisms equipped for survival, as agents for sensing value they have degenerated.

The creative event works against great difficulties in developing organisms that can react with fine discrimination, diversification, and feeling. One difficulty is to keep alive the organism with the sensitivity and responsiveness required for any high level of value. Such organisms must live in the presence of frequent death and constant danger; they can have no security except by riding on the backs of tougher organisms.

The creative event, it would seem, can produce great values only with the most sensitive organisms living dangerously, surviving only by mutual support, by intercommunication, and by letting the tougher forms of life take the impact of inert and sterile lumps of existence.

It may be that man's present organism is not fit to undergo the transformations which the recurrent creative event must achieve in order to reach higher levels of value than we can imagine today. The organisms which we now have are not capable of reacting appreciatively to as many different sorts of people as we meet in the complexities of modern life. Our organisms do not have the resources of diverse and complex feelings sufficient to absorb appreciatively the many rich meanings that we might derive from creative interchange with one another. Perhaps the human organism does not have the nervous energy and capacity for diversified and complex feeling that is required to enter appreciatively into the riches of other races and cultures in a manner necessary to avoid destructive conflict. In any case, further creative advance seems to call for capacities beyond the reach of most human organisms as we know them. It may be that disciplines in sexual reproduction and hygiene of the body will have to be practiced to bring forth a better human species. Many other rigorous conditions may have to be met before we can realize the potentialities of value in our present situation and avoid the destruction which this situation brings when the values are not realized.

Even more obvious is the need for change in social and psychological conditions, if we are to move up the steeps of greater good under the transformative power of the creative event. If we have not the physiological, moral, and religious capacity to mount these steeps, one of two things is likely to happen. Either these capacities will be developed by searching out the conditions whereby they can be created in us, or else we shall fall back to lower levels with much suffering and destruction. If we cannot go along with the creative process, we shall suffer the fate which other cultures and civilizations have suffered when they reached a like limit in their capacity for further creative transformation. They sank into decline with a spreading sense of despair and cynicism.

Men recoil from the breaking of comfortable stereotypes, from the often painful stretching of perceptions and appreciations, from the reconstruction of the world relative to themselves and their interests. Men sense the loss of customary values in this breaking and remaking and cannot apprehend the values yet to be created which lie beyond the reaches of imagination. A kind of religious faith is required by which one commits himself to the creative event with a final devotion.

CREATIVE GOOD IS SUPRA-HUMAN

Serving the creative event that renews itself is the work of man—the supreme vocation of human history. Innumerable things can be done by men to remove obstacles and provide sustaining conditions which release the power of creative good to produce value. Every serious practical and theoretical problem finds its solution in clearing the path for creative transformation, and there is nothing else to be done that is worthy of man. Meeting the demands of this source of human good calls for all the moral rigor, all the labor and sacrifice, all the religious commitment of faith which human capacity can afford. There is, therefore, plenty for man to do in helping to create a better world.

The emphasis just made is important because of a persistent misunderstanding that arises when it is said that man cannot do what the creative event does. All we mean to say is that the creative event produces a structure which could not be intended by the human mind before it emerges, either in imagination or in the order of actual events.

Human effort cannot accomplish anything which the human mind cannot imagine. If something results from human effort which was not intended and which the human mind could not imagine prior to its occurrence, it is an accident relative to human effort. It is not, of course, an accident in the absolute sense of being without cause. But, even though the existence and the labors of men are part of the many causes issuing in this consequence, the consequence is not the work of man if the human intent sought a result different from this consequence.

The structure of value produced by the creative event cannot be caused by human intention and effort, because it can be produced only by a transformation of human intention and effort. We saw how the creative event transforms the human mind, the reactions of the human organism, the community of associated individuals, and the very structure of events as they occur in the appreciable world. Obviously, this cannot be the work of man in the sense that he can foresee the structure yet to be created. He cannot strive to achieve it before he has sufficient imagination to conceive it and the required hunger to seek it.

Many protest when we claim that man cannot be creative. Of course, man in many senses of the term is creative: he exercises his imagination to envision something that never was in existence and then proceeds to construct it. But man cannot exercise his imagination to envision what is inaccessible to imagination prior to the transformation which gives his mind the added reach. Man can do only what lies within the scope of the imagination that he has; he can seek only the good that he, to date, is able to appreciate. To do what lies beyond the reach of his imagination, a greater imagination must be created in him. To seek a good beyond what he can appreciate, a greater appreciation must be developed in him. The creative event, not man himself, creates this greater imagination and this more profound and discriminating appreciation.

What we have said demonstrates that man cannot be creative in the sense in which this term applies to the creative event we have been describing. Man's creative ability is something produced in him as a consequence of the prior working of the creative event. To fall into controversy over whether or not man is creative is to use the same word for different things. Such an argument is as futile as a merry-go-round.

The creative event is supra-human, not in the sense that it works outside of human life, but in the sense that it creates the good of the world in a way that man cannot do. Man cannot even approximate the work of the creative event. He would not come any closer to it if his powers were magnified to infinity, because the infinite increase of his ability would have to be the consequence of the prior working of the creative event.

The work of the creative event is different in kind from the work of man. Any attempt to measure the power of man against the power of the creative event is defeated at the start because one cannot compare the two. It is true that man can set up conditions that obstruct the work of the creative event so that the good it produces will be much less than it would have been if men had met its demands. Also, he can serve it by removing obstacles. Men can do this in their personal conduct, in the organization of society, in the physical and biological regime which they maintain. When men do meet its demands, the creative event faithfully produces a far greater abundance of human good. But the actual creative event is never the work of man and cannot be. In that sense it is supra-human and transcendent, but the transcendence pertains to its character as creative of the appreciable world created to date. This appreciable world contains the meanings and the things, the goods and the goals, which are subject to human control. It is the world in which man lives his conscious life for the most part. Since creativity is not readily accessible to awareness, we can speak of creativity as "transcendent." But it is not transcendent in the sense of being nontemporal, nonspatial, and immaterial. It can be discovered in this world by proper analysis.[2]

Since this creativity has the character just stated, it was almost inevitable that man should think it supernatural. Nature, for the ordinary man, is his appreciable world. Therefore, what is not accessible to his appreciation must be supernatural, especially when it is creative of this world which he appreciates. Creativity is not beyond all human appreciation. It can be appreciated, and, when proper social conditions and required knowledge have been achieved, it can be known as a part of the temporal, spatial, material world. But, generally speaking, it has been mythically represented as supernatural; and, if the creative event be of the sort we have described, the human mind could hardly have approached it otherwise until certain cultural conditions and scientific knowledge had been achieved, especially knowledge in the fields of biology, psychology, and social

[2] See chap. x for the difference between functional transcendence and metaphysical transcendence. Creative good is functionally transcendent but not metaphysically so.

psychology. Expert specialists in these several fields might not find it, but one who can draw from all of them and from other cultural conditions might well do so. Many have done so in recent years.

Like the ancient supernaturalism, and in opposition to almost all religions and philosophies that stand over against supernaturalism, the naturalism here defended repudiates the supremacy in value of all the goods and goals of the created appreciable world and turns to what creates them for the sovereign good of life.

INSTRUMENTAL VALUE

"Instrumental" refers to what man can use and control as a means to an end. As we have seen, man cannot use and control the creative event because the structure of value it produces can never in its specific character be intended, desired, or sought by man. Man can, of course, know that the creative event will produce good and can welcome the need of his and the world's transformation; but he cannot know the kind and form of good it will produce, and if he could foresee, *per impossibile*, with his untransformed perception, what the creative event would produce, it would at times seem hateful and fearful and the opposite of good. The kind and form of good actually produced by creativity inevitably transcends, and in some ways runs counter to, the present order of human desire; for one of the necessary subevents of the creative event is precisely this transformation of the previously existing order of human desire. The primary demand which the creative event makes upon man is that he give himself over to it to be transformed in any way that it may require. Obviously, man cannot use as a means or instrument the generative process which transforms him so as to create values which he cannot in their specific nature anticipate or see or desire.

[78]

CREATIVE GOOD IS ABSOLUTE GOOD

The claim that creative good is the only absolute good can be defended only after we are clear on what is meant by "absolute" in this context. When we speak of "absolute good" we shall mean, first of all, what is good under all conditions and circumstances. It is a good that is not relative to time or place or person or race or class or need or hope or desire or belief. It is a good that remains changelessly and identically the same in character so far as concerns its goodness. It is a good that would continue to be so even if all human beings should cease to exist. It is a good that retains its character even when it runs counter to all human desire. It is a good that continues to be identically the same good even when it works with microscopic cells prior to the emergence of any higher organism.

Creative good meets all these requirements pertaining to absolute good. Its goodness is not relative to human desire, or even to human existence, although it is also good when desired and when working in the medium of human existence.

On the other hand, created good—the structure of meaning connecting past and future that we feel and appreciate—is relative value in all the senses that stand in contrast to the absolute as just described. The particular chains of qualitative meaning having value for man do not necessarily have value for microbes. The structure of interrelatedness pertaining to events which increases quality and meaning relative to one organism or race or class or culture will not ordinarily be equally good for another. Thus created good does not retain the same character of goodness under all circumstances and conditions and in relation to every different sort of organism, human person, or social culture. The creative good which does retain its character of goodness under all these changing conditions is, then, the only absolute good.[3]

A second mark of absolute good is that its demands are unlimited. A good is absolute if it is always good to give myself, all that I am and all that I desire, all that I possess and all that is dear to me, into its control to be transformed in any way that it may require. If there is some point beyond which the cost is too great to justify the claim that a good makes upon me, then it is relative in that respect. Creative good is absolute in this sense for there is no amount of created good opposed to it which can diminish the claim that it makes upon me. The value of the creative source of all good is immeasurable compared to any particular instance of good derived from this source.

Thus in a third way, inseparable from the second, creative good is absolute. It is unlimited in its demands because it is infinite in value. Its worth is incommensurable by any finite quantity of created good. No additive sum of good produced in the past can be any compensation for the blockage of that creativity which is our only hope for the future. And the created good of the past sinks into oblivion when not continuously revitalized by the recurrent working of the creative event.

Fourth, absolute good is unqualified good. There must be no perspective from which its goodness can be modified in any way. Always, from every standpoint, its good must remain unchanged and self-identical, whether from the worm's view or the man's view, whether under the aspect of eternity or under the aspect of time, whether viewed

[3] "Absolute" in any intelligible sense cannot mean "out of relation." It is relative to conditions, circumstances, organisms, and the like; but its character of goodness does not change when these relations change. Instead of being out of all relations, it is rather the one kind of goodness that, without losing its identity, can enter into all relations. It is good always and everywhere, therefore relative to everything.

from the standpoint of the beginning or the ending, whether judged by its origin or by its final outcome, whether viewed as means or as end. In respect to created good one can always find some standpoint from which its value disappears or changes; it must be qualified. But in this sense, too, creative good is absolute.

Finally, creative good is absolute in that it is entirely trustworthy. We can be sure that the outcome of its working will always be the best possible under the conditions, even when it may seem to us to be otherwise. Even when it so transforms us and our world that we come to love what now we hate, to serve what now we fight, to seek what now we shun, still we can be sure that what it does is good. Even when its working re-creates our minds and personalities, we can trust it.

We can also be sure that creative good will always be with us. When all other good is destroyed, it springs anew; it will keep going when all else fails. In this dual sense creative good is absolutely trustworthy: it always produces good; it never fails.

A further claim might be made for an absolute good, but this claim cannot apply to the creative event. Neither can it be applied coherently to any other interpretation of the nature of absolute good. This claim is that absolute good means all-powerful good. It means a good that overrules all evil so that in the end everything will come out all right, no matter how long and how great the intervening evils may be. According to neo-orthodoxy, this blissful outcome is postponed to "the end of history," whatever that may mean. There is a transcendent realm, so it is asserted, where perfect and almighty good reigns supreme; but in our world of time and space and matter and history this almighty power of good is only partially regnant. Life may be a valley of frustration, but nothing can prevent ultimate, absolute, and complete regnancy of supreme value, somehow, sometime, somewhere, although the human mind cannot know how this may be.

The claim that any kind of good is almighty cannot be defended. Creative good is not absolute in that sense, but neither is anything else.

CONCLUSION

Creative good will be our standard and guiding principle in dealing with all problems concerning good and evil and better and worse. Anything is good if it sustains and promotes the release of that kind of intercommunication among men termed the "creative event." It is evil if it does the opposite. One act or course of conduct is better than another if it provides more amply the conditions enabling the creative event to produce qualitative meaning; it is worse if some alternative would be more favorable. Kinds of legislation, types of economic order, methods and goals of education, habits and moral practices, forms of religion—these and any other proposals for changing or maintaining the established state of affairs are evil if some practicable alternative should enable men to communicate more fully and freely in a manner fostering creative transformation. They are good if they facilitate this event more fully than anything else under the circumstances.

According to this standard, one good is not better than another because it contains a greater quantity of good in itself. One might be much greater in value so far as concerns its content of created good. But if the lesser served to release more fully the potency of the creative event, it is the one to choose. The Roman Empire, with all its culture, may have contained far more qualitative meaning than the little Christian sect. Nevertheless, if the latter could release more widely and deeply among men the kind of intercommunication creative of all good, the latter should be chosen and the

Empire rejected. Thus the quantitative standard by which one created good is measured against another is not the standard directive of wise choice.

The problem of choice involves not only good but also evil. Neither can we fully understand the nature of good until we see it in silhouette against the fact of evil. So we turn to a study of evil as one kind of value no less important than good.

CHAPTER IV

Good and Evil

THE consideration of positive value cannot be carried further without an examination of negative value. Evil is not negative in the sense of being the mere absence of good; for particular instances of evil are powerful and aggressive. But there is no general principle which characterizes all instances of evil except the negative principle of being opposed to the good. When instances of good are analyzed, they all display a substratum of positive identity, being either creative, created, or instrumental. But evil at one time and place may be totally different in character from evil at any other time and place.

No single event, such as a particular war, is either good or evil when taken by itself. To discover the evil or the good of the war one must either relate the total event called the "war" to other events or break the total event down into subevents. If one breaks a war into subevents, he finds both good and evil. Some of the subevents are so related to one another and to the past and future of human life that we must call them "good." Even the pacifist who denounces war as evil in every respect would at least have to say that some of his own activities are good. These are as truly a part of the war as the soldier's acts of heroic devotion and would not have occurred without it. War calls forth the best and the worst that can issue from the hearts of men. Causes both good and evil, along with ends and consequences, become inextricably tangled and intertwined as wars run their course. This is one of the primary evidences we have of the mixed character of life. So it is with every complex occurrence. One must always analyze it into sub-events to see how these are related to one another and to the good, or else one must trace the relation of the total event to other happenings external to itself.

What is really good or evil generally lies hidden in the context of the thing bearing the name of a good or an evil. An organization of gangsters may be called evil, but the structure of interrelated happenings which is the real evil is much more complex and pervasive than the gang itself. Hence it is more difficult to draw the boundary lines precisely about the evil than it is to specify the limits and character of the gang. Good and evil include and cut across other things like gangs and wars, which are more simple and easily distinguished.

As long as conditions remain the same, generation after generation, things like gangs and wars that bear the name of evil but are not truly identical with evil serve, nonetheless, to guide conduct fairly well because they signalize the context in which evil lies. They are the red lights which indicate the evil presence. But in times of rapid innovation, especially in a time when men move from small slowly changing societies to a swiftly changing Great Society, these old "taboos" become a source of confusion and error. Evil has changed its locus and its character, and the old signals mislead. In such a time men are chiefly engaged in getting rid of these "senseless" constraints, "provincial" prohibitions, and "puritanical" scruples which hinder the free exercise of intelligence.

Such a time is peculiarly dangerous. The labels of "evil" are taken off the things which are not in themselves necessarily and always evil, but the real nature of the evil is not brought forth. Men forget that evil is a definite and specifiable character of events; it is what obstructs or destroys the good. Though evil is still present and may be worse than ever, people have no reliable guides to lead them from it and to the good. It is not enough to distinguish the good; one must also be able to distinguish the evil. Indeed, the one cannot be set forth in clear outline except against the background of the other. Let us, then, try to clarify some of the characteristics of evil.

SOME DISTINGUISHING CHARACTERISTICS OF EVIL

Since intrinsic good is of two basic kinds, opposition to good is also of two kinds. The evil opposing created good is destructive; the evil opposing creative good is obstructive. Created good can be destroyed and always is being destroyed in some measure; creative good cannot be destroyed, but it can be obstructed and always is to some degree. Of these two general kinds of evil, the most deadly by far is the obstructive, even though the word "destructive" carries a more evil connotation in common usage. This is natural. Men are usually more concerned about created good than about creative; they are more disturbed over the evil that attacks what they have in their hands than over the evil which opposes the creation of what they cannot envision and do not yet specifically want. But creative good is the only ultimate and absolute good. Therefore, what opposes it is more basically evil than what opposes created good.

It is important to note that creative good is obstructed but not destroyed; for creativity can be driven down to lower and lower levels of existence, and it can be forced to work with lower levels of created good. If all the more highly sensitive and responsive organisms were destroyed, creativity would have to develop qualitative meaning by way of more brutish organisms. If the human level were wiped out of existence, the creative process would occur only at the levels of life that still persisted. If all living organisms were destroyed, creativity would have to work at the level of matter from which the first new living

[86]

organisms might once more be created. But creativity working at the lowest possible levels of existence is no less good
than it is at the higher. The "lower level" applies to what
it must work with, not to the creativity itself. Creativity
carries the hope and the potency of all the highest good
that ever will be. It has this absolute character just as fully
at the lowest level as at the highest.

One might speculate with the idea that everything in
existence might be so destroyed or transformed that nothing
whatsoever remained which could be the standing ground
of creative good. If that should occur, creativity would be
destroyed; but such speculation is idle because we have no
more evidence concerning ultimate endings than we have
about ultimate origins. All that we know is that creativity
always has sprung anew from lower levels when the higher
levels were destroyed. Thus, so far as we know, evil can
destroy created good but can only obstruct creative good.

ABSOLUTE EVIL

Many insist that evil must be eternally overruled and
mastered by an omnipotent deity, a God both all-good *and*
all-powerful. This claim is very doubtfully supported by
evidence. Many devices have been used to solve this "problem of evil," namely, how there can be so much evil in a
world in which a benevolent God is absolutely in control.
The desperation, diversity, and constant change in the ideas
that have been used to "solve" this problem of evil should
be warning enough that this is only a pseudo-problem.
Such pseudo-problems are common not only in religion but
in all areas of human living. The problem actually posed is
not to find the truth but to find some way, by hook or by
crook, to hold fast to a belief when evidence is insufficient to
support it.

Any claim that divine power must overrule evil denies the
reality of evil. The neo-orthodox and the transcendentalist,

the absolute idealist and those who believe in the conventional "Heavenly Father," all explain evil away, although they may not so intend. Evil is not truly evil if it is predetermined to be overruled or if it is bounded above, below, before, and after by an eternity of perfect good. If this is true, then our war against evil becomes a kind of sardonic joke. All these interpretations deny the most important distinction in human existence—the distinction between good and evil.

Many who thus deny the ultimate reality of evil proudly take the titles of "pessimist" and "realist." They talk at length about the evils of the world and the sin of man. This "realism" helps to conceal from themselves and from others their romantic optimism on ultimate issues, since they claim that evil must sometime, somehow, be overruled by good. They refuse to face the ultimate reality of evil, and they cover the evasion by means of a vociferous pessimism about this present world.

There is no conscious hypocrisy or insincerity in these "pessimists" and "realists." They are driven by the coercion of a faith they have inherited, which drives them to hold to the belief in a good that is absolute in the sense of keeping all evil subject to its power. Belief in the overruling power of good is tied so deeply into their faith that they would have no faith at all if this were taken from them. Their personal attachments, all the work of their lives, the zest and courage and hope, the very structure of their minds and personalities, would tumble to ruin if this were taken away.

The unintentional, yet no less pernicious, consequence of this overbelief, held against the evidence, is that it sickens the spirit. Men drugged with this belief cannot live with power in the face of things as they are. When the belief is threatened, they turn desperately to some new device with which to defend it against the evidence; for, without this assurance that good will surely prevail in the end, "life is meaningless," so they say. Yet many have lived and do now live courageously and constructively, without any injections from this belief. Hence the alleged meaninglessness of life without this belief is only a confession that one has become addicted to the drug and cannot live without it.

What ground for hope is left when evil is no longer kept surely under the control of an almighty power by means of a belief? Obviously, the first reply is that a belief determines nothing. The only ground for hope is the evidence. Let us survey very briefly the evidence on the fortunes of good and evil through the centuries.

People often deny that there has been any increase of good. Of course, they are correct if they specify something to be good which has not increased. If by good they mean what they like, then it may well be that the world is becoming less to their liking. But we have stated what we understand good to be, and, with this understanding, the world has certainly been growing better. To be sure, not every year and not inevitably does good increase; but since our planet began to cool and the first specks of life appeared, qualitative meaning has certainly increased.

Still others claim that, no matter how much good has been gained, far more has been lost in the process. The more widely and richly the world is structured with quality and meaning, the more of such good is being destroyed. They say that, when no such good existed or only a little, very little destruction could occur. Likewise, as creativity develops organisms more capable of undergoing transformations leading to rapid increase of good, the greater becomes the obstruction to such increase relative to what might have been. The issue succinctly stated is this: The greater the possibilities for good, the greater the possibilities for evil. When nothing existed making possible great and rapid increase, there could be no obstruction to great and rapid increase. But to make such a complaint the basis for saying that the world is getting worse seems like a whining child that will not accept the stern conditions of growing up.

Furthermore, this increase of good that has occurred upon the planet is not an accident. It is the working of a known and definite reality we have described as creative good. This creative good works against obstacles and overcomes them with a power qualitatively and immeasurably different from man's.

The second ground of hope is even more reliable than this empirical fact of the increase of good throughout millions of years. We have no knowledge of any evil that can destroy creativity. It can be obstructed. The good that it has created can be destroyed. It can be thrown back to begin again at lower levels of created good. But all available evidence indicates that it can begin anew at any level and construct again the good toward higher levels. Creative good is absolutely universal good, unlimited in its claims, infinite in its worth, unqualified in its value, and absolutely trustworthy in the sense that it abides with us through all things and will always produce good. Such good is enough to give fighting hope to any man unless his spirit has become flabby through habituation to a belief which denies the reality of evil.

If all this is true, it follows that evil is definitely real. There is no kind of reality called "ultimate" or "absolute" which does not have its opposing evil along with its good. Creative good is absolute good, and the evil that opposes it is absolute evil. Let us once more make clear what we mean by "absolute."

Opposition to creative good is absolute evil, first of all, because it is evil everywhere and under all circumstances. Its evil is not relative to time and place and person, to interest, need, social situation, or culture. When creative good is obstructed, the obstruction is evil, regardless of what people may want, regardless of what may be the prevailing standards, regardless of what benefit may be derived from this obstruction in terms of conserving some created good. On the other hand, the destruction of created good is not absolute evil. There are times and places where it is good to destroy created good. At least, there are many occasions when created good must be transformed in order to provide for the creation of some further good, and this transformation may seem to be destruction to the persons involved. There are many instances of relative evil in the sense that certain people are deprived of some created good. What is loss for one is often gain for others. But when it comes to creative good, such judgments do not apply. When creative intercommunication is hindered, that hindrance is evil, no matter what other issues may be involved.

Of course, obstruction to creative good is a matter of degree. Obstruction is never complete in the sense that creativity cannot operate at all or ever again. Such obstruction would be almighty evil; but there is no almighty evil, any more than there is an almighty good. "Absolute" in that sense does not apply either to good or to evil.

The evil that assumes the form of obstructing creative good is absolute in a second sense—it is unqualified evil. That means that it is evil from every standpoint. Whether one takes the viewpoint of the cosmic whole or the view of some part; whether one views it from eternity or from time, as a condition promoting freedom and moral responsibility or any other alleged end, from every angle of vision it is evil to obstruct creative good. It only magnifies the evil to try to interpret opposition to creativity as somehow from some view not really evil after all. On the other hand, destruction of created good is not unqualified evil. It is relative evil in this sense of being qualified when the perspective is widened or otherwise changed.

Obstructive evil is absolute in a third sense: It is ultimate. There is no original source of good that "permits" it;

here is no deity that opens the way for it; neither is there any end of history or other consummation of good into which it will ultimately issue. However, this ultimacy does not mean that there is anything discoverable in the world which predetermines its everlasting existence. It may go on forever, or it may not.

Final outcomes, as well as all original beginnings, are entirely beyond the scope of our knowing. Anyone who claims to know by revelation or otherwise the ultimate beginning and ending is deceiving himself and others. If we speculate at all about the final outcome, we are doing so not to support any alleged knowledge but for the opposite reason—to demonstrate that no one knows. For example, suppose that in time all evil were driven out of existence and everything was perfect in its goodness. If evil still hovered as a possibility over the existing world (and it seems probable that it would), there still would be work to do. If evil were not even a possibility for our world, the very fact that there would be nothing to do would be evil. We do not mean that evil in existence is a necessary component of a good world; we are speaking of evil driven not only out of existence but also out of possibility. However, these speculations are cognitively worthless, being of use only to show that the outcome is indeterminate and that there is no necessity that evil must always exist, although it probably will. In any case, the evil of obstructing creativity is absolute in this third sense that it neither originates nor ends in good necessarily. It is not an episode of time rounded out by an eternity that is perfect in its goodness. If good should reign supreme and all evil disappear entirely, that would be only a possible outcome in the face of great hazard and would depend on the uncertain victory of an undetermined struggle.

Finally, the evil under consideration is absolute in the sense of being unconfined. It is not held down to certain limits by a power which is so mighty that we can be sure evil will never cross those limits. This must not be interpreted to mean that evil will rage rampant forever, reaching ever further into new areas of existence; the assertion is only that it is not necessarily bound to any limits. How completely it is kept down, how closely it will be confined, how narrowly restricted, will depend on the fortunes of the great struggle. The outcome is not predetermined by the nature of reality.

We can state the issue in other language. Evil is not a domesticated animal, kept inside a pen by a power which holds it under control. Evil is a wild thing; it wanders abroad because the creative power of good has not been able to confine it or annihilate it. All other views represent evil as kept by the Almighty in a pen to do what the power of good may require of it, until the time comes when it shall be slaughtered. When we say that evil is absolute in this last sense, we mean to contradict this view of evil as inclosed within bounds beyond which we can be sure that it cannot pass.

Thus obstructive evil is absolute on four counts: it is universal, unqualified, ultimate, and unconfined. Destructive evil, on the other hand, is relative because it is just the opposite in all these respects.

ARE PAIN AND SUFFERING EVIL?

Suffering is one of the evils of human life in the sense that it bears that label in common usage. The label is justified in the way that other labels are: evil often lurks hidden in the context of suffering. Nevertheless, in the contextualistic interpretation of good and evil, suffering is not necessarily and intrinsically evil. In some contexts suffering is a good. Our point, speaking as contextualists, is that suffering in itself is neither good nor evil, it may be the one or the other

[93]

according to the way it does or does not serve the creative event.

The suffering we have to confront and endure is divided into two kinds: the relatively simple kind of suffering which we experience in physical pain coming from, and consisting primarily in, stimulation of pain-nerves; and that other more complex kind of suffering commonly called "mental," which plagues the higher reaches and more subtle depths of the human spirit. Pain and suffering both have a psychological component; but when we say that suffering only is "mental," we point to a spiritual significance in suffering which is ordinarily absent from the physiological disturbance of pain.

It is clear that the simple event of pain, which we feel in the form of smart and sting and throb and ache, is not an unmitigated evil for human life. Pain of this kind can serve instrumentally to warn us against greater evil. It has an important biological function in commanding and focusing our attention upon the source of pain in order that the organism will so act as to escape from danger. Besides this elemental protective function, pain also serves to stimulate the human organism to energetic and varied action. In this way it reduces the propensity to sink into a routine stupor. This propensity to contented stupor, which is certainly one of the automatic drives in human life, would be far more deadly than it is if pain did not serve recurrently to deliver us from it. The pain of hunger, heat, and cold arouse the organism ever anew to varied action by which qualitative meaning can grow. Without pain as a goad, this growth might never have achieved the dimensions it now has.

In fact, under some conditions, pain can even serve the growth of qualitative meaning by way of intercommunication. When pain becomes significantly endowed with communicable meaning, it may be woven into that web of meaning that carries the good of life. Pain does not often

[94]

serve the creative event in this way, but under some conditions it may; and when it does, it takes on the character of intrinsic good.

However, in other respects and in the large, pain is an evil, destroying the created good of life and obstructing the working of its source. This simple event often becomes a burden and a curse, assuming a uniquely obsessive guise. It chains attentive awareness to itself and cuts off the range and depth of meaning which the mind can entertain. For all its simplicity, pain becomes a tremendous evil when it persists and recurs so stubbornly that it cannot be escaped and holds awareness upon itself. The individual may then become so obsessed with his pain that he turns away from all interplay of thought and feeling. He wants to hear nothing of the wants and needs and joys of others; he becomes a complaining, bitter pulp of tormented flesh. Physical pain, sheer and simple, has served through the ages as a blunt reminder of the fact that so mundane and undramatic a series of events as pain can strip us of our humanity, walling us up within ourselves, cutting us off from the creativity that alone can save.

Suffering is very different from pain. Pain is an event or series of events and may not bear any communicable meaning beyond the barest minimum; suffering, on the other hand, is a meaning or system of meanings and may not be an event at all to the sufferer beyond that minimum event which serves as a sign. Sorrow is a kind of suffering; when some dear one dies, it is not the bare event of death that generates the sorrow; it is the meaning of that event. The meaning of that event is that I shall no longer be able to communicate with that individual. All that interchange which enriched our lives will no longer occur. All the memories of past events rise up with new vividness when connected with this event of the death.

As sorrow pertains not to the present immediate event

that is happening to me but rather to the meaning of that event, so also with regret, despair, sense of failure, shame, humiliation, sense of loss, disillusionment, and all the other forms of suffering. Meaning, let us remember, is here defined as that relation between events whereby a present happening enables one to feel the qualities and discern the interrelatedness of many other happenings and possibilities which do not physically impinge upon the organism at the time. Pain impinges upon the organism here and now. It is a present physical modification of the organism, whether it carries any meaning or not. Suffering always is a meaning with only that minimum present physical modification of the organism required to serve as a sign.

This difference between pain and suffering is of basic importance in our interpretation of value as qualitative meaning. Increase of value is increase of qualitative meaning. Pain may add no qualitative meaning to the world and frequently diminishes it by hypnotically focusing the mind upon the quality of the present event of pain to the exclusion of all else. Suffering, on the other hand, always adds some meaning, since it is essentially the meaning and not the present event alone that is the suffering.

Since suffering is a meaning, it can be communicated readily, as pain cannot. Through intercommunication, suffering can be woven into a growing web whereby the qualitative meaning of history increases. The legends and the folklore, the art and the story, the recorded history and the celebrations of a people, are almost always communications about past events in which suffering has played a considerable part. They concern heroism and devotion, struggle and triumph. These can scarcely occur without suffering. It would seem that suffering, even more than happiness, leads to that kind of communication whereby creativity increases the good of life. Certainly, the intermixture of suffering and happiness rather than happiness without suffering is re-

quired for this. If great art teaches us anything about the
nature of man and the good of life, it tells us that suffering
is intrinsic and essential to the increase of qualitative meaning.

It seems that human living without suffering always con-
geals into complacent contentment at the lower levels of the
social order and complacent arrogance at the higher. In
both cases this complacency resists that intercommunication with others which yields the greater good. Furthermore, in all intercommunication that is free, full, and
honest, we expose ourselves to the criticism of others and
are forced to criticize ourselves and acknowledge in ourselves often much that is evil. This cannot be done without
suffering. Then there is the humiliation and misunderstanding, the treachery and betrayal of trust, to which one always
exposes one's self in such openness. There is the ridicule and
the shame, as well as the honor and the love, the disillusionment and loss of what was loved, the learning to appreciate what was alien or even hateful at first. This and more
must be encountered if one enters the full tide of life and
moves through the creative transformations whereby qualitative meaning increases.

Not all suffering under all conditions is good. It is good
only when it enters as one essential ingredient in creativity.
When it opposes the creative event, as it often does, it is
evil. Whether or not an instance of suffering is a barrier to
creative good depends in great part on how the individual
treats it and reacts to it. One of the outstanding marks of
maturity is the practice of seeking value in the face of suffering. The immature individual cannot do this. The small
child cannot and should not be expected to do this, except
in respect to small doses of suffering. Maturity, of course, is
not merely a matter of years. Some people of fifty and sixty
seem less able to seek value in face of suffering than some
children.

MATURITY IN SUFFERING

"Emotional maturity" is the term used to indicate that way of dealing with situations involving suffering whereby life may be enriched rather than impoverished by what is there encountered. The mature man will put himself and all that he can command under the control of what generates value to be transformed in any way that it may require. Putting one's self under this control means seeking to know what this creativity may demand and striving to meet these demands. Obviously, this may bring suffering. The immature person turns away from this control and from these demands whenever they bring suffering in the form of disillusionment, self-criticism, criticism by others, acceptance of what one dislikes or fears, labor, loss of prestige and popularity, financial deprivation, and the like. The amount of suffering one can take, when creativity makes that demand, is one of the clearest marks of maturity. This does not mean that one should prize suffering for its own sake or seek it as an end, but the mature person takes it in his stride when it is a part of the growth of qualitative meaning.

A second mark of maturity is the amount of labor and sacrifice one will undergo in seeking to know and to provide the conditions which must be maintained for the increase or conservation of human good. The experimental probing and earnest searching will often make severe demands, and only the highly mature will meet them.

Accepting criticism of others and undergoing the transformation demanded when the criticism is based on evidence is a third indication of maturity. Plainly this acceptance will often bring suffering because it will force one to acknowledge some very disagreeable facts about one's self. People so frequently refuse to accept criticism because they will not endure the suffering of self-disclosure. One can gauge a man's maturity by this. This does not mean that the

[98]

mature man accepts all criticism. Ability to distinguish criticism based on evidence from criticism based on irresponsible malice or distorted points of view is itself a part of maturity.

Submitting all beliefs to be determined by evidence rather than by desire is a fourth characteristic of the mature man. Here again the great obstacle to relinquishing beliefs unsupported by evidence is the suffering thus encountered. Certain beliefs bolster one's prestige. It would be humiliating to submit them to evidence and find them false. If the group with which one has identified himself is not the chosen people, if the religious tradition which renders one a bearer of salvation is not the most important heritage of man, then the comfort and the complacency, the prestige and the power, which seemed to accrue to one's self by right are right no longer. If one cannot claim supreme importance for one's message, the personal loss is exceedingly heavy. Hence, beliefs are not submitted to evidence, or a special method is devised to carry them through the test. Some of the most important undertakings in human life are possible only when evidence is allowed to prevail. Therefore, holding beliefs against the evidence is one of the serious obstacles to creative transformation.

Appraising correctly one's own abilities and virtues and any institution, group, culture, or tradition with which one has allied one's self is a fifth mark of maturity. Unless one does seek correctly to appraise one's worth, including all with which one has identified one's self, one cannot meet the demands of the creative event or communicate freely and fully with others. But correct appraisal cannot be carried through without suffering, and the immature will not endure it. Hence they appraise themselves wrongly, either too highly, for obvious reasons, or too meagerly, in order to escape responsibility or compensate for something else. Incorrect appraisal due to lack of skill or lack of evidence sincerely sought should be distinguished from incorrect appraisal due to the refusal to undergo the suffering.

Keeping open the avenues of communication between one's self and other individuals, other cultures, other races, and other classes is a sixth indication of maturity. Almost everyone is ready to do this so long as no suffering is involved; but when suffering is encountered, the immature close the avenues. Loss of prestige, criticism and ridicule, and limitation of monetary advantage may be the price of keeping open these avenues of interchange. Then the immature will not do it.

Assuming responsibility for the consequences and implications of any commitment, promise, act, affirmation, or choice; for promoting good and fighting evil within the limits of one's knowledge and power; for increasing the range and accuracy of one's knowledge and power in order to serve more effectively, are further marks of maturity.

Accepting the disciplines that transform likings and sources of satisfaction into those other likings and sources which yield greater value is another.

Treating personal and social breakdown as an opportunity for creative transformation is still another characteristic of maturity. When the order of life in which one has lived begins to disintegrate, the mature person knows that danger is at one hand and opportunity at the other. Suffering cannot be escaped in such crises, but the creative event may be released and qualitative meaning may increase. The measure of a man's maturity is the amount of suffering he can take in searching after the way leading to greater good in such a time. The mature person will not be turned back from creativity by suffering in personal and social breakdown.

Participating in a group not as an ultimate recipient of service rendered but as agent for the realization of values is another indication of maturity. The mature person, the

[100]

group, and all members of the group are agents in the service of a good that is beyond them all, yet a good in which they may participate, provided that they do not interpret the value of it primarily in terms of what it can do for any human being or human group. When the Christian idea of *agape* is interpreted to mean that any human being should be the recipient of my unmeasured love and devotion, it becomes highly pernicious. The statement that individual human personality is of infinite worth is false if and when it contravenes the principle of service to a good greater than any individual participant in the creative event. To repudiate any human individual or group as ultimate brings suffering, and hence the immature reject this demand made on human living by the sovereignty of creativity over every man and group.

All these indications of maturity sum up to the first of them: Putting one's self and all that one can command under the supreme control of what generates all value and not under the supreme control of any good that has, to date, been created in existence or envisioned in the mind. The mature person finds his ultimate security and stability not in any created good and not in any vision of ideal possibility but solely in that creativity which transforms the mind of the individual, the world relative to his mind, and his community with other men, so as to increase the qualitative meaning of the world.

Thus, to reject every basis for ultimate security and stability other than the creative process itself is to meet the final test of maturity. Rejection of apparent security and stability in any kind of created good whatsoever involves suffering. But the suffering is transmuted from an evil into a good if one finds through this rejection a deeper and unfailing basis of security in the creative event.

Maturity is a matter of degree, and there is no final point beyond which further maturity is impossible. Yet there is a high level which the great of the earth have reached in meeting suffering. This level might be called for man his "maturity."

We have discussed the problem of suffering at considerable length in this treatment of evil, not because we equate suffering with evil, but for exactly the opposite reason. Suffering is often identified with evil, but we have declared that in our interpretation of value it is evil only under some conditions and not under others. Hence it was required of us that we show when and how suffering is evil and when and how it is not.

THE ALLEGED EVIL OF CREATIVITY

Since the creative process produces cultures, personalities, and social systems refusing to accept its sovereign control, it produces evil, so it is affirmed. This confusion is cleared by looking again at the basic moral and religious demand and the consequences that issue from man's failure to obey it.

This demand is for man to use all his science, technology, and other achieved good to provide conditions most favorable for that intercommunication which produces a richer appreciable world, a more highly developed personality, more extensive and profound community. The more good that creativity produces in the life of man, the more evil he can do by turning against these demands. Thus creativity is given the character of evil because man uses created good to throw off its control. In this sense, if one wishes so to put it, creativity produces evil. But the moral and religious demand remains the same. This alleged evil of creativity only makes more imperative the demand that man serve it first and all else second, because the evil comes from men's refusal or inability to do this. If the "evil" attributed to creativity is used to justify man's refusal to serve it above all, the claim is obviously fallacious. If, on the other hand,

one still insists that creativity is evil, the dispute is purely
academic and dialectical and is not worthy the attention of
a serious mind, so long as the truth is clearly seen that all
this "evil" heaped upon the creative power at work in
human existence only makes more compelling the First
Commandment, which is that we give ourselves to it in
absolute commitment of faith. This is the meaning of the
commandment that we love God with heart and soul and
mind and strength and our neighbor as ourselves. The
neighbor must not be loved more than self, but God must
be. The neighbor must not be loved more because self and
neighbor are equally servants of the creative power which
produces all the good of our existence. Any moral quibbles
which obscure this plain fact are dangerously pernicious.

Again it may be said that creativity is evil because it
creates evil perspectives or meanings. But when is a perspective evil? Only when it resists integration with other
perspectives. But this is not intrinsic to the perspective as
such. It is what man does with the perspective he has. The
meaning may emerge in my mind that tempts me to steal or
murder. But here, again, the evil lies in allowing the meaning to dominate the demands of creativity. Any careful
analysis of an instance of evil will show this to be the case.
Always the evil lies not in the meaning as such but in the
use of it to block the avenues of creative interchange between persons or between the organism and its physical environment. Proof that the evil is not in the meaning appears when we note that a supremely good man is one who
has most profound sympathetic understanding of the evil
man and so entertains in his own mind the meanings in the
mind of the other. But thus by love to have in mind the
meanings of the other cannot be evil. Therefore, the meanings themselves are not evil, even though the evil man
operates in evil ways by means of them.

Still again it is said that the fellowship of a common per-

spective is often evil, this fellowship having been produced
by creative interaction. But the fellowship of a common
perspective must be sharply distinguished from fellowship
of commitment to creative intercommunication. This second kind of fellowship can include perspectives of utmost
diversity, provided only that the members give first place to
the creative event, finding ultimate security in the keeping
of it and not in any achieved perspective. In some cases this
second kind of fellowship will have a common perspective
as an over-all canopy for their diversifications. But if it is
truly a fellowship of commitment to creativity and not to
the common perspective, what they have in common in the
way of a shared perspective will be incidental and second-
ary to the demands of creative intercommunication not only
among themselves but also between themselves and others
who have totally different views. In the fellowship of commitment to creativity the common perspective, if there be
one, will always be used to promote and nurture that transformation which makes the world more meaningful and
will be relinquished whenever the deepening of creative
intercommunication so requires.

After discussing the general nature of evil under the negative category of opposing creativity, we must now try to
get at some of the more specific instances of evil. These are
so multitudinous and diverse that we shall resort to a device
for classifying evils into certain major kinds. These kinds
do not state a positive nature common to all instances in
each class but are classifications of expediency for getting
before us an array of instances of evil that cannot be examined individually.

CHAPTER V

Kinds of Evil

THE most general classification of evils distinguishes between those rooted in the nature of things not caused by man and those that originate in human life. In our analysis the first will be subdivided into the "inertias" and the "protective hierarchies." Evils that originate in human life we shall call "sin," "immorality," and "demonry."

THE EVILS OF INERTIA

The opposite of inertia, in our usage, is not change. We do not assume that all change is good and all changelessness evil. By "inertia" we mean two things: lack of that sensitivity and responsiveness necessary to get the thought and feeling of another or to participate appreciatively in a more complex community; and resistance to that kind of transformation whereby the individual organism, the world relative to that organism, and the associated community are all re-created so as to increase qualitative meaning. This insensitivity and this brutish resistance to creativity constitute the inertia here under consideration.

We shall discuss this kind of inertia—insensitivity and resistance to creativity—in three rough categories, according to its causes: inertia due to lack of vital energy, inertia due to the running-down of energy, and inertia due to the canceling-out of conflicting energies.

Inertia of insensitivity and unresponsiveness pervades inanimate matter, meaning by "matter" not the individual electrons and protons but that statistical average of their impact which we experience in the form of clod and stone,

Kazantakis "The cry."

[105]

dust and wind, earthquake and fire. Up from this inertia through millions of years, energy has gradually been built and stored in forms available for life—first in plant spores, then in more complex vegetation, next in the lowest forms of animals, and finally in more sensitive and responsive animals like man. But this stored energy is quickly exhausted in vital use, and inertia drags us down once more.

Creativity could do far more with life and created good would doubtless be far more extensive than it is if we did not so quickly become exhausted. When weary, we are inert and unresponsive. We cannot undergo the transformations which a new creation requires. Much irritation, anger, violence, and destruction (the organism is simply unable to respond in more constructive ways) can be traced to fatigue and frayed nerves. The supply of energy for any one individual is very limited, and he sinks into inertia when it fails.

Restricted vitality and impoverishment of life due to lack of energy are manifest in many forms. Specialization, biological and mental, is a kind of inertia. Organisms specialize because they lack the energy to do everything. Heavy shell and protective coloring, tusk and claw and poisonous bite, are ways to conserve vital energy. They turn energy into a single channel, where it can have more concentrated power. But these devices render the organism less sensitive and less responsive, and they cut down enormously the qualities and meanings otherwise accessible to life for its uses and enjoyment. The human organism, unlike all the other forms of life, has not developed organs thus narrowly limited to a specialized and unvarying function. Thereby, man has become the medium through which creativity can produce a world relatively vast in its richness and expanse. But the human organism escaped the inertia of biological specialization only to be beset by a more drastic kind—specialization of the mind at higher levels of civilization, where men cannot communicate creatively with freedom and fulness across narrowing lines of concern.

Anything is evil which drains the precious and limited supply of energy for life, so painfully and slowly stored in forms available for creative living. Much pleasure, otherwise harmless, is dissipation because it wastes the store committed to us by the many ages of the past. Pleasure is not evil simply because it is pleasure; in fact, some pleasure is a great good. But many instances of pleasure drain away energy that might have been used to rear a further range of value but is now lost forever in a triviality. And this is no little thing that we waste in triviality—it is the most sacred trust, the most precious legacy, we have, a gift rescued from the perishings and inertias of time by the sufferings of the millions of shoulders on which we stand.

Routine habit is another form of inertia resulting from a limited supply of energy. In the grip of habit the organism cannot respond to innovation and loses awareness of the quality in events as they happen. Yet not all habit is evil; for a complex system of habits can conserve energy and keep our minds and bodies in a fine balance of equilibrium and readiness for creative response. But if it does not serve the creative event, habit obstructs it, because we lack the energy to break free of the routine.

Increasing magnitude, both in the organism and in the social group, seems to bring on inertia. Much more energy is needed to vitalize the bulk of the organism or to respond to the complexities of the larger group. Dazed confusion and a sense of futility result from attempts to deal with the complexities of the Great Society. The individual takes refuge in calloused insensitivity to its demands. Reorganization and special devices may cope with this difficulty, but inertia due to limited energy is always there to drag us down.

Other instances of inertia are not so largely due to a lim-

ited supply of energy as they are to a steady running-down
of the supply available. In its greatest cosmic dimension this
is the second law of thermodynamics. Dynamic energy is
flowing down to a dead level, where it cannot be used for
the upward thrust of creative advance. This is not always
and everywhere evil. Obviously, all we do makes use of this
running-down of energy; but, like everything else, this
running-down becomes evil when it obstructs creativity or
destroys created good. In the end, dispersion and dissipation of energy might destroy all created good, and we do
not have sufficient evidence even to speculate upon what
this would mean for creativity itself. But whether or not
the whole universe is headed for this level of death—experts dispute the point among themselves—in any case we
have millions of years to go. The way of life for us remains
the same whatever this outcome may be. Always our task is
to provide conditions most favorable for that kind of sympathetic intercommunication which creates the qualitative
meaning of life. The following lines express this:

> I can be kind
>   Although I know
> The gods are blind
>   And planets go
> Untended, lost,
>   On chartless gyres
> Of lifeless frost
>   And lawless fires.
>
> I dare be kind
>   Although I know
> The clanging, blind
>   Eternal snow
> Shall swell from out
>   The dark at length
> In undevout
>   Indifferent strength,

And each by each
Our planets fold
In tranquil reach
Of level cold.[1]

Old age and death are examples of inertia due to the running-down of energy; yet death might not be an evil if one could keep his sensitivity and responsiveness to the end. Medical science has done much to improve health and vitality, but, so far as the writer knows, it has not been able to hold back the creeping paralysis of the aging organism or to sustain its capacity for further growth. We struggle against the fading of the last loveliness from the lives of those we love; against the waning of their capacity for human fellowship; and, finally, against extinction itself. Human shrinking from death does not make it evil; but, when death obstructs the increase of qualitative meaning, it is to that degree and in that relation evil.

When cut off from external communication, any cultural group seems to drift toward uniformity and inertia. Peoples in isolation from other cultures have either remained primitive or degenerated to a lower level. Every form of life, when not goaded by pain, suffering, and danger, seems to undergo the same fate. Apparently all existence is under the threat of this propensity to uniformity, repetition, monotony, and inertia. Every created good seems in time to turn against its creator in the sense of resisting the creative event to the point where it must either be destroyed or shrivel to a dead shell by losing its qualitative meaning.

There is still a third source of inertia. It is due to diversifications and other changes that cancel out. It has its cosmic dimension in the form of inanimate matter and its social dimension in a kind of liberalism that cancels out to a final sense of futility and indifference.

[1] Part of an unpublished poem by Donald Carey Williams, professor of philosophy at Harvard University. It bears the title "Credo."

What we call "inanimate matter" in the world of common sense is the statistical average of innumerable atomic activities that cancel out in their total impact upon us. The particular atoms and molecules seem to be highly dynamic, even organized. But the organizing and creative process at the submicroscopic level does not seem to be able to rise to higher levels except in those rare instances in which life has emerged. The living cell is the first triumph of the creative event over the inertia due to this canceling-out of the diverse activities in the atom and molecule. Throughout most of the universe, creativity seems to have been halted at the level of matter's inertia. Since our knowledge of remote space is very limited, it would be rash to state that only on this planet has creative fulfilment risen above the molecule. But even this planet, the moon, other planets, and the sun give evidence of the rarity with which this impasse has been surmounted. The crushing and destructive drift of matter in the form of wind, earthquake, fire, and flood and the vast sterilities in which life cannot survive and where drought, famine, cold, and heat destroy—all exemplify this sort of inertia.

The neutralization of creative action by one innovation's canceling the other appears very widely in modern society at the top, as well as the bottom, level of existence. The supreme problem of the Great Society is to organize and direct the activities of individuals and groups so that the good of one will not frustrate the good of others and the striving of one will not cancel out the effects of the striving of others. The great economic depressions that become progressively worse are examples of this kind of inertia. In more simple societies the equilibrium of competition in business enterprise could sometimes be creative, although perhaps it was never so creative as Adam Smith and others claimed. Certainly, in the Great Society of today it is not.

Finally, we come to that inertia which is perhaps the

most deadly threat in our society today. It issues from a kind of tolerance, where tolerance is made the sovereign good.[2] Under the regime of this kind of tolerance, every individual, class, or group is permitted to value most highly anything it likes for itself, providing others are allowed to do the same. This kind of tolerance reduces to the triviality of a private preference every value which the individual exalts; it destroys all profound devotion and kills all sense of lofty value. The first generation or two may stand out against the deadening inertia that is bound to creep over all society when this sort of liberalism prevails. Toleration becomes triviality when it denies that any value is great enough to be regnant over all human living. When every highest good for the individual is his own affair alone, he cannot help feeling in time that anything he or any other may hold supreme is nothing but a private liking. The persistent question becomes: Who is going to say what is good and what is bad? As though it were merely a matter of someone's saying! When the individual is constantly meeting people who live by private preference under the control of an order of value utterly different from his own and are justified in so doing simply because it is *their* system of value, all high dignity becomes dust. Even the supreme concern of religion becomes "religious experience," peculiar and private to the individual and the group, and the business of no one else.

This thrusting of the individual back upon the littleness of his own private preference drives the race to violence if no other way is open to the amplitude of greatness. Life becomes so inane and empty that men will turn to war or revolution or any other fury that will lift the pall of triviality. In our society it is not primarily injustice and hardship which drive men to madness. It is rather hunger

[2] See *The Diagnosis of Our Times* (Oxford: Oxford University Press, 1944), by Karl Mannheim.

for a towering majesty that will deliver them from the
inane; men seek it in illusion if they cannot find it in reality
—for instance, that of racial destiny. Men must find greatness somewhere, else the humanity dies out of them.

Under the kind of tolerance and liberalism here described, men lose the sense of any real deity. Many will
continue to talk about God, but God becomes a name used
to apply to anything that one happens to prefer. One's
preference may be shaped by tradition inherited through
belonging to one group rather than to another or by a need
to believe this rather than that in order to live in the way
one wants. "God" may become private to the confessional
group. So people begin to speak not of God but of "my
God" and "your God," "the Christian God," "the Mo-
hammedan God," "the God of the nineteenth century,"
"the God of the philosophers," "the liberal's God."
Plainly this is not God at all. This is simply anybody's private preference masquerading under the name of deity.
Nothing is more arbitrary and nothing can drag down to
such depths of triviality the ruling concerns of human living
than giving the name of deity to what anybody may happen
to prefer, with the added understanding that anybody else
can choose something entirely different and with equal
right call it "God."

The issue is only confused when it is asserted that the
ultimate decisions concerning what is supremely important
are not rational and are determined by tradition, interest,
and much else beyond the reach of any empirical and rational test. This only says that men are subject to error in deciding what shall command their last devotion and that one of
the causes for such error is the nonrational, arbitrary, and
accidental compulsions which drive them to choose this
rather than that. If I have inherited one tradition, my
choice will move in one direction; if you have another tradition, your choice will move in another. But, as long as

[112]

a "superhistorical reality" which assures the ultimate meaning and worth of human existence despite all appearances to the contrary. This is blind credulity forced by desperation. The third way is absolute commitment to a creativity that is more than human, which works in this temporal world and can always be trusted to bring forth richer good beyond the human vision of any time.

As insight and power increase, anticipatory vision is not sufficient to sustain the sense of meaning and hope in life and to ward off the threat of inertia arising out of the sense of futility, because human anticipation never comprehends the growing good that is now being created. In this sense, hope based on anticipation is always illusory. In time all men who observe keenly and learn the harder lessons of life discover this. Then they become pessimists unless they find some other basis of hope and driving propulsion. If we are to survive the insights that dispel illusion, we must learn to live by self-commitment to the creative might that works for good beyond the vision of the immediate participants.

This demand, opening the way to unfailing hope, runs even deeper. Our lives, our plans, and our persons must be broken to gain access to the depth of creative power where alone hope can securely take its stand, because our plans and purposes and the organization of personality are too restricted. They are too self-centered; too much confined to the concerns of our own local group, our own culture, age, race, class, and vocation; too biased by the perspective of our own place and person. If our envisioned plan, if our cherished order, fitted to the purpose and desire of our group—white race, American people, or whatever it be—if that plan and order of life were not broken, if it were carried on to continuous success and imposed upon the world in unending triumph, it would be the imposition of death. Our chosen plan and order, if not broken, would cramp and kill the growth of human good. This holds, no matter how righteous and noble our plan and order of life may seem to be, so long as it is shaped within the limits of our perspective and bias, and it always is so limited. If maintained triumphantly to the end, it would suffocate hope and destroy fulfilment and leave life a barren waste. Such is the limitation of human vision and human plan by reason of the essential and inescapable nature of man's existence.

We must be broken because there is a good so great that it breaks the bounds of our littleness. We must be broken because there is a power which works in our lives to achieve a good we cannot compass and cannot discern, until some later time in retrospect reveals the form of the new creation now invisibly emerging. Our own anticipatory vision is always too narrow, biased, and self-centered to comprehend it. We must be broken because there is a God who works for righteousness so great that it cannot be confined to the limits of our control. We must be broken because there is, day by day, the creating of a kingdom of goodness in depth and height and scope so far beyond the reach of any human plan that it must not be constricted to our imposed directive. We must be broken because above us, above the breakdown and the ruin of plans and persons and ages and nations, there is a beating of great wings.

How to make the transition from the drive of biological propulsion and the lure of anticipatory vision over into the power and keeping of a creative might that works beyond the plans of man is the problem of our existence. If we do not make this transition, sooner or later the inertia of disillusionment overwhelms, and we sink into the drift and roll of inert and meaningless existence. If we make not this transition, we shall be engulfed in the void of the inane.

This threat of inertia and loss of meaning is not peculiar to human life. It hangs over all the world. It seems to be a cosmic drift and threat, but it can be conquered. There is a power more than human which works against it. Several times since this planet cooled, it seems, this power reached a level where further advance was precarious, where defeat was imminent. The transition from inanimate matter to the living cell may have been such a time. The transition from lower animal existence to man may have been another such dangerous and difficult passage; and now the end of one period of history and the beginning of another, marked by change from hand-technology to supertechnology (the atomic age), is another such time of precarious transition.

Hope and the sense of meaning and purpose in life will be drained away when this new power and widened perspective compel us to see the bias and limitation of every human purpose—they will be drained away unless we find hope and impulsion in a creativity which works beyond the scope of human plan and purpose and which, therefore, man must serve with his new power and widened vision instead of trying to make *it* serve *his* perspective and goal. He must see and he must accept the way of being broken as the only way to recover again and again the depth and power of new creation, reviving life forever with growing abundance of value.

We have sketched the evil and the danger of inertia as one of the basic evils of the world, arising from sources beyond the control of man. Another evil, derivative from this of inertia, is the evil of protective hierarchy.

PROTECTIVE HIERARCHIES

There are many kinds of hierarchy, but here we are concerned only with what could be called the "hierarchy of sensitivity." The graduated levels of sensitivity and the graded capacity to undergo creative transformation impose a hierarchy on existence in which only the few at the top can be the medium through which the creative event works most fully. This ordering of life is a hard necessity, but it is evil. It is evil because not all forms of life, not even all human organisms, can share equally the supreme fulfilments of qualitative meaning; it is evil because some forms of life must support other forms by enduring hardships or other stultifying effects that render them less responsive and less sensitive.

In biology this hierarchy of sensitivity begins with tiny plant-spores of life which draw nourishment directly from inanimate matter, and it rises at the top to man. For all his maximum sensitivity and capacity to undergo creative transformations, man could not endure the impact of raw, inert matter uncushioned by all these lower levels.

This hierarchy of sensitivity is also found in every human society. The less sensitive and the less responsive must do necessary kinds of work and live under conditions rendering impossible that growth of qualitative meaning which sometimes occurs at the top levels of capacity for appreciation and creative transformation.

The apex of the hierarchy of sensitivity is not, however, the people who exercise most power or most intimidation or have most wealth or prestige. We must distinguish the hierarchy of sensitivity from the hierarchy of executive control, the hierarchy of social prestige and status, the hierarchy of intimidation. A class or an individual that stands at the top in one of these may be near the bottom in another. A mob may be able to intimidate all others, but it may have no ability at all to administer the course of events. A monarch who does nothing but serve as a symbol and thereby stands at the top in the hierarchy of prestige may be near the bottom in the hierarchy of sensitivity and creative value. Nevertheless, he may render very important service to those at the top in capacity for qualitative meaning. The great executive does work necessary to sustain the more sensitive and yet may himself be quite incapable of entering into the interchange of deep, rich, and creative meanings. Perhaps, in his time, Jesus stood at the top in capacity for creative transformation but certainly was far from the top in every other kind of hierarchy.

Sometimes the perspective of history may give top place in the hierarchy of prestige to those who were also at the top in sensitivity. But if we keep to the hierarchies of the living, this almost never happens and for good reason. Prestige produces an arrogance that destroys the capacity to undergo creative transformation in free and open interchange with all sorts and classes of people, including the mean and the outcast. It would seem that those with whom creativity is to work most freely and potently must be excluded not only from great social prestige and power of executive control but also from that undue ease and comfort which produce in man the inertia of complacency and frivolity and arrogance.

Perhaps in the future no one need suffer the inertia that comes from possession of disproportionate wealth. But another kind of inertia may be increasingly manifest—it is the inertia in respect to creativity that settles upon the man who exercises enormous executive power and social prestige. Perhaps in the future no great number need endure the sort of manual labor and material impoverishment that kills capacity for sensitivity and creative transformation; but I do not see a time when great numbers will not be exposed to the inertias of arrogance and frivolity, which is perhaps just as deadly as the inertia imposed by hard labor and impoverished conditions. Arrogance in the high places and frivolity in the low may be the inertias deadening many in the days ahead.

The hierarchy is both a necessity and an evil. It is necessary to enable the creative event to produce the richest fulfilment of value with those most capable of engaging in that kind of communication. It is evil because it imposes upon many an undue protection from pain and discomfort; upon some an undue fatigue from hard labor; upon others impoverished organisms; upon still others the irresponsible existence which puts on the throne of life what they happen to like, without demonstrating by any reliable method that it is truly most important.

The evil of the hierarchy of sensitivity is mitigated, but not corrected, if those at the top are truly provided with conditions most favorable for the work of creativity. The basic evil is this very difference in capacity when it cannot be overcome by anything which might be given to the individuals concerned. Unequal native capacity to undergo the transformations of the creative event exemplifies the evil of inertia in the form of physiological limitation. The social hierarchy of sensitivity is better if it corresponds to the levels of physiological capacity. It is better if the optimum conditions for creativity are given to those that are physiologically best fitted for it. But the evil of the hierarchy of sensitivity, as well as the necessity for it, still remains.

In truth, the hierarchy of sensitivity never does correspond perfectly with physiological capacity. Optimum conditions for creative transformation never are given to all that are most capable, with less favorable conditions graduated downward to fit every other level of capacity. We shall never know how many of the most sensitive by physiological endowment were caught at the lower levels of opportunity and had their capacity beaten out of them before they or anyone else ever discovered it. Sir Isaac Newton was a farm hand up to his budding manhood and perhaps would have remained there, had not a nobleman discovered him by accident and given him opportunity. Such happy accidents probably do not befall every potential Newton or mute inglorious Milton.

Nor is the necessity for exercising great executive power, thus removing the opportunity to reach great values in creative intercommunication through books and converse and meditation, any less evil because many would choose it as a way of life. The arrogance and the frivolity, the ease and the comfort, the dull routine and the social strain, are not less evil because people like them. But services must be rendered which seem inevitably to bring on these evils. The evil of the hierarchy remains after man has done his utmost to correct it; for it is an evil arising out of the nature of things.

Our claim that the people to be pitied and delivered from the fate of serving in the lower levels of the hierarchy of sensitivity are men living in great comfort and ease or exercising magnificent power or possessing social prestige or engaged in works of scholarship or other highly specialized achievement may seem ridiculous. But this ridicule is evidence of cultural lag. We are most concerned and fight hardest against evils dominating the age that is passing, while the worst evils of our own time are discounted as not so pressing and important. Certainly, a great fight still remains to distribute the wealth more equitably and provide the masses of men with material goods. But this is on its way, less through any work of idealism or good will than through impersonal social coercions; but to think that the evil of our time will be diminished when material abundance is available is a great blunder. The evils that run through an economy of abundance are different from those pervading an economy of scarcity, but being different does not make them any less evil. To fight windmills because the knights of old were heroes at jousting is not heroic in an age when jousting is no longer the way to rid the world of evils which are very different from small groups of wandering bandits and evil men on horseback.

At times the social hierarchy of sensitivity undergoes shifts that are like earthquakes breaking and remaking the social order. These occur when advancing technology, along with more leisure, opulence, and social interchange, endow people at the lower level with capacities for a higher place in the hierarchy of opportunity and awaken in them the desire for it. The present moment in history is such a time. Modern technology has made it unnecessary for toiling masses to live in a brutish state of inertia in order that others may undergo creative transformation in rearing a world of qualitative meaning. At the same time, this technology has given to these masses more leisure and more appreciation for the values to be found at the higher levels of creative interchange, from which in the past they were not only excluded but for which also they had little desire because they could not appreciate them. Above all, modern technology has thrust upon these masses a power and a responsibility for the conduct of society which they never had before. For the most part, they do not as yet realize the full measure of power accruing to them, and even less the measure of social responsibility now resting upon them. But they are awakening both to the power and to the responsibility. Almost month by month—certainly year by year—one can see spreading among the industrial workers of the world this awareness of their own power and their responsibility for the common good.

All this spells one thing. The social hierarchy is undergoing one of the major shifts of history, perhaps the greatest of all because of the number of people involved and the magnitude of power at their command. People at a lower level in the pyramid of opportunity are rising to a higher level, where creative transformation can work upon them with more freedom and power. This shift cannot occur without breaking down and remaking many institutions, habits, and customs, fitted to the established hierarchy of the past but unfitted to a society in which great numbers of industrial workers and farmers will have powers and opportunities never before open to them. This is the meaning of the disruptions occurring in the world today.

[122]

The point is not that this shift from a lower level of creative interchange to a higher for large numbers of workingmen all over the planet will be successful. The shift is in process, but it may not be consummated. It might be blocked by some new kind of tyranny or some devastation of war. It is not inevitable, but processes are under way that might achieve it. Also, even if the workers should gain access to the larger opportunities, it must be remembered that they might not participate in the kind of interchange which enriches life and might not permit others to do so. But the opportunity will be theirs, and it is probable that they will make as good use of it as other classes have done.

Progress in history (when it occurs) might be measured by progression in the following: (1) widening the upper levels of the social hierarchy to include more of the people, (2) increasing the diversity of intercommunicating individuals and groups, (3) each apprehending more of the meaning which others have to communicate, and (4) each integrating more of this communicated meaning into his own life and personality. These four must be combined if there is social progress. The shift that brings more people to the level at which creative transformation can work upon them with freedom and power is one of the necessary conditions for social progress, but it is not in itself alone sufficient, since people thus exposed more fully to creative transformation must also undergo it.

Generally speaking, they who have lived at the higher levels of creative transformation in the established hierarchy which is now being broken and remade can see no good in the reconstruction now going on. They see the old values in jeopardy, they cannot see how creative transformation might bring forth new and possibly greater good with the remaking of the social order. Hence they exercise all their power and prestige to resist the change or to direct it so as to conserve as much as possible of the good they cherish. This is natural, perhaps inevitable, for most; but there are some at the top levels of the old social order who are not so blind. These few, however, are often frustrated and confused by finding powerful forces working to achieve partial and opposing goods, which, when taken in their partiality and opposition, become evils. So they find themselves unable to work wholeheartedly with any group or with any movement. Here again the only deliverance from inertia is to give final priority not to any striving group or goal but to the creative process itself, measuring the worth of each project and each direction of effort according to the service it can render in opening the channels of creative communication between each and all. To this service one can give one's self wholeheartedly with unabating fervor if one sees that creative interchange is the true source of all human good.

Through all these shifts and with all these liftings of more people to the higher levels of creative opportunity, the hierarchy will still continue, precariously sustaining human life above the blind drift and moil of a welter indifferent to values. There must be government and economic order along with educational, fraternal, and familial institutions, opening opportunities for the richer fulfilments of life according to the individual's capacity for sensitivity, diligence, and discipline. The high peak of creative transformation will continue to soar far above the mass of people, with only a very few finding a place there. This is a hard necessity, an evil inherent in the cosmic situation, so it seems. If this claim should be mistaken, none would be more happy than we; but if it is true, we must face the fact and order our lives accordingly.

The distinguishing feature of our time is the enormous power exercised by man today to direct the subhuman processes of nature and to produce an abundance of goods and services beyond any limit that has yet been definitely and finally set. The problem is to discover and to enforce the way to use this power so that it will not bring on the inertias of inane comfort and ease; of frivolity; of arrogance and complacency; of superficial communication between every sort of individual, class, group, and culture; or the inertia of continuous change, blocking or canceling out every creative transformation; the inertia that issues from a kind of tolerance that hands over to private preference the ultimate decisions concerning matters of supreme importance; the inertia of the cultural crisis that comes when growing insight discerns the relative futility of every high human purpose.

In discussing the evil of the hierarchies we have come back to the evil of the inertias, because the one rises out of the other. The hierarchies are necessary to lift beyond the reach of the great inertias some few individuals with whom creativity can produce the greatest good.

SIN AND IMMORALITY

The evils thus far treated are thrust upon man from sources outside of human living, and they seem to reside in the nature of things. They are great evils which we must fight, and we must understand them to fight them; but they have their source in subhuman regions, and we must fight them there. It is true that these evils pass over from the external source to the internal affairs of man, and it is hard to draw the line precisely determining the place where human responsibility begins. We unquestionably do have responsibility for many of the inertias, particularly for that neutralizing tolerance which arises because we have not as yet developed any method of determining objectively and independently of private preference and accepted tradition what truly is most important for all human living; we also have responsibility for many of the evils that develop in the hierarchies. Nevertheless, the inertias and the hierarchies

[125]

are, primarily and in the large, thrust upon us from sources external to human life.

We now examine evil in respect to man's responsibility. Sin, immorality, and demonry are the three kinds of evil originating with man. Sin is any resistance to creativity for which man is responsible. If we make the inquiry, it is difficult to determine the place where man's responsibility begins, although, actually, it is not important that it be precisely determined. What is important, however, is that man recognize that his responsibility is not limited to instances in which he is consciously aware of obstructing creativity or deliberately intending to do so. Unintended and unconscious resistance is sin, too, because it is the consequence of many past decisions for which the man is responsible. Also, when we speak of man's responsibility, we refer not only to the individual but to society and the race. Much resistance in the individual not intended by him is due to choices made by other human beings. Thus there is a collective responsibility in many cases in which the individual cannot be held solely responsible as though he lived in isolation from all others, as he never does. In fact, sin is always social, even in cases in which a particular individual must take primary responsibility. It is social because creativity is essentially and necessarily social. To be sure, the creative event includes in one of its four phases the creation and progressive integration of the individual, which is just as uniquely and exclusively individual as anything can be. But even this cannot be cut off from the other three parts of the creative event, and these other parts are interactions between individuals.

When we say that sin is man's resistance to the creative event, we refer to what was meant by the theological statement: "Sin is man's rebellion against the will of God." The language and the ideas are different; but the way a man thinks of the creative event, the names he uses, and the ideas he may entertain about it are not the primary consideration. Modern men are as responsible for sin as men ever were, even though they use utterly different language and mental pictures.

Another way of describing sin is to say that it is the creature turning against the creator—it is created good turning against creativity. Man's personality is a created good, and so also are his society, his culture, his ideals. He, with his society, culture, and ideals, is forever refusing to meet the demands which must be met if the creative event is to rule in his life. This is sin. He refuses to provide the conditions which he could provide and which are necessary to release the freer working of creativity; he holds onto conditions that obstruct its working, and he refuses to fight the conditions which oppose it. All this is rebellion against God. The "will of God," so far as it prescribes what man should do, is the demand of creative power that man provide conditions most favorable to its working. God's will in this sense is the imperative demand that men remove or fight the conditions obstructing creativity and that they relinquish what must be cast out of their life if the creative event is to have free way there. To sin is to refuse to do any one or more of these three things when they lie within one's power.

Most sin is unconscious and unintended. To be unconscious of one's sin when he could be conscious of it is itself a darker sin. Though this touches on the problem of free will and the limits of man's responsibility, we here point only to the fact that man can, if he will, be far more fully conscious of his sin than he generally is. To be conscious of one's sin is to be that far in the direction of deliverance from it; for the deepest enslavement to sin is the state in which one is not conscious of it. When one becomes conscious of it, one achieves, thereby, a degree of freedom and independence and mastery over it and is in some measure delivered from it.

It has been claimed that all sin can be reduced to pride. Plainly, this is not true. Frivolity is no less a sin, and it may be as free of pride as anything can be. The most frivolous, the most indifferent, and the most inert are rarely men of pride. Interpreting sin simply as pride reveals a blindness to the full scope and depth of sin in human life.

DEMONRY

The evil of immorality will be discussed in the chapter on morals. The evil of resisting creative transformation for the sake of a vision of human good remains. Here the interpretation of a traditional religious symbol is illuminating. The devil, like all other religious symbols, must not be interpreted in terms of the ideas entering the minds of men who first used the symbol. The symbol can be correctly interpreted only by examining the context of its usage and determining what it was that men were actually struggling with when they used the term. The "devil" has stood for many different things and is found in other traditions than the Christian. Here, however, we wish only to discover what reality was involved when it was used in one of the classic strands of the Christian tradition.

In this strand of tradition the "devil" has meant the archtempter. The devil is what tempts man to sin in the most dangerous and evil way; also the devil is the most glorious of the sons of God. Furthermore, he tempted Jesus in the wilderness, where the devil showed Jesus the kingdoms of the world and suggested that Jesus rule them for the good of all men. Also he suggested that Jesus cast himself off the top of the temple and bring the forces of nature under control in service of man, and he tempted Jesus to turn stones into bread and feed the hungry.

Apparently, the devil is the beatific vision. The devil is the most glorious vision of good that our minds can achieve at any one time when *that vision refuses to hold itself subject to creativity*. This is the most subtle and dangerous and obstructive sin that man can sin. No vision of any man, race, or culture at any time can be lifted up and made supreme against creativity. And no sense of destiny for the individual, family, or culture can be so exalted without refusing the demands of the creative event.

When the power of man increases by leaps and bounds, as it is doing today with the intensive industrialization of the planet, when the complexities of organization increasingly demand centralization of authority with delegation of power under a ruling body, some group will surely rise to a height of power that no men ever before enjoyed. It will be tempted to use its power to achieve what seems to it good and refuse to use it to serve the creative event.

In this discussion of evil we have made no attempt to cover all evils. That would be impossible because, as said in the beginning, evil is essentially multitudinous and diverse. The best that we could do was to make certain fundamental distinctions, such as obstructive and destructive evil, absolute and relative evil, the nature of suffering in relation to evil, the inertias, the evil hierarchies, sin, and the devil.

PART II

Specific Kinds of Value

CHAPTER VI

Beauty

BEAUTY is brought to human awareness when reactions of the organism distinguish and relate events within a sharply delimited whole and in such an order that the qualities of these events are vivified by mutual reference of each to the others. The structured whole displaying beauty must be a unity in the sense that each part directs attention to every other part but not to anything else beyond. To this end, the form must be precisely fitted to the use—plowshare, sentence, song—and precisely fitted to the materials used and the methods of construction. To lift from the depth of organic response, on the one hand, and from the fulness of the object, on the other, the qualitative abundance potentially there, a rhythmic recurrence of form is required, with a dominant theme binding all together in graduated accents and variations. The whole structure must have equilibrium and stability which so balance tensions that the organism can react with all its sensory, muscular, and glandular resources. The eye, the ear, and every other organ of response must be directed to follow this theme and this rhythm from part to whole and from whole to part until the fulness of quality is elicited. Every aesthetic situation is created by this vital vibration of organism and physical object.

The imagination may wander, but everything that enters consciousness must refer back to the one order of mutually vivifying parts. Each event, whether imaginative, perceptual, or deeply organic, must vivify the others. Nothing must lead the mind on beyond this internal cross-reference of part to part. Thus beauty holds attentive awareness to itself; it fascinates and brings to maximum vividness the apprehension of the qualities which are the events within a bounded whole.[1] In every other instance of awareness the mind is either led on to something else or loses interest.

Qualitative meaning, as we have interpreted it, is closely akin to beauty; but there is a difference. In instances of beauty the reference of meaning may play from event to event, but it must not wander off beyond a single whole. In qualitative meaning the reference of each event to the others must, in like fashion, play back and forth from part to part, eliciting the quality of each in vivifying contrast to the others. Consequently, if one wishes to extend the meaning of beauty to include all aesthetic richness attained by this reference of events to one another, then all qualitative meaning is beauty. But this, it would seem, extends the meaning of beauty beyond the common usage. More strictly and narrowly, beauty is aesthetic richness achieved within a unitary structure of events by sharply separating it from all others. Qualitative meaning, on the other hand, is aesthetic richness not so limited but produced in an order of meaning leading on indefinitely and creatively. We shall treat beauty in the narrower sense; otherwise beauty would include all intrinsic created value.

The work of art in the narrow sense is to render qualities vivid and richly variegated by delimiting a structure to the compass of human capacity to comprehend the qualities appreciatively as a single whole. Viewed in one way, works of art are exploratory ventures of the human spirit, conducted under narrowly controlled conditions, to discover

1 My most recent and very deep indebtedness in this discussion of aesthetic value is to S. C. Pepper, *Aesthetic Quality* (New York: Charles Scribner's Sons, 1938), and to Eliseo Vivas, "The Natural History of the Aesthetic Transaction," chapter v in *Naturalism and the Human Spirit*, edited by Yervant T. Krikorian. Also much is owed to Walter Dorwin Teague in *Design This Day* (New York: Harcourt, Brace & Co., 1940).

the possibilities of qualitative abundance in the world. In time this richness of quality may be opened to the wider expanses of human living beyond the bounds of the fine arts. To this end we might design our houses and cities, our group and personal relations, our government and economic order, and the daily intercourse of man with man. Railways and highways; kitchens, cellars, and bathrooms; river and woodland; dress and posture; movement and form of the human body—all might be developed to create a world rich with meaning and vivid with quality. The fine arts will always range ahead as scouting parties, but the practical arts will follow after, and the whole world open to human awareness might unfold the fulness of quality actually there.

BEAUTY AND REALITY

All experience, even the common and ordinary experience of every day, is made up of a myriad of events infinitely rich with quality. Each moment, even the simplest of moments, is a new event defined by uniqueness of quality. Perhaps we might be more accurate if we said that the common world of everyday experience is only potentially rich with quality, because we are usually too distracted or too torpid to note what is there to behold. It is only in the experience of beauty that we are actually aware of the full quality of events. In every other instance of awareness our mind is either led on to something else or loses interest. We may be so tired or so busy washing dishes or reading the paper in the evening that we miss the full glory of the sunset. But in beauty the focus of attention is held steadily to one limited order of events without loss of interest until the full richness of the quality is apprehended. Otherwise, pragmatic activities or diffuse wandering of attention reduce to a minimum the qualities we feel. Aesthetic form is created by, and waits upon, proper organic responses, and with the creation of aesthetic form a new structure of events emerges.

[135]

Therefore, it may not seem quite correct to say that the same infinite abundance of quality discerned in beauty is always present or that the common world of every day is substantially and ultimately a world of qualities infinitely rich in variety, calling only for aesthetic form to make us aware of them.

Nonetheless, no activity or fatigue can completely drain events of their quality, since quality is always there, felt more or less vividly. Something is delivered to feeling and sense, no matter how meager or vague it may be. Careful discrimination of what we are experiencing at any time, even in the most dull and routine of moments, will reveal many subtle and fleeting qualities on the fringes of aware-ness. So abundant is the quality of any moment that no words can exhaust its fulness. Therefore, it can be said with-out qualification that the substance of the common world of experience is infinitely rich with qualities. The world is actually a rich fulness of quality, with each event a quality and the world a myriad of events. Quality is the substance of events, more or less vividly apprehended, waiting upon aesthetic form to direct attention to it and discriminate its uniqueness and richness. Not until aesthetic form so orders what is here and now presented to thought and feeling and sense that the mind is continuously led back to the same structured whole, illuminating it, rendering it more fully disclosed to awareness, with all the subtle nuances and dis-tinctions laid bare, is the full quality of events apprehended. But it is always the substance of the common world of ex-perience that is thrown open and exposed to awareness by aesthetic form.

So strange and startling, so vivid and rare, so different from the usual meager reach of attention may be this dis-closure of quality in aesthetic form that men sometimes are led to think that it is a visitation from a metaphysical realm beyond the real world of temporal experience. They may even speak in their excitement of "eternity erupting into time," whatever that may mean. They construct a transcendental metaphysics to account for this marvelous extension of their world. They pay homage to a "Reality" beyond time and space and matter in revering the quality they confront in beauty. The matter actually is much more simple. The quality they feel is really the substance of events, and structured events are the ultimate nature of existence. Beyond existence there can be nothing, unless one wishes to speak of the possibilities always carried by existence. Distraction and torpor simply render the full quality of events inaccessible until aesthetic form directs attention and discriminating awareness to the richness of the world.

What is required for the enhancement of human living is an ordering of ordinary life—physical, biological, psychological, and social—permitting organism and physical environment, mind and mind, to interact creatively, producing a world pervaded with aesthetic form. The greatest cultures, in the age and with the class in which they culminated, produced such an ordering of life and circumstance. Aesthetic form enabled events to stand forth with clarity and vividness and to pass by in tragic majesty and comic sport. Perhaps an unimaginable richness and intensity of quality might be elicited from the world if we ordered it aright and if we had the faith to undergo the creative transformations required. Reality with a capital R might be used to designate that potentiality in the world, provided that the term is purged of reference to a timeless eternity and that it points to an inexhaustible creativity at work in the world of events.

BEAUTY AND THE UGLY

In beauty we become vividly aware of the substance of this common world. This is equally true of the ugly. Experience of the ugly is as vividly and truly aesthetic as is experience of the beautiful. Art not infrequently is designed to produce this aesthetic experience. In the ugly there is the same vivifying cross-reference between parts within a delimited whole, so that the mind is fascinated with quality rather than distracted. The ugly, even as the beautiful, focuses attentive awareness upon contemporary events. But in ugliness one shrinks away even while he is fascinated. In beauty the mind is willingly enthralled, while the ugly thing enthrals the mind against its will.

The shrinking of attentive awareness from the fascination of qualities may in some cases be due to conventional associations, which render a particular kind of object disgusting to people shaped by these conventions. In other cases some deep instinctual reactions having an ancient biological function may compel an effort to escape from the fascination. Still again it may be an ancient social function; one may react to the enthralling object with horror or disgust because a long sequence of generations has developed a pattern of response forcing such a reaction in the presence of any object having this character. Thus, what is beautiful to natives of one culture may be ugly to people inheriting a very different tradition. Again, certain psychological associations peculiar to the individual may cause him to struggle against the fascination of aesthetic quality. Perhaps some occurrence in his childhood, now quite forgotten, produces in him an ineluctable aversion to the object.

While ugliness may derive from accidental conditioning of this kind, there is an ugliness more basically evil. It is the repulsiveness of aesthetic form so ordered as to distract attention from further aesthetic form and to hinder the wider and deeper exposure of quality in the world. This must not be confused with moralistic repulsion. Art is not created to teach the principles of moral conduct; but aesthetic form can be ugly if it directs appreciation into channels that prevent the more ample creation of aesthetic form. True beauty is aesthetic form meeting with inevitable precision the demands of function, materials, methods of use, and construction. It is aesthetic form releasing the freedom of human action, the range and keenness of human appreciation, the fulness of intercommunication, and the creative transformations that unfold the depth of quality in the world. Ugliness basically evil in character is aesthetic form hindering all this. Good taste is taste which approves aesthetic form fitted to release the creativity of life, and pronounces ugly any aesthetic form of the opposite sort.

Ugliness understood as aesthetic form obstructing creativity is one of the great evils of the world. The obstruction may be at the level of physical manipulation. The beauty of good design facilitates the hand, the eye, the whole body in dealing with physical things. Or again the beauty (and its opposite, the ugly) may be at the level of intercommunication between persons and cultures. We can understand the devastation wrought by ugliness in aesthetic form if we are sensitive to the way great art opens the gates of communication from one age to another. Nothing out of the ancient past speaks so profoundly to the present as the great art created in that far time. What men in other ages suffered and achieved can reach us by way of their art if it is truly beautiful. Otherwise, the ages of the past are silent and cannot speak to us from the inside of their appreciative awareness. They cannot speak to us at all in any form distinctively human except by way of their art. "Art" is here understood to include their utensils and weapons, their songs and folklore, and all they constructed of aesthetic form.

Perhaps nothing creates history more effectively and profoundly than beauty, and nothing obstructs its creation more drastically than ugliness, because beauty continues through the ages while ugliness dies. Appreciative consciousness achieved in the past and communicated to the present is history. Aesthetic form is the only medium through which this communication can occur. Since beauty is cherished through the ages while ugliness is rejected, beauty creates history while ugliness prevents its creation. Creation of history is the creation of human existence and the only possible source of its enrichment. Therefore, ugliness, being obstructive to this creation, is an evil striking at the sources of human existence and all human good, and therefore ugliness must be fought by all the resources at our command, and beauty must be fostered. In beauty the ages speak in gathering eloquence one to the other; without beauty they die in silence. The Greeks live in our midst today because they fashioned their world into aesthetic forms of undying beauty.

BEAUTY AND LOVE

One of the most common cases of beauty is the beloved in the eyes of the lover. The lover sees beauty where others do not, yet he is not necessarily subject to illusion. In the presence of the beloved he reacts to distinguish and relate events pertaining to the loved one in such manner that they really do have vivid qualities, and each event is a sign referring not to anything beyond this person but always directing attention back to events intrinsic to this object and none other. Each perceptual event and organic response occurring in his experience as he stands before the beloved has interplay of reference. All is so structured that maximum awareness of the other personality is achieved. This is aesthetic form. It is not a work of art in the technical sense, but it is a creation of aesthetic structure achieved by interplay between the lover and the beloved when conditions are so ordered that attention is not distracted and the range of reference of any event is strictly delimited to the individual contemplated.

In this interplay the structure of events brought forth will generate many qualities derived from their past experiences together and many anticipations that are inarticulate. Aesthetic form is present if the events display a sharply delimited unity with internal meaning, each event directing attention back to what is contained in that unity and to nothing beyond.

In love the intricate organic responses of sex play their part; but that is true in many cases of beauty not ordinarily associated with erotic love. Perhaps all instances of great beauty awaken organic responses which in other contexts would be called sexual, just as they awaken other organic responses of fear, hope, joy, sorrow, remorse, and hate. But in the context of aesthetic form these biological and psychological responses are necessary constituents in the situation if there is to be conscious awareness of the qualities associated with these responses. Having this function of rendering the individual aware of aesthetically structured quality, and not the function of meeting the demands of ordinary living, it is scarcely accurate to call them the responses of sex, fear, hope, or sorrow, even though the same resources of the biopsychological organism are brought into play.

In love between the sexes the beauty that enthrals the lover may awaken responses more predominantly sexual than in other situations. The sexual embrace, however, need not be the outcome or the direction of the order of events. If it be a genuine instance of beauty, the events may be so ordered as not to lead to sexual fulfilment or even to suggest such an outcome. On the other hand, when lovers have established the sexual relation, the sexual embrace and erotic play may well be intrinsic to the whole order of events bearing the character of beauty.

There is almost always some profound aesthetic quality in love between the sexes. One in love will experience a rich undercurrent of qualitative events running through the days and hours, sometimes dominant in conscious awareness, sometimes like a substream. Beauty and erotic love are closely allied and properly belong together, although they may also be separated, each running its course without the other. When this last occurs, each is impoverished, and the good of life declines.

FEELING IN AESTHETIC CONTEMPLATION

Feeling in one sense of the term drops away when all resources of the organism are brought into harmonious action, whether it be in absorbed attention or in absorbed exertion of movement. Feeling which attracts attention to itself appears in consciousness only when the organic response is more or less disorganized and equilibrium is disturbed. When every bit of energy is released in utmost exertions of flight or attack, we do not feel the emotions of fear or rage. After we cease the strenuous exertion or just before we begin or when some blockage arises, so that all energy cannot flow in perfect harmony of dynamic action, emotions surge into consciousness. Lack of feeling in a time of full and unobstructed release may be only a theoretical ideal never perfectly achieved but approximated to all degrees. Yet retrospection seems to support the claim that conscious awareness of feeling fades to a minimum when unrestricted release of all resources is given to contemplation or to action.

On the other hand, to be aware of all the qualities in aesthetic form, one must have the organic responses yielding such awareness. Feeling in the sense of apprehending the qualities of the object is certainly present in aesthetic contemplation. The difficulty seems to be a matter of definition. Feeling, as apprehension of the qualities presented in aesthetic form, must be distinguished from feeling which distracts attention to itself and away from the object. To the degree that absorbed attention approaches perfection, we have no "feeling" in the second sense but may have the greatest abundance of feeling in the first sense.

[142]

BEAUTY

The folklore and myth of a people convey in aesthetic form the quality of events critically determinant of their history. Men encounter individually the wonder of new birth and the breakdown of death. In high hope they undertake some enterprise, only to find that, when power and wisdom ripen toward fulfilment, the body fails, the mind declines, the high swing breaks in mid-flight. Some caprice of circumstance blocks endeavor when plans and action are moving toward anticipated outcome or when, from disaster, some new hope arises and surprising fulfilments ensue. Thus men encounter the rise and fall of fortune. They brood over it, and one tells another what he thinks and feels concerning it; the other has encountered something like it, and he elaborates the account—so the story grows. The account of events bringing joy and sorrow, hope and failure, life and death, occurring through many years and through a sequence of generations, takes on aesthetic form with the telling. Occasionally, some Homer will gather it all together and create a more magnificent form for the relating of this story. The story shared creates a profound community of the people. What happens to each individual, giving redirection to his life, is then interpreted as an exemplification of what the myth relates. Hence the community of people is not merely imaginative. It is found in the creative and destructive events which men encounter in the actual conduct of their lives. Through the medium of the myth all the most important events are woven into the web of the common life and are felt to be moving toward some obscure outcome, dimly felt with horror or exultation or some commingling of these with many other emotions.

The outcome of the common life is always in the making. No one understands it, although it may be presented in vivid pictures of mythic symbolism. Not by intellectual understanding but by feeling together the quality of transformative events do people live under the control of a creativity which is shaping their history. This achievement of community and sense of a meaning unfolding in the common life through the interpretation of events in the aesthetic form of myth and folklore has been set forth by a number of writers. I do not know a better statement of it than the following:

Mythology, in the widest and most general sense, is that living body of uncriticized and fundamental notions, that largely unconscious yet undergirding theory of interpretation, or that broadly imaginative ordering or giving shape to experience that arouses the activity, elicits the feeling, and crystallizes the meaning of a people's collective existence. Mythology of this order operates at levels far deeper and richer than the mind, and exercises an urgency of control more compelling than the intellect can ever command. It provides and defines the vision of the world and of man with which they see.

In a stricter sense, mythology refers to that concrete body of stories and legends preserved in the popular memory which is the unconscious creation and inheritance of the common life. Myths in this sense are a recording, a distillation, and a celebration of the facts of ordinary human experience. Myths of this kind are the fragmentary fossil remains of the grass roots of human thought and feeling, the most sensitive index to the story of human striving that we have. They are the products of that marvelously assimilative faculty a people possesses whereby they can transform ordinary events into symbols far more concretely allusive and imaginatively real than the wooden abstractions of propositional statement can ever be. They keep alive the hidden strivings of the human spirit by giving them telling shape, deliver men from the narrow bounds of private worlds to endow their lives with a wider meaning and a deeper sanctity, express the elemental traits of human character and constantly, beneath varying guises, capture the primitive cyclic patterns of birth, death and renewal, and enable a people to re-enact their past and reaffirm their common lot and destiny. Myths of this character release the magnificent and unsuspected energies for expression and action lying far behind and beyond the small circle of man's educated consciousness. They are the preconscious means whereby the vast and obscure reaches of common humanity participate imaginatively and concretely in realities far more complex and important than they ever know.

An example of a myth with this curiously specialized character is the body of stories and folklore and song which have clustered around and cast a glow of significance about the simple, obscure figure of John Henry. No one knows for sure where John Henry was born. All we know is that he died while building a tunnel for a railroad shortly after the Civil War. The songs that have grown up around him are work songs, wrung from the simple but compellingly concrete rhythms of heavy toil, rhythms responsive to the rise and fall of the hammer. The pattern of the verses is unmistakable, though not consciously designed by its many makers. John Henry, backed by his white boss in a contest against the new steam drill, won the bet but died from the strain. The story provided a plastic symbol for many things. Many a man, in singing its simple refrains, has been enabled to participate in processes and realities more rich and full in scope than the symbols taken literally by themselves apprehend. For the myth of John Henry dramatized and made accessible to the human heart the dark tragedy of the black man subjected to the power of the white; the inexorable fate of the worker in the early, desperate stages of industrialism, when he blindly felt that survival depended on matching his strength with that of the encroaching machine; the violent gutting of nature, which ruthless exploitation of the west could bring; the mingled glory and horror in existence, whereby all good is inextricably mixed with evil and whereby the arc of man's rise to his ripest, most full and heroic stature, is a broken arc, ending in death. For the rhythms and meanings of the John Henry refrains are those of an exultant chant, undercut by a deep strain of haunted sadness. They strike at the heart of human existence, catch elemental patterns of recurrence, evoke the typical and the universal, root life in its communal basis, join men together in an imaginative order, invest the hard realities of daily life with a ceremonial dignity, and convey an enlarged sense of the way what happened to John Henry once upon a time can happen to any man at any time.

The value of myth for a people therefore is this: its unexcelled expression and celebration of community, wherein all achievement is a collaboration and where a thousand think and feel as one.[2]

This statement suggests the historic, creative significance of aesthetic form when it assumes the character of a myth. The myth distinguishes and relates events creative of the life of a people in such manner that they can be apprehended as one unitary movement. Thereby each individual becomes a conscious participant in the fulfilment of the vast accomplishment of the people as a whole.

Every distinctive culture transmits from individual to individual and generation to generation a structure which shapes the organization of personality from infancy. This organization is of such sort that the psychosomatic individual, down to the glands and cellular tissue and nervous system, is rendered deeply responsive to certain objects, happenings, and goals. He is so organized by this transmitted structure that he is receptive to, and integrative of, the massive accumulated stimulus of many people living and striving and suffering together. This psychosomatic structure determines the scope, order, and meaning of the appreciable world for the people of this culture; it shapes their desires and aversions, their interests and inquiries, their problems and aspirations. If the culture has the potencies of greatness, it will release the utmost capacity for sensitivity and responsiveness, for striving and appreciation in the individual who most fully acquires it. How profoundly a man can respond, how deeply appreciate, how finely discriminate and abundantly apprehend, will depend (1) upon the

[2] This statement is taken from an unpublished paper by Preston T. Roberts, Jr., a Divinity Fellow in the Divinity School of the University of Chicago. It represents a condensation of what F. O. Matthiessen, Harry Levin, Thomas Mann, and other literary figures have had to say about myth in our time.

[146]

kind of culture he inherits, (2) upon the completeness of its acquisition by him, and (3) upon his native endowments.

This subrational structure, which is the substance, power, and richness of a culture, cannot be intellectually formulated or reflectively analyzed except at superficial levels. Therefore, it must be transmitted and quickened to power by noncognitive symbols; a cultural myth such as we have been describing is precisely such a symbol. What it symbolizes is the very structure of life for the people of this culture; and this structure extends far beyond the reach of intellectual understanding. The myth, so long as it continues in the living context of that culture and so long as the culture retains its coherence and potency, awakens these deeps of response and quickens into living awareness that scope and richness of meaning which this culture provides.

Great art has the same identical function as the cultural myth which we have described. Indeed, great art and cultural myth are the same, except for one qualification: As a culture becomes more sophisticated, reflective, and diversified, the cultural myth breaks up into the several diversified arts and becomes the work of individual artists, thus losing the conglomerate anonymity of a myth. Nevertheless, great art serves the same function in human living when culture becomes critical, analytical, and diversified, as myth serves when culture is more homogeneous and less critical; it communicates and quickens to living power those subrational feelings whereby a person becomes aware of that depth, scope, and richness of qualitative meaning made accessible to him by his culture.

A culture may lose this power; in fact, we have come to such a time in our own history. The social structure of creative interchange (our culture) will not fit into the channels to which it must conform if it is to provide security, richness, and meaning to life as shaped by our technology. These two shaping powers—the cultural matrix and the technological order—do not fit each other. The social structure of creative interchange, when not distorted by other demands, gives enrichment and support to human personality at levels too complex and too spontaneous for administrative direction or intellectual control. Working at these subrational sources, it engenders meanings which give zest for living. It is maintained by myth and art and all the innumerable symbols of daily life which arouse the nonintellectual depths of interresponsiveness between people and between them and their physical environment. Social order and human good must always rest basically upon this kind of interresponsiveness. Consequently, serious evils break forth when another order is imposed upon the people, such as the technological, requiring them to interact in ways not sustained by the underlying structure of interresponsiveness, here called the "cultural matrix."

There is one example often noted of this evil which arises from conflict between the cultural forms providing channels for creative interaction and some other order, which creativity cannot sustain because the cultural forms do not fit into it. This appears when a complex civilization is imposed upon a people with a primitive culture. At first, the primitive people fall into destructive vice or destructive violence, because the subrational structure of mutual interchange can no longer regulate their desires and aversions in constructive ways. Later a deadly apathy falls upon them, and they are likely to die and dwindle away as a people and a culture.

These consequences also occur when a new technology of power and complexity rather suddenly develops and imposes forms of behavior into which the established cultural forms of creative intercourse will not fit. This new technology then operates as though it were imposed by a civilization alien to the people; their own culture is then "primitive" compared to their own technology. This is what has happened to us, first to European-American culture and then, as technology spread around the planet, to modern men generally.

The twelfth century in European history was an age when the matrix of creative interchange, working by means of art and other noncognitive symbols, was fairly well fitted to the demands of the technology of that time. But with the thirteenth and fourteenth centuries a new technology began to arise, and to it the structure channeling the course of sustaining creative intercourse was not fitted. The people of wealth, power, and prestige and the agencies of social control all conspired, whether consciously or unconsciously, to conserve the structure of enriching interresponsiveness in its established form and in opposition to modifications required to fit it into the demands of the new technology. This has continued up to our time, with the development of technology gathering momentum continuously and the cultural matrix becoming less fit to give meaning, richness, and sense of personal security to those who live under the control of the technology. Our major social ills can be traced to this maladjustment between two major structures of our existence: on the one hand, the cultural matrix with its sustaining interactions working through art and other noncognitive symbols and, on the other hand, our supertechnology with its operations demanding an order of life unsustained by creativity, because creative intercourse is confined to cultural forms alien to this technology.

This failure of the order which regulates human desires and aversions at levels beyond the reach of human management cannot be rectified by more efficient administration or by extending the scope and power of political control. No doubt, these must be extended and made more efficient to avoid social confusion when the subconscious cultural matrix is unable to do the work that it should; but this is a crutch and not a cure. Intelligent administration has its place in every society, but that place is not to do the work of the cultural matrix in regulating psychosomatic reactions at subrational levels. These interactions are too complex, intimate, and imperative for intelligence to construct, for reason to direct, or for administrative devices to control. Yet we are not helpless in the matter; we can provide conditions favorable to the working of those processes which create community and determine destiny for good and not for ill at noncognitive levels. The most important of these conditions is the self-giving of men to these creative processes under the guidance of art.

If art is to fulfil this high office in our time, it must be an art which fosters mutual support and creative interchange first of all among the industrial workers who operate our technology. The reason for this is not that technology produces economic goods and economic goods must be the base on which every other good depends. The reason for this is that our technology nullifies the efficacy of our inherited cultural matrix with its mutual support and mutual enrichment and will nullify every other unless the matrix is woven into the very working of the technology itself. This can occur only if the workers who operate the technology find in their work such relations to one another and to the rest of society that a subrational system of mutual support develops throughout society to sustain them and to give to each a sense of importance and meaning in life, not apart from his work but in his work.

The conclusion of all this can now be stated: The only art able to shape the destiny of our age toward the good and away from the evil is proletarian art. It must be proletarian not in the sense of promoting propaganda (although it may do this incidentally), but proletarian in the sense of awakening among industrial workers who operate our technology those interactions which create the subrational matrix of culture, thereby leading them to assume responsi-

[150]

bility for the social order and the good of all human living. This they will do, not because they understand the good of all human living (no one does), but because their lives are directed to this end at levels which understanding cannot reach.

The supertechnology of our time will be either the destroyer or the constructor of human good. It can be constructive only if it becomes the creature and servant of the creative process, whence springs all the good of life. But if this is to happen, those who operate the technology must find in the very operation of it that growth of meaning and that deep sense of social security and social responsibility which only the creative process can give. But if all this is to occur, we must have a proletarian art combined with other conditions to be discussed in chapter ix under the head of justice.

An art thus serving the industrial worker and through him all the rest of us can be the voice of destiny leading the blundering steps of man through the confusion and danger of this transition into an age of fulfilment. Art is the expression of creative powers, which the artist himself does not understand, which no human mind can shape or master, but which transform and lift to new levels the subrational substance of life upon which all rational structures must be erected and which all agencies under human control must serve. To fulfil this high office in our time, art must be proletarian in the sense noted; it must create substance, richness, and meaning in the lives of industrial workers.

This proletarian art may not be great art in its early stages according to certain aesthetic standards; great art requires a cultural matrix potentially rich with qualities of deep and complex human responsiveness. It will take time to develop such culture among the industrial workers. Proletarian art may become great, however, even according to these aesthetic standards; and, in any case, it will have that kind of

[151]

greatness which shapes history and social destiny in such a way as to bring forth the supreme potentialities of our age. Men who scorn such art because it is not great in some other sense are irresponsible snobs and parasites.

BEAUTY AND EVIL

Beauty, like every other instance of created good, can at any time become greatly evil. When beauty enthrals and love adds rapture to the enthralment, men may become deaf to the marching orders of the creative event. Here is a good so dear, here is a time and place so sweet, that time must end. Space must be bounded where the borders of this good world reach. Out beyond lies the lesser good. So here we must remain. When the aristocracy of a great culture in the days of its ripe maturity have achieved aesthetic form pervading all their lives, beauty tempts in this manner. To be sure, agencies other than aesthetic form are at work to bind the aristocracy to some completed fulfilment. Pride and love of power, comfort, and brutish inertia play their part in building up the reactionary who fights social change. Yet, despite economic and political interpreters of history, we venture to suggest that the charm and beauty of the aristocratic way of life may often be the stronger motive for a large group, even though the aggressive leaders of reaction are driven by other desires. These leaders who loudly vocalize the action may not represent a love of the old ways for the sake of qualitative richness found in them, but the greater body of aristocrats may cling to the established order on this account.

The greater the gift of created good given to man by creativity, the more completely and decisively is he likely to repudiate the demands of creativity when it requires a transformation of the old ways. The greatest gift is beauty pervading a magnificent culture with all the arts of courtesy, friendship and love, poetry, painting, and song—each person cultivated and tuned from infancy to respond like a violin to the touch of a master. But all this, exclusively restricted to a few men and to one locality, becomes an evil when it resists a widening and deepening of qualitative richness throughout subsequent history. The resistance to creativity and the repudiation of its demands by the beneficiaries of such a culture bring on the kind of disaster which has been called "the judgment of history."

Never in the past could the whole planet be organized against creativity in this manner; now, with modern technology, it can be; and there lies the danger. In the past one group might resist, but other people would attack and undermine its power before it went too far in obstructing the creative movement of time. In the past, moreover, only a thin layer of aristocracy had access to the qualitative riches which tempt man to resist the transformations of creativity. The dispossessed would always rise up in time and throw off the constraint. But if the whole planet should be organized against creativity for the sake of an achieved fulfilment, if the riches of life were sufficiently distributed so that all were exposed to the great temptation, if none were so dispossessed as to force the others to heed the demands of the creative event, then the greatest judgment of all might come upon us. Our human race might then live voluptuously, with time made sterile to prolong the sweetness of a honeymoon.

If this should happen, either of two consequences might ensue. The creative event might disturb the established order, first here, then there; and in time the whole system would crack and break. But since so many had lived so long with a minimum of creative interaction beyond the demands of their established order and since there would be no large body of the dispossessed to take over leadership at the spearhead of creativity in rearing a new order, none would be able to develop a new order fitted to the new conditions.

The other alternative would be for the resistance against creativity to be so well knit and universal as to prevent any such breakdown. In that case humankind would cease to be the medium through which the creative event might work to achieve progressively a world of maximum value. Human beings in an order securely established against creative transformation would then decline, in bliss, to the level at which creativity could no longer work with human minds to make a world of widest and richest meaning. Some other species would become the spearhead of creativity, and man would become extinct or would settle into an obscure and degenerate existence, despised or ignored by the life that moves triumphantly.

Perhaps what we are saying is only a myth to suggest by exaggeration the nature of an evil that may threaten us. Just now we are moving over one of the great humps of history. The two demands that seem most imperatively to drive us are the right of every man to work when he wants and the release of the power of technology for industrial production. But if these should be achieved and the age of conflict should pass into an age of world-wide peace, utopia will not necessarily be with us. The time of peace and plenty might bring a danger as deadly as any we have known.

TRAGEDY

Tragedy is the contrast between what might have been and what actually occurs. The good excluded by tragic events may not be explicit, but it must be in awareness sufficiently to bring out the contrast. By this contrast tragedy forces into fuller recognition and evaluation the greatness otherwise hidden and ignored. Events, to be tragic, must also determine the destiny of some individual or group or other span of history. They reach deep into issues basic and constitutive of human existence. Therefore, tragedy, more than anything else, brings to the level of human appreciation the quality of events rich, stirring, and compelling beyond all others. It generates meanings that are common to all those who can reach the required level of discernment, because the issues explicated by tragedy are continuously creative or destructive of human life. In great tragedy we stand at the brink where the struggle goes on forever between creativity, generating man hour by hour, and the destructive conditions which threaten his continued existence and not infrequently drag him to ruin. Except by way of tragedy we do not become conscious of the titanic struggle and the ever recurring triumph of creativity over the destroyers of value and the life of man. The loss, the failure, and the destruction adumbrating the glory that might have been, and some day may be, make us realize the enormous issues at stake and the magnitude of the struggle involved in human life. Apart from this awareness generated by tragedy, we are like children at play in the midst of war. Tragedy sends a shaft of light down into the depths, where creativity is always struggling to sustain and lift life against its foes. Hence tragedy opens the way for man to find the meanings most rich in quality, most important for human living, and most universal—universal because they are generated at the level at which creativity is always snatching man from destruction and lifting him to higher fulfilment or failing to overcome the obstacles.

This gateway of tragedy into life's deepest and most universal meanings is, for the most part, closed, because man cannot undergo fateful events with sufficient poise, discernment, and understanding. The desperate straits of practical emergency distract attention. The fear and hate, the suffering and despair, the danger and imperatives of action, are too obsessive. They will not permit man to apprehend the meaning of what is transpiring and the levels at which destiny is determined. Hence the problem arises: How can man ride these fateful events, sufficiently free of compulsions and distractions to learn what they have to tell of the deepest and most universal meanings of human life?

Tragic art solves this problem. It mediates through symbols the impact of events too severe for man to endure in direct encounter. It presents in dramatic form events that break and remake the order of human life, where suffering, fear, and hate would overwhelm man's interpretive power if he were in the midst of the actual happenings. Hence tragic art enables creativity to surmount man's limited capacity to undergo creative transformation. Through symbolic representation in tragic art the human animal can walk through devastation and the remaking of the order of life and, in the midst of breakdown, be sufficiently free of obsession and compulsion to undergo the transformation producing a world more rich with meaning. Thus equipped with tragic art man may be the recipient of meanings emerging from the fateful depths of human existence, more comprehensive of human fate and possible fulfilment than any others. They who share these interpretations of life through tragic art are a community growing through history.

The most common instance of tragic art serving in this manner is the story of the Cross of Christ. This story sets forth events of suffering, despair, and triumph which transformed the lives of men and the meaning of history. Yet the records indicate that the men who encountered the events did not appropriate their meaning as fully as did Paul, who received them at second hand by way of the tragic Gospel story. This story has given to the whole of human history a new meaning and direction by interpreting events in relation to the Cross.

Thus tragic art provides a way for man to undergo happenings beyond his capacity to interpret in direct encounter. It awakens the deepest responsiveness of the human organism, releasing its capacity for feeling quality and liberating the human mind to undergo the transformations of creativity. By way of tragic art, creativity can produce meanings that speak to every man in every age who will undergo the disciplines required to understand and appreciate. These meanings tell the story of human existence from its beginning to its ending: the story of its continuous creation, dangers that threaten and destroy, salvation hardly won, glory dimly felt of a greatness yet to be and of a goodness narrowly missed. The community of those who walk through the Valley of the Shadow of Death under the guidance of tragic art may span the ages and grow through time. The men of this community feel one another's feelings and understand one another's meanings at levels deeper than any group created by economic interdependence, political control, race, class, kin, custom, or locality.

One who has joined this community by way of tragic art and commitment of faith will be empowered to undergo creatively what he could not otherwise encounter without impoverishment. For him futility will be lifted from defeat, for the quality of his failure can be added to the qualities of events which are significantly connected throughout history by tragic art and religious faith. For him arrogance will be taken from triumph, bitterness from suffering, poison from despair, selfishness from the intimacy of love, and triviality from the hour of joy. The deep and solemn tones that sound through ages of struggle will not be altogether absent from his laughter. The narrowing moment of each supreme fulfilment will always have two gates open, one to the long trail that comes from the endless past and the other to the road that leads into the growing future. He will be lifted from the confining pit of his individual existence to a place where he can feel and live the story of man and the spiritualizing of the world. By tragic art spirit may reign where beasts would rule. The deepest tragedy of human life is confinement of human appraisal and striving to

[157]

some one perspective and to goods seen and prized out of that relation to creativity which renders them good. From this predicament we cannot escape, ordinarily, unless the artist enables us to see, not through his eyes necessarily, for he himself may not understand, but through his selection and vivification of the most fateful events in human life.

The greatest of tragic art is always religious in nature, even when it is not consciously so and even when it professes to repudiate religion. When it does repudiate religious symbols and practices, these have generally lost their true function and are misdirecting faith. Under such conditions, tragic art is our best guide back to a saving faith. Theology can learn more from tragic art, perhaps, than from any other source. We have already mentioned the Gospel story of the Cross, but that is not the only instance. All great tragic art proclaims this truth: Man is beaten and destroyed if he gives first place to any other good save what creates all good, and he finds the trail leading to indefinite increase of good by way of the frustrations, futilities, and destructions attendant on seeking the good of life in any other way. Tragic art sets forth this truth not by stating it but by portraying the most dramatic events of human existence as they truly are.

COMEDY

Comedy is closely akin to tragedy. We laugh when perspectives seemingly incongruous and irreconcilable are swiftly integrated. Thus in laughter and in humor we are caught up into the creative event and delivered from enthralment to any given perspective. The perspectives are not, ordinarily, very profound and compelling, and their integration is not very profoundly transformative; but the joy of laughter is the joy of the swift triumph of a new creation over an obstacle that seemed, for a split second, insurmountable. Within the bounds of its involvement, laughter for a little time frees us from bondage to any other com-

[158]

pelling concern except the creative integration of meanings. This lift, this freedom, and this joy show how profoundly we are made for the creative event. If we could live in its power down to the roots of our nature and if we could move with it triumphantly, our lives would have a joy which deep belly-laughter can only suggest. If the torpor of the flesh did not bind us, if the pride, fear, and triviality of the mind did not hold us so fast, the joy and freedom of laughter, merging with the depth of tragedy, would make life magnificent.

No suggestion is made that we shall reach such heights in any foreseeable future. Only it is important to note that comedy and tragedy both demonstrate the nature of human good; both make plain that creativity is the way of man's fulfilment. All good claiming to be more important is an illusion into which we fall because we have had so little experience of those moments when the creative event surged to power. In comedy, creation does not take control of all of our lives, but it does dominate and direct all that is relevant to the comic occasion. When we have what is truly "a good time," the limits may be narrow and great evil may ensue; but, within the bounds circumscribed, the joy is the joy of creative transformation.

Some comedy borders close on the depths of tragedy; the satires of Molière and the fools of Shakespeare sometimes reach this depth. Humorous art spontaneously created by great men in the midst of fateful events reveals the uplift of creative power, as it frees them from the overwhelming fate of inevitable outcome or confining circumstance.

Humor shows what the creative event might do with human life if we could live in its power and for it above all. In humor we live at the breaking edge of life, where worlds are torn down and remade. This quick breakdown and new creative synthesis is what makes us laugh. In wit and satire these worlds do not include the ultimate grounds of se-

[159]

curity. If they did, we should reach the ecstasy of the saint and the martyr in the supreme moments of their sacrificial devotion. But the joy of humor at its best reveals the nature and destiny of man more clearly than most other moments of human life.

BEAUTY AND TRUTH

Truth we understand to be a system of propositions specifying a structure of relatedness pertaining to events. When this truth becomes knowledge, we are able to observe events occurring in the specified order and are therefore able to infer the past and predict the future with some measure of probability.

Any order of interrelatedness which the human mind can know with precision must be rather simple. Events which yield much richness of quality require a structure too complex for the human mind to make accurate inference concerning its past and future. Hence a complex structure of events with rich quality can be felt, but it cannot be clearly and correctly thought. The cognitive search for truth, therefore, seeks always for the greatest simplicity in the structure of events. In contrast, aesthetic form must have structural complexity sufficient to present rich and vivifying contrasts of quality. Aesthetic form has its own simplicity, but it is the clarified simplicity of quality for feeling rather than the clarified simplicity of structure for knowing.

These considerations explain why intellectual inquiry long and rigorously pursued reduces existence to bare abstractions. The philosophy of logical positivism is a striking example. Positivism sought, above all, to be intellectually rigorous and clear, and it has succeeded in portraying the world in so barren and worthless a form that some of its ardent devotees in the days of its beginning have turned away from it and its leaders are beginning to transform it considerably.

The long search of science, logic, mathematics, and logical positivism for structures of utmost clarity and precision is of inestimable value. Accurate knowledge is indispensable. But the demands of beauty are not the same as the demands of knowledge. Truth and beauty do not coincide, even though each has much to contribute to the other. Beauty supplements truth, for structures too barren of quality cannot even lure the cognitive search. Truth supplements beauty, for beauty must have a structure which can be known in its more abstract features. Most important of all, their mutual reference appears in the concrete situation of value, since beauty and truth are always present together in every concrete situation that has great value.

When science and philosophy seek truth in disregard of that qualitative abundance which value demands, they run dry. They taper off into abstractions which, for a time, a few specialists may pursue with ardor but in which, in the end, even they lose interest. Truth as one component of value must serve qualitative abundance, even as abundance must meet the demands of truth.

Bertrand Russell's autobiography is a striking illustration of the fate which threatens man when he is dominated by a passion for precision and clarity to the exclusion of qualitative richness. Russell's parents died when he was three, and he was reared by his grandmother and by tutors in a library. His associations with other children were negligible. He had remarkable skill and great interest in mathematics. "A great event in my life, at the age of eleven, was the beginning of Euclid. . . . . I found great delight in him. Throughout the rest of boyhood, mathematics absorbed a very large part of my interest."[3]

As an adult, Russell considers the world as known by the sciences the surest and most reliable reality we can know.

[3] *The Philosophy of Bertrand Russell*, ed. Paul Arthur Schilpp ("The Library of Living Philosophers," Vol. V [Evanston, Ill.: Northwestern University Press, 1941]).

The rich flood and flow of experience thronging upon us in the world of common sense and in artistic and religious appreciation seem to him less real, less sure, less satisfying, if they cannot be put into mathematical form. ''And so my intellect goes with the humanists, though my emotions violently rebel . . . . the consolations of philosophy are not for me.'' The only happiness that he has found in philosophy is the happiness of achieving a logical analysis that approximates the clarity and precision of mathematics. ''In this respect my philosophic life has been a happy one.''

Bertrand Russell represents one direction in which modern life might go. Science and mathematics may come more and more to dominate our lives and shape our minds. Technology enables us to select from the massive impingement of common reality those abstractions which happen best to meet the demands of scientific precision and technological control. Thus man may come to seek and love these only and miss the qualitative abundance of the world and the most important realities.

When this happens, great personalities like Bertrand Russell will say ''my emotions violently rebel,'' because they will sense that they are missing something. Small personalities will be quite content. But those who rebel will be helpless to make good their loss. The only escape from this fate is tragic art, together with an education, religion, and morality which direct us to qualitative meaning and to that which creates it. In previous ages the richness of the world thrust itself upon the appreciative consciousness of man because he had not the power to evade it. In our time, mathematical science and technological control, brought to superb perfection, will blind us to the creative source of human good unless we have tragic art guiding religious commitment and an education directing the appreciative consciousness to the sources of life's richness.

Although intellect alone can discover truth, what truth

it discovers depends on the reality it seeks. It can search only that reality in which men consciously participate with vital concern for the problems inherent in it. Tragic aesthetic form, in combination with religious commitment to creative transformation, renders one consciously participant in, and vitally concerned with, problems involving the qualitative abundance of life and the deeper issues of human destiny. Without such art and faith the intellectual pursuit deals with problems progressively more barren of human value.

Thus, while it remains true that art does not give us truth, we never seek and find the truth about matters of great importance unless we have tragic and religious art.

CHAPTER VII

Truth

TRUTH rests upon the foundation of value, not value on the foundation of truth. Organic reactions with conscious awareness distinguish better and worse long before propositions are formulated and distinguished as true and false. Also the issue of true and false, when it arises, is always incidental and subsidiary to distinguishing the better and the worse. After the philosophical and scientific apparatus of truth-seeking becomes highly developed, this order may seem to be reversed for some specialists, truth taking priority over value. But this is a false appearance. Truth cannot be chosen as a goal and lifted above all else unless it be valued above all else. This valuation may be mistaken; and we shall try to show in subsequent discussion that it is. But now we are only making the point that the problem of value precedes the problem of truth and always encompasses and underlies it. Truth is one branch that buds and grows very late on the tree of value. Value pervades all of life, truth only one small part of it.

Truth, we shall try to show, is any specifiable structure pertaining to events and their possibilities. Truth is not knowledge but must be potential knowledge. Hence the structure must be specifiable. When specified in relation to actual events determining the structure, the truth becomes known and is called "knowledge."

A serious problem immediately confronts us. The structure pertaining to events undergoes change when the mental reactions, devices, and implements needed for acquiring knowledge are introduced into the situation. In such case is

[164]

truth the new structure assumed by events when knowledge is achieved? Or is it the structure which the events had when the inquiry was initiated prior to the changes caused by the reactions, methods, and implements of inquiry? Or is truth that abstract totality of structure residing in the realm of possibility, waiting to be actualized progressively in events, as proper inquiry achieves correct knowledge?

Given some established interpretation of value, the relation of truth to it will be determined by answers to these questions—answers which cannot be settled by an appeal to truth because they concern the very nature and status of truth itself. Or, putting it otherwise, the affirmative and the negative answers to all these questions are equally true. The answers are determined by our initial definitions. Whatever answer one gives to these questions, one will acknowledge the same matter of fact as the opposite answer would do, except that one will apply his labels differently. What one calls "truth," one's opponent will name by another term; but, apart from the name, what is acknowledged in each case will be much the same. Our choice of initial definitions and our application of labels will be determined not by truth but by utility and other value. This again shows that the problem of value runs much deeper than the problem of truth and that truth is ancillary to, and derivative from, value.

VALUE AND TRUTH

Living organisms at all levels of existence experience value, but they are not concerned with truth until linguistic signs can be used to specify the order of events. Even after truth becomes a concern for the minded organism, the events having quality as determined by the feeling-reactions of the organism are enormously more complex and numerous than those relatively few events precisely specified by linguistic signs, and thus known. Every reaction in the organism and in the society of associated organisms is an event. All these associated organisms determine one another and also determine a vast complexity of events in the environment lying between and around them. All are events having quality because of the feelings involved.

This vast complexity of events with their possibilities is not known or knowable save in small part; but, in so far as the organism ever comes to know anything at all, it is some part of this structure of happenings. When it engages in any cognitive inquiry, some part of this structure of events and their possibilities is what it seeks to know. As it comes to have more of a mind and develops the methods and instruments of cognition, these distinctions and connections pertaining to events come progressively into the range of known fact. Finally, and most important, this complex of events involved in organic behavior is what each individual and the group need to know for their own good. Therefore, if truth is what man *needs* to know, what he *can* know as mind and method are perfected, what he *seeks* to know, and what he *must* know progressively to meet the issues of life and death and good and evil, then the specifiable structure of events and possibilities, determined by the feeling-reactions of the organism prior to knowledge but waiting to be known, is the realm of truth.

Whether we apply the label of "truth" to the structure of qualitied events determined by interactions between associated organisms and their environment or whether we reserve this exalted term for the structure which events assume as a consequence of successful cognitive inquiry and relative to that inquiry is a question of utility, as said before. Certainly, the organism reacts differently when it comes to have a mind capable of conducting inquiry than it did prior to the achievement of such a mind. Also it undoubtedly reacts differently when conducting inquiry in quest of knowledge than it does when not. Furthermore, events are demarcated differently when all the apparatus of highly developed scientific research is brought into play, along with the complex civilization which must always accompany such apparatus and research. Consequently, the structure of events finally known cannot be identical with the total structure of events as initially determined by the noncognitive feeling-reactions of the organism. We can know by scientific research that this is the case, even when we cannot know the specific structure characterizing all these events at the time of their original emergence relative to noncognitive feeling-reactions. Thus to know that something must have been the case, without knowing the specific details of its occurrence, is so common that no quibbling paradoxes need be raised, except for the sport of playing with puzzles that have no consequence of importance.

If the structure of qualitied events and the possibilities relevant to them, as determined by noncognitive reaction of the organism, must undergo change in the very process of achieving knowledge of them, the objector might say that they are never known. Only that modified form of them is known which can reach knowledge. But if this modification is precisely what must always occur when one knows anything at all, it is a useless quibble to say that this modification renders knowledge of them impossible when, in fact, it is precisely what must occur when any knowledge is ever achieved. So we conclude that it is quite proper to say that we come to know the structure of events determined by noncognitive feeling-reactions, even though this structure is modified by the inquiry issuing in knowledge.

While we believe that truth can in this way be identified with the total value-structure of events relative to the noncognitive feelings of associated organisms, we shall not adopt this alternative. The complexity of existing reality so far exceeds any competence of language to designate it that we must simplify whenever we can. It is much more simple, and hence less staggering to our limited abilities, if we identify truth with that possible structure which is actualized in events to the degree that correct knowledge is achieved but does not characterize events completely and perfectly until complete and perfect knowledge of them is attained. Even after truth so defined has been attained, a great many events distinguished by noncognitive reaction of the organism are never characterized by the structure of truth and never can be. A simple illustration of this can be given. The standard acceleration of a falling body is the rate of fall in a vacuum at sea-level. But no body ever is in a vacuum at sea-level. Therefore, the truth about falling bodies is never descriptive of actual falling bodies. We compute the actual falling of bodies by estimating their deviation from this ideal way of falling; but even the computation introduces features which render the description only an approximation to the actual falling of bodies. It follows that the deviations of most falling bodies, since they are infinite, can never be computed.

In sum, truth is an artificial and abstract version of that infinite complexity of structure characterizing actual events and their possibilities when these events are determined by interaction between associated organisms and their environment. Therefore, truth is never the whole of any concrete embodiment of value but is always one abstract feature ingredient in concrete value as experienced by human beings.

The specifiable structure called truth becomes more and more remote from value as it is lifted out of the concrete matrix of qualitied events to which it is relevant and treated as a goal of endeavor independently of this vast, unmanageable matrix brought forth by creativity. As the technology of scientific research, industrial production, and political control becomes more dominant, with the rest of life subordinated to its demands, a gap forms and widens between these specified and specifiable structures demanded by technology and the deep, complex matrix of events, which matrix alone can yield richness of quality. This matrix has complexities beyond the coverage and penetration of specifiable structure. Least of all can it be comprehended by structures specifiable to that degree of precision demanded by efficient technology, whether in scientific research, in industrial production, or in political control.

Thus the totality of all structure includes far more than can ever be specified. Furthermore, the totality of all specifiable structure includes far more than can ever be relevant to any inquiry conducted by the sort of mind and world created to date. Hence it would seem to be the part of simplicity and economy to identify truth not with all structure but only with specifiable structure that is relevant to any inquiry within the bounds of possibility for the human mind and its world as now created.

If we take this position, truth is created by the creative event, but it is not created by the inquiring mind. When creative transformation produces a world containing minds capable of inquiry, in the same act it also produces a world having the kind of possibility called "truth." Prior to the existence of such a world containing such minds, no such possibility was relevant to existence. But when minds exist which conduct inquiry and achieve knowledge, the creative event producing such minds, along with the necessary sort of encompassing world, in the same creation likewise creates truth, namely, structures of possibility relevant to the world which sometime may be discovered by these minds.

As inquiring minds with their encompassing world are transformed by the creative event, new possibilities come into being. The new possibilities under consideration are those structures which *may* characterize events with some degree of approximation and *will* do so if existing minds conduct successfully the inquiries of which they are capable.

Thus truth, according to this interpretation, is both created and discovered. But no contradiction is involved.
Truth is *discovered* by the inquiring mind; it is never created
by the inquiry or by any performance of the mind. It was
created by the event that created the mind and the world
capable of sustaining the kind of inquiry that might issue
in events having the structure which is a possibility prior
to such inquiry. But even as a possibility it had to be created, because there could be no such structure relevant to
the existing world until after the proper kind of mind and
world had been created.

When the world with its inquiring minds is so transformed by the creative event that new kinds of inquiry
become possible, which inquiry was previously impossible,
then new truth is created. This truth may never be discovered. The inquiring minds, while capable of conducting the
search that might lead to the discovery, might never do so.
Or, while undertaking the inquiry that might lead to this
discovery and while capable of doing it successfully, they
might, nevertheless, fail. According to the metaphysics here
defended, there is indeterminacy in the world, as well as
determinant structure. Possibility is not the same as necessity, and new possibilities can be created that had no prior
being of any sort.

Thus truth is created by the creative event, but truth is
antecedent, coercive, and determinant for all inquiry. It is
ineluctably imposed upon the mind and its world. Truth
is so imposed, but knowledge is not. The truth is a possibility waiting to be discovered, but the discovery depends
upon the initiative and action of the existing minds.

What we have said about structures of possibility in the
form of truth might also be said about aesthetic form. As
forms of truth are created and yet antecedent and coercive in
determining what knowledge shall be to the human mind,
so it is with forms of beauty. In the chapter on ''Beauty'' we

said that it was created in the existing world by interaction between the organism and its environment and between it and other minded organisms. But this structure was
a possibility relative to such organisms and their encompassing world. In creating such organisms with their world,
the creative event created these forms of beauty as possibilities. They may continue to be possibilities only; but if some
organism with its mind and its inherited culture should
undertake the proper kind of vibrant interplay with the
proper portion of the world, this aesthetic form would become embodied in actual events. Thus forms of beauty are
created but are, like forms of truth, antecedent, determinant, and coercive for the individual who seeks and achieves
beauty. They are there to be discovered and brought into
the actual world of events. The most glorious of them are
most rare and difficult and are the eternal quest of high
artistry. But all were first generated as possibilities by the
creative event, and in some phases of their achievement the
artist or the aesthetic discoverer of them must himself undergo further creative transformation along with some portion of his encompassing world. Yet, if the basic structure
of a culture contains these forms as possibilities, they are
there to be achieved by men through constructive action on
the world.

In some measure our minds and their appreciable world are
continuously undergoing change by creative interaction.
Hence some structures are being added to that ideal realm of
specifiable structure relevant to any inquiry and any artistic
or aesthetic achievement we may undertake. Also some are
being lost. But this gain and this loss are gradual. Through
long periods of time the more general and comprehensive
structures persist without change. Those structures which
are definitive of the human mind itself and any appreciable
world it might have remain identically the same throughout the entire period of human existence. What change, if

any, may mark the transition of the human mind into something else we cannot say. Here again is a matter of definition. Not merely is it a matter of definition that some change may occur beyond anything we can imagine, putting our present state of existence beyond the pale of kinship with that new creature coming into existence; but it is a matter of definition whether or not we call that new creature "man." Some structure characterizing his existence will remain identical with ours, if it be nothing more than creaturehood. Doubtless, much more than that will be identical and common. But whether or not we choose to call the structures that creature may have in common with us by the name of "humanity" is a matter of terms only.

PERVERSION OF TRUTH

Specifiable structures (truth) and structures specified (knowledge) can have richness and depth of qualitative meaning only when they keep close to the matrix of structured events as determined by the feeling-reactions of the organism. Here we encounter a fateful problem always emerging with civilization and never more acute than it is today. As knowledge and knowledge-getting become increasingly dominant over human living and as man superimposes upon events more and more that abstract, quality-impoverished structure which is sufficiently simple for him to specify with his limited mental ability and set of linguistic signs, a dichotomy and conflict arise between the demands of that uncomprehended complexity of organic feeling-reaction, on the one hand, and the demands of this cognitive structure of control, on the other. Relative to the infinite complexity of feeling-reaction, the appreciable world is infinitely rich with quality but unmanageable and unknown except in small part. It lacks form, as the Greek thinkers would put it, when form means what can be precisely specified with linguistic signs. On the other hand, the

structures of truth, both those known and those that can be
known by further and better inquiry, are relatively barren
in quality even when they are established in events as their
actual structure, because so much must be omitted in order
to reduce them to the simplicity which the knowing mind
requires.

Here is one of the most serious conflicts in human existence and one of the most fateful decisions which man
must make as he approaches the higher levels of civilization. Will he give first place to the structures of truth progressively knowable by scientific and philosophical inquiry,
holding in servitude to the demands of truth the vast and
uncomprehended complexity of qualitied structure relative
to feeling-reactions? Or will he give first place to this vast
and uncomprehended complexity of structure, which is rich
in quality, and hold the relatively barren structures of truth
in servitude to it? One kind of human life, one kind of culture and civilization, one outcome of human existence, as
over against another, will issue from this decision. Our
Western civilization, dominated by Plato and Aristotle, has
tended to choose the first alternative. If there is any truth in
our interpretation of value, this is the way of progressive
impoverishment until life becomes unendurable and man
breaks forth with unthinking fury to liberate himself from
the inane efficiency of human control and the impoverished
abstractions of precise cognition.

While Western civilization has tended generally to follow
the way of progressive impoverishment, leading to fury and
destruction so far as deliberate choice is involved, the
deeper propulsions operating noncognitively have driven in
the other direction. Also, strong elements in the prophetic
tradition of Judaism have tended in the opposite direction.
Hence the final decision has not yet been made. The Western
world is today again at the crossroads, to which it periodically returns because of this inner conflict and undeter-

mined choice which someday it must make finally and fatefully. One difficulty is that the issues have never been made
so clear as they might be. The Greeks have dominated our
philosophy so completely that the deliberate, philosophical, and scientific analysis of the issues has been unfairly
weighted. The Greek scorn for the uncomprehended and
unspecifiable richness of quality in the world has carried
over into all our thinking. On the other hand, those who
have striven for the priority of concrete value over abstract
truth have done so blindly in great part. At times they have
reared great speculative systems like that of Plotinus and
other semimystics, but they have not made plain the indispensable importance of truth as a servant of concrete value.
We can never outgrow the need of the services of truth.
Rather, we must have more and more of this service as
civilization advances. But always it must be kept in servitude. Not the ideals of man, not any specifiable structure of
truth, whether it be scientific, metaphysical, moral, or aesthetic, should be master of our lives. Known truth must be
magnified to the utmost of our ability but always in service
of something more important.

Again we repeat, the tragedy of man and his generic sin
is to try to put all existence into servitude of specifiable
structures of truth when truth is defined as those structures
which the human mind can know with precision under
optimum conditions of inquiry and can use to shape the
course of events. Such truth is a great good but only when
it is used to set up conditions which magnify creative intercommunication of perspectives along with creative interaction between sensitive organism and environment. The
rightful function of truth is to regulate the rhythm and behavior of the organism so that noncognitive feeling-reactions can be more finely discriminating and richly qualitative.

When truth is sought and used in any other way and to

any other end, it becomes an evil that mounts as civilization advances. It becomes an evil because it impoverishes the richness of quality which is accessible to human awareness. Destruction, hate, and fear abroad in the world today will come again with greater fury if man continues to subordinate, restrict, and impoverish the unknowable richness of qualitative events by subjecting them with increasing rigor to science, technology, industry, and scientific philosophy. All these—science, technology, industry, philosophy—are servants of creativity when rightly used; but, when they try to dominate and control creativity, hell breaks loose. If we prefer a tamer phrase, no less popular, life becomes progressively "meaningless."

A decision must be made to serve what is deeper than truth—the encompassing structure whereby events have quality for the feelings of the organism and, on beyond that, the creativity which generates this unanalyzable richness along with the structures of truth. The mind is created, in the first place, to discover and more clearly to specify whatever structures can be used to release this creativity for bringing organic responsiveness to the level of qualitative meaning. But qualitative meaning fades when the structures of truth no longer continue in the service of the unknown matrix of value which has creativity deeply and obscurely imbedded in it.

When this perversion occurs—the attempt to build value on the structure of truth instead of truth on the structure of value noncognitively apprehended—an astounding interpretation of value arises, astounding even though it has become almost commonplace in our time. Instead of interpreting value as the generating matrix, far exceeding anything the intellect can know, value is declared to be the abstract structures of possibility rationally specified as goals sought by human living. These abstract forms are then set up as an essential value which is contrasted with existence.

Thus we hear of value and existence being opposed. When men speak thus, they are trying to build value on the foundation of truth. This is perversion; for truth must be built on the foundation of value, and value is in existence to the degree that events are (1) so structured as to be richly qualitative and (2) so structured as to create more richness of quality.

This opposition and conflict between values as abstract possibility specifiable by linguistic signs, on the one hand, and the vast, deep structured well of existence infinitely rich with quality, on the other, is wrecking human existence. The fathomless deeps of qualitied structure have been built through countless ages of noncognitive interaction between cells, complex organisms, and nonliving things. Our existence is rooted inextricably in these depths of value. We cannot really live for and by and with anything else. Therefore, when we artificially reverse the order of reality and set the most important values high in the empyrean of abstract possibility, we produce a hopeless conflict of striving. Cognitively and volitionally we strive after the abstractions as goals and ideals, but organically we strive after the rich content of quality in actual events. Each way of striving frustrates and impoverishes the other. One theory of psychopathology claims to trace most psychic ills chiefly to this conflict[1] and also says that it is the basic source of social conflicts and frustrations. Whatever other causes there may be for social and psychic trouble, it would seem that there is no surer way to dry up the wells of value than to magnify this conflict between two opposed ways of striving after the good of human life, one directed to linguistically specified structures of possibility, the other to the structure of events made rich with quality by feeling-reactions of many organisms in association with one another.

[1] See the writings of Alfred Korzybski and his followers

[176]

This perversion of truth has assumed still another form, even more grotesque. Truth concerning the heavy events which determine our existence by giving us value has been confused with truth concerning those rarified events which are nothing but linguistic symbols, namely, marks on paper and vibrations of the air when ordered and used for communication. Often the term "truth" or "knowledge" is applied to both indifferently, without distinguishing the two. But true knowledge about specifiable structures that do not pertain to the life-shaping events of our world is not at all the same as knowledge about structures that do. The former are about events, to be sure, but they are about linguistic events only. Linguistic events may shape our lives, may destroy us, may even make us insane, but only by way of illusion, only when we mistake these specifiable structures for the heavy realities that make a difference through impact upon us and upon one another.

Since the confusion is so subtle and persistent between specifiable structure which pertains to nothing save linguistic events and specifiable structure which pertains to the heavy events of existence, let us reserve the term "true knowledge" for the latter only. There is no issue here for debate or disagreement. If one wished to use the word otherwise, we should not object. We only ask to be permitted our chosen usage because we believe it will avoid one of the most treacherous confusions arising in discussion of truth and knowledge.

Error is fruitful when it concerns the structure of events directly generating richness of quality or its opposite by way of feeling-reactions. Such error can lead to knowledge of truth because the error can be discovered through experimental interaction between organism and environment. The discovery may require observation throughout a sequence of generations and so call for historical research evaluatively conducted, or it may be compassed within a single generation. It may require co-operative inquiry of many people and so become a social enterprise, or it may be conducted by a single individual or small group. (The T.V.A. is an excellent example of inquiry conducted as a social enterprise.) Thus error can be fruitful when it concerns the structure of events which generate value directly or impoverish and destroy directly.

But there is another kind of error which is not fruitful. It tends, rather, to be cumulative in its evil consequences. It is the error of thinking that a structure precisely specified by linguistic signs is designative of some important, value-generating reality beyond the world of events, because no events can be found having that structure. This error cannot be discovered by any perceptual event whatsoever because the assertion claims to be about something that is not an event. Therefore, the error can be developed to produce more and more illusion. One specifiable structure is built on another, one generation passes it on to the next, more people come to accept it, tradition sanctifies it, religious authority is given to it, the social order comes to depend upon it because it provides the community with a common perspective even when the perspective is of nothing save an illusion, people are persecuted or ridiculed if they do not accept it, political and economic authority join with the religious to enforce it, children are reared from infancy to accept it so that the sense of personal security comes to depend upon it, any doubt concerning it producing psycho-pathic symptoms.

Sooner or later this structure, supposed to characterize a reality having causal efficacy beyond the world of events but truly about nothing save conceivable possibility, begins to crack and break beneath the weight of social and personal organization built upon it. Then social confusion and personal pathology break out, spreading and deepening until the loss of meaning and frustration drive people either

[178]

to build another illusion or, haply, to abandon illusion and turn to the world of real events.

This kind of progressive error is called "insanity" when it is not subject to social criticism. When socially accepted and shared by many, the illusion does not isolate the individual and cause insanity, but it may become a grand illusion held in common by the culture and transmitted in a great tradition. In this guise it may be even more deadly because its dangers are not revealed by the symptomatic pains of personal pathology. Its illusory character persists undetected because it is accepted by so many, each finding community with others in sharing it with them. The hidden evil of it can then grow until a whole people are led to confusion and frustration.

Here we have what some may think is an evil produced by creative intercommunication. But this springs from a misunderstanding. There is nothing evil in the creation of these specifiable structures that reach far beyond the actual world. Instead, we must say that this is the greatest gift of creativity to man. The evil lies not in what creativity does in giving the structures to man; it lies, rather, in what man does with them, namely, treating them as descriptive of some kind of important reality when they are not. These specifiable structures that are not yet descriptive of anything give to man his glory and power and make him supreme over all the rest of creation because these, when properly used, criticized, and experimentally modified, enable him to explore the actual world and discover the order of actual events. With specifiable structures so used, man can range far back over history to learn how creativity has worked through time to create the present. He can reach far out through time and space, deep into the hidden intricacies of existence, through the feelings of the human heart, and up into the splendor of imaginative construction.

Man would not be man without these specifiable structures as resource and arsenal. The evil arises only when man misuses them. His greatest sin is to put the creature in place of the creator, and this is precisely what he does when he worships some allegedly hidden reality supposed to conform to specifiable structures embodied in nothing but linguistic signs. He may even go into mystic rapture about this hidden reality. Or, again, he may worship the structures themselves in their bare abstraction as ideals more compelling than any actual reality in this world of time and space and matter. This was the great sin of the Greeks in contrast to the Jews, who kept their speculations pruned close to the creativity that works in history. This is the sin many Christians have taken over from the Greeks. When one proclaims an alleged reality, supposedly timeless and changeless, comprehending all the past and future in one total simultaneity, he is guilty of this idolatry, because nothing is timeless, covering past and future, except these specifiable structures treated apart from any actual events which they might describe. He who identifies God as "the ground and goal of history" or "super-history" is perpetrating this sin. This is perverse arrogance of reason, and none have been so guilty as certain religious teachers and leaders, who have set up this idol and worship it.

When creativity is used to identify God, we are saved from this perversion. Then we know that God is working in actual events and is not a mere construction of human linguistic devices, set high upon a cosmic throne. Plato and Aristotle, many mystics, perhaps most Christian thinkers in modern times since the Renaissance, even those who have inveighed most bitterly against the humanism of the Renaissance, have committed this sin of putting the creature in place of the creator, the ideal in place of the actual God, abstract structure allegedly representative of a hidden reality in place of concrete events having structure.

TRUTH AND MYTH

We have already described myth. It is the forerunner of truth. It is not truth, but it is the first step in the direction of truth. It is a construction of the imagination, not specifying the structure of events as they truly are but directing the organisms and the social process in service of creativity and the matrix of qualitied events relative to feeling-reactions, so that this matrix yields qualities more rich and vivid. This is myth at its best. But myth can be misused, even as truth, technology, and all other created goods. We shall not elaborate the importance of myth, since much has already been said about it. Only this should again be said: We never outgrow the need of myth along with truth. But when it is confused with truth and men begin to use it in the way that truth alone can be used, it produces the evil consequences which we have just been describing.

TRUTH, KNOWLEDGE, AND OBSERVATION

Structures of possibility, here called "truth," are brought down into actual events and so become knowledge by way of observation. Observation is the gateway through which truth must pass to become descriptive of actual events. Through observation, structures of possibility become structures of known events. Observation always includes some measure of experimentation, even though the experiment is nothing more than turning the head and focusing the attention. We must examine observation with care, for it is crucially important, in part, as the source of much misunderstanding.

Observation, as here understood, is a series of perceptual events. The perceptual event is not merely sense data. We do not deny the reality of sense data; and if one wishes to identify observation or perception with them, there is no denying one's right to do so. But here again we come to a nominal problem. However we define our terms and apply our labels, we all must acknowledge the same problems and realities. The issue is not to prove the validity of any one set of definitions and labels versus another but to choose the set most useful in solving the problem under consideration.

The perceptual event, as here treated, includes everything within and without the biological organism which experiment can demonstrate makes a difference to conscious awareness when the perceptual reaction occurs. Complex and intricate as the perceptual event is, when so interpreted, it is only an infinitesimal part of the total universe. Experiment easily shows that innumerable happenings can occur in the wide reaches of the world, and even in close proximity to the organism, perhaps also in it, which make no difference whatsoever to the conscious awareness accompanying the perceptual reaction of the organism. All this, which makes no difference, is excluded from the perceptual event.

Innumerable structures are ingredient in every perceptual event. Far fewer are common to a sequence of such events. From these that are common, selective attention picks out one, and that is what we perceive. Under other conditions, attention might select a very different structure from all those that are common to the series. For example, instead of perceiving a table in this series, I might perceive firewood, if I happen to be perishing with cold; or it might be simply a bulwark against an onrushing foe, if I am seeking protection. In such cases I might ignore the "tableness" that is resident in those same events because selective attention is otherwise directed to meet the emergency.

All knowledge is achieved by way of perception, because all structures whereby events are distinguished and related can be sought and found in perceptual events, and there only. Metaphysical knowledge is achieved by a more elaborate analysis of perceptual events to the end of discovering structures not merely common to a selected series but those essential to all perceptual events whatsoever. Time and space, for example, are essential ingredients in every perceptual event. This we discover by analysis of perceptual events. So also are identity and difference, change and permanence, existence and possibility, structure and quality, mind and matter, substance and form, better and worse, right and wrong, good and bad, God and man—all the categories sought by metaphysics or other philosophical inquiry can be uncovered by proper analysis of the perceptual event.

It is true that philosophical and scientific inquiry demand a much more elaborate analysis and more precise selection to discover in perceptual events the structure sought. In ordinary perception the analysis and selection are often made by automatic, habitual reactions of the organism, focusing attention upon some one structure which is pertinent to the interest of the moment. But even in ordinary perception, the analysis is sometimes made deliberately, and the selection may be tested with care to learn if it truly is in the events under consideration. Science and philosophy carry this deliberate analysis much further, with all manner of techniques and instruments, to probe more deeply into the complexity of structures common to perceptual events, searching after a structure to meet the need that concerns the inquiry. But in principle there is no essential difference between knowledge by ordinary perception and knowledge sought and found by philosophy or any other kind of valid inquiry. In this sense it can be said that when God is known truly, he is known by way of perception, even though it is perception wherein the analysis and the search are carried much further than the automatic and habitual analysis and selection made by automatic reactions of the organism. These suffice for perceiving hills and houses and spoons, but not for perceiving God (the everlasting creative event). However, when one first learns to perceive these common objects or enters a culture wherein very different objects are observed from those to which one is native, even ordinary perception must do a good deal of deliberate analysis and selection together with elaborate testing.

It is claimed that mind other than my own cannot be observed. We can observe the body and its behavior, so it is said, but the mind cannot be known by way of observation. It must be known by intuition or inference or self-communication, whatever that may mean.

This claim arises from a misunderstanding of the nature of observation, on the one hand, and the nature of mind, on the other. We observe the mind of another when we observe symbols (words, gestures, and the like) so ordered as to communicate meaning. The ordering of such symbols so that they communicate meanings in response to our communications is the mind of the other. A phonograph does not order the symbols into meaningful structures but only reproduces what has previously been ordered by a mind. Mind is the communicating and interpreting of meanings by use of symbols. When we observe such communication and interpreting by the appropriate ordering of symbols, we observe the mind of the other. Meanings thus being generated, communicated, and received by an organism, *is* a mind, not merely the physical manifestation of mind. The mystery, complexity, wonder, and value of it are not augmented in the least by representing it to be something different and independent but running parallel to all this. Since this meaningful ordering of symbols by an organism is the actual, present existence of a mind and since this ordering can be observed as a complex event, we do, in truth, observe other minds.

Intuition must be examined, both because it is claimed to be the way we know other minds and because it is often held to be a unique way of getting knowledge different from observation. Intuition is the creative integration of diverse meanings to form a new, more ample meaning. It is the second subevent in creativity; or, if one wishes, one can call it the first subevent, the emergence of a new meaning, because creativity works in a spiral, so to speak. When integration of old meanings forms a new meaning, the new one can always be considered the first step leading to a further integration with others, and so on without end.

Intuition in the sense noted is going on all the time and is another word for creativity. We take note of it and so label it "intuition" only on those rare occasions when it becomes spectacular. But those spectacular instances are not different in nature from the common process continuing all the while at some minimal level. Intuition is what Whitehead calls "concrescence" when it is lifted to the level of conscious awareness. Diverse influences pour in upon the organism from different sources and are ordered and organized into a unitary system of reaction. At the level of conscious mind this unitary system of reaction assumes the form of a meaning more or less complex. This newly emergent meaning may carry with it a profound sense of conviction and importance, and this sense may be justified. It is justified when innumerable data acquired in the past are now seen sufficiently to fit into an ordered whole, thus providing evidence for the truth of the new meaning. Of course, elaborate testing may at times be required. But in our time certain irrelevant kinds of scientific inquiry are often applied with great ceremony to some of these intuitions, until the whole procedure becomes ridiculous and certainly adds nothing to the relevant evidence.

If this interpretation of intuition is correct, there is a sense in which we do know other minds by intuition, although the same is true in knowing anything else which requires creative integration of diverse and fragmentary meanings. Intuition is most prominent in the intercourse of minds because only in communication between minds do we give and receive so many different meanings requiring creative integration. Intuition, in the sense that we have interpreted it, does, therefore, play a larger part in knowing other minds than in most other instances of knowing; but by no means is it a peculiar way of knowing restricted to our cognition of minds.

There is a sense, also, in which it can be said that we know God by way of intuition. If God is the creative event and intuition is a spectacular instance of creative integration of meanings re-creating the mind and personality, then God becomes spectacular in such radical instances of intuition. Obviously, we cannot get firsthand knowledge of God until God does something that attracts our attention. Spectacular instances of intuition are instances of God's doing something to attract our attention, hence providing the occasion when knowledge of God becomes possible. But, here again, intuition is not a peculiar way of knowing. It enters into all instances of knowing where some new meaning is generated by integration of previously acquired data, these data being meanings of minor scope relative to the new meaning produced by their integration.

Mystical experience, in one of its many forms, is an instance of intuition. It is called "mystical" only when it is radical and revolutionary in transforming the mind and personality (as in the case of Paul on the Damascus road). This, however, is not the only kind of mystical experience. Mystical experience, most generally speaking, is a breakdown of the organization of the mind. It may be induced by drugs, by excesses, or by diverse and conflicting meanings with strong driving propensities. When this last is the cause, the breakdown may be transitional to a new integration of the mind and personality, with more scope and richness of meaning and more power of action. In this last kind of mystical experience, we have a direct experience of God if God is the creative event. If the individual is properly equipped with traditional symbols and interpretations, he may recognize this seizure to be the direct apprehension of God, although the theology with which he interprets the deity he has apprehended may be quite mythical. These spectacular instances of creativity, compulsively attracting attention to themselves, do not equip the mind with concepts for interpreting correctly what is there and then undergone. Nevertheless, this is the divine presence and the divine work and, when properly analyzed and interpreted, yields knowledge of God, if God is creative.

We have tried to show that observation enters into all cases of getting genuine knowledge. We have glanced at knowledge of other minds, self-communication, intuition, and mystical experience only because these are often alleged to be ways of knowing without observation. On analysis, we see that they are not. Reason also, when attempted without observation, can yield no knowledge of events. Reason apart from observation can do nothing more than specify structures of possibility, which may or may not characterize events. Observation and experiment alone can inform us if they do and when they do. Authority, also, is no exception. Valid authority merely transmits to us from some original source the knowledge that we acquire from it. This original source must be observation and experiment or analysis of perceptual events.

TRUTH AND CREATION

Truth, we have said, is any structure of possibility which becomes descriptive of actual events when observation and experiment are applied under required conditions. Only specifiable structures relevant to the kind of mind and world now existing shall we entitle "truth." When this kind of mind and world have been transformed by new creation, other structures will be relevant.

This does not make truth relative in any pernicious sense.

[187]

The specifiable structures called "truth" are definitely constitutive of the very existence of the mind and its world. The human mind, as there and then existent, and the existing world relative to that mind could not be what they are without this structure of specifiable possibility, which is the truth concerning them, being precisely what it is. This holds regardless of whether any existing mind ever achieves knowledge of these specifiable structures or ever operates in such a way as to render them descriptive of actual events. As said before, the order of truth is not constructed by any mind or dependent on any mind, but it is constructed by prior creation. When new creation transforms the mind and the world, new structures become relevant, and some old structures, relevant to the preceding state of affairs, no longer have relevance to the world. But the specifiable structures of truth are there to be discovered and are the truth, no matter how unknown they may be. They never are discovered in their entirety, and even the meager parts that man may come to know are not known with absolute certainty and precision. Nevertheless, the specifiable structures composing truth become different as creativity changes the mind and the world. They are a part of the essential nature of the mind and the world. They are not constructed by human endeavor and choice. They are ineluctably the truth, no matter how we strive to make them otherwise. They are the truth just so long as the mind and the world continue to be what they are.

A substratum of the structure of truth is never changed by creativity so long as the human mind and its appreciable world continue to preserve any identity whatsoever. This statement is a tautology, for identity can be nothing other than identity of specifiable structure pertaining to the matter under consideration. When this matter changes in some respects but continues to have the same specifiable structure relevant to it, we say the two situations (before and after change) are similar. This is the nature of similarity in all its instances, and this interpretation of similarity removes some of the baffling contradictions besetting it when otherwise interpreted.

Many of the structures known to common sense as descriptive of certain situations will sometime cease to be relevant to any actual state of affairs. Nothing in existence has the structure of Babylon in its glory, but once Babylon was a familiar object. Structures now known to science will cease to characterize anything at all when the methods, theories, instruments, and civilization of one age have been supplanted by others radically different. But the basic structure essential to human existence must remain self-identical and changeless throughout all transformations that man can ever undergo. This affirmation, we repeat, has the truth of a tautology.

When truth is identified with structures of specifiable possibility which are relevant to actual existence but does not include all structures which might sometime become relevant, a basic metaphysical cleavage emerges between, say, the metaphysics of Whitehead and the metaphysics here upheld. The primordial order as defended by Whitehead is necessary if every structure that might ever become relevant is to have some kind of reality prior to that creation of a world to which it would be relevant. Apparently, Whitehead upholds the idea of a primordial order precisely to provide some ground for asserting that all these structures (eternal objects) are eternal and have some kind of reality even when irrelevant to anything in existence. But when we understand that new creation in producing any kind of world does thereby also create the structures of possibility relevant to it, the idea of a primordial order becomes indefensible. Also God then ceases to be identifiable with an inactive primordial order and becomes an active, creating reality.

This brings us to further metaphysical issues that call for clarification.

METAPHYSICAL ALTERNATIVES

The materialist says that matter gives to all reality whatever structure it may have and does this independently of the human mind. The subjective idealist claims that the human mind gives to all reality whatever structure it has and that there is no structure antecedent to the human mind. Other idealists teach that a cosmic mind provides this structure, and they assert it to be antecedent and coercive to human existence. The organicists make this same claim, except they say that it is organism that provides the structure, either the biological organism or some cosmic organism. Others, who have been called "formists," claim that structure itself is eternal and uncreated and imposes itself upon existence, giving to matter, mind, organism, and everything else whatever structure they may have. According to this philosophy, structure is not provided but is eternal with no source beyond itself.

The metaphysics here defended is different from all the foregoing. It is not materialism in the traditional sense, which asserted that pellets of matter accidentally fall into combinations to form all the objects of the world as we behold them, or at any rate to produce such illusions. On the other hand, if matter is identical with energy and if energy in the form of the creative event, working against the resistance of other forms of energy, produces all the good in the world, the evil being precisely this resistance to the creative event, then the metaphysics here upheld could be called a kind of materialism. But this kind of materialism must be sharply distinguished from everything bearing that name in the past. Since it must be so distinguished, it is misleading to call it materialism. Inanimate matter as known to common sense is *not* what creates all else, accord-

[190]

ing to this philosophy. Rather, matter as known to common sense is merely one level in that progressive creation which generates all the levels of order. Furthermore, matter, in many of its forms, seems to be peculiarly resistant to the demands of further creative transformation.

Our metaphysics certainly is not idealism, organicism, or formism, as these were described above.[2] The structure that we find in the world does not come from mind or organism. These are themselves creations of that kind of energy having the structure of creativity. Neither is the structure we find in the world derived from some realm of eternal disembodied structure, as the formists assert. The structures of possibility are themselves created, as we have been saying.

Structures are created by progressive creation of the world. Each level of creation has not only a structure of existence peculiar to itself but also structures of relevant possibility which had no relevance to existence prior to this further creation. Structures of possibility having no relevance to the existing world are round squares. That is to say, they are self-contradictory concepts and are meaningless. There are no such possibilities; hence structures of possibility are created when a new kind of relevance is created.

While structures are created, there is one kind which cannot be. It is that minimum structure which energy must have to be creative. What that is we can know only by an infinite series of approximations as we search the process of creation down to lower and lower levels of origination. As we said before, we do not know if there ever was a time when this lowest level was all that existed. There is nothing in the logic of this metaphysics which demands such an affirmation. Also, it is foolish to ask if there ever was a "time" when "nothing" "existed," at which "time" the structure of the creative event originated. These ideas are

[2] This classification of types of metaphysics is derived from S. C. Pepper's book, *World Hypotheses* (Berkeley, Calif.: University of California Press, 1942).

all self-defeating and contradictory of themselves. Further-more, even if the inquiry could be so formulated as not to contradict itself, it would seem utterly impossible to con-duct any kind of search that might inform us of a "nothing-ness" whence all things originated or whence the creative source of all had its beginning.

The form of the creative event working at the higher levels of value is created by its working at the lower levels. Whether or not it ever did begin at some lowest level, mounting upward ever since; whether or not there are, even now, levels far higher than the human; whether there are a rise and fall of levels throughout the cosmic whole of things or an upward march forever—these and many other such matters we do not know and consider it futile to speculate about. All we know is what has happened upon this planet, and even that we know but slightly. But we do know enough to live in absolute commitment of faith to the crea-tive event and to serve it above all else by striving to pro-vide whatever conditions it may demand, whether these be physical, biological, personal, or social.

We do not accept Whitehead's primordial order in the sense of an order distinguishable from the creative event, nor do we interpret creativity as Whitehead does. As stated above, in the metaphysics here upheld there is a primordial order intrinsic to the kind of energy which works creative-ly, but it is not the primordial order presented in White-head's philosophy. According to Whitehead, the primor-dial order waits helplessly for creative events to embody in themselves the eternal objects which are presented to them as possibilities by this order. The primordial order serves merely to provide a habitation, so to speak, for structures that otherwise would have no relevance to the existing world and thus to keep them in storage until the transfor-mations of the existing world bring about a situation which might entertain these structures as possibilities relevant to its own operations. The primordial order, according to Whitehead, is not the order of any one kind of creative event but rather the all-encompassing order which prevents the totality of creative events from falling into confusion and becoming utterly aimless.

When Whitehead identifies God with the primordial order as just described, we have something which might command religious commitment of faith if there was nothing better. But it cannot respond to man or meet the needs of human life as does the creative event we have been describing.[3]

The consequent nature of God, as set forth by Whitehead, is the consequence of prior creation. On that account it is called God's "consequent nature." It gathers up, so to speak, all that has been produced by the totality of creative events as they occur, so that nothing may be lost. As the primordial order provides a receptacle for storing all structures that may ever become relevant to the existing world, so the consequent nature provides a receptacle for storing all that has ever existed, so far as it can have any value whatsoever.

Here, again, we must part from Whitehead's teaching. There is certainly some conservation of value, not only in human life but in the world generally. There is a building-up of structure in the existing world of such sort that events can take on vivifying contrasts of quality and then, at a higher level, qualitative meaning. Under favorable conditions all this may render the world progressively meaningful and rich with quality. But this is not inevitable. There is loss as well as gain, and some losses are irrecoverable and irreparable so far as any evidence at our command is concerned. If the consequent nature of God means anything

[3] This criticism is made specifically of Whitehead because we are so profoundly indebted to him that we fear our thought will be confused with his in every particular. This would be a misunderstanding.

more than this kind of uncertain progression in the increase of value (with Whitehead we are sure it does), it seems to us a fabrication of the imagination to comfort the human heart in its sore distress over the perishing of precious values. To assert this perishing to be an illusion by reason of the consequent nature of God is to come very close to denying the reality of evil.

We have pointed to three major differences between Whitehead's metaphysics and our own: We do not interpret the primordial nature of God as Whitehead does, nor do we agree with him in his account of the way values are conserved or in his portrayal of creative events as having no order among themselves except an order imposed upon them by something that is not an event at all—the primordial order of God. In our own account the order or structure of the creative event is not imposed upon it but is intrinsic to the very nature of such an event and has no source other than the creative work of some lower order of creativity.

Our indebtedness to Bergson is almost as great as to Whitehead. Hence there is likely to be confusion in this quarter also. Consequently, we must distinguish creativity as here interpreted from creativity as set forth by Bergson. According to him, creativity has no structure and creates no structure. This, plainly, is exactly opposite to what we are saying about creativity, although here, again, in Bergson we recognize a source of insight beyond measure.

Also we must point out differences from Dewey. According to him, the creative mind of man gives to the world the structures discovered there by inquiry. The very process of inquiry creates the structure, which is the product of its search. In respect to narrowly scientific knowledge there is some truth in this, although not to the degree that Dewey sometimes seems to assert. But the basic structure found by philosophical inquiry and much that is vaguely known to common sense are produced not by human inquiry and not

by human experience but by creative energy, as previously
described. Here again what we say will sometimes sound
like Dewey, and at times Dewey almost seems to talk this
way. But when challenged, he refuses to go this way.
Furthermore, the creativity which he upholds is that of the
human mind, not a creativity working antecedently to the
mind, creating it along with its world.

There is a determinate order of existence at any given
level of creation. There is also a determinate order running
through all levels. The latter is the minimal structure of
creative energy, the former the structure of the world as created at that level. The primordial order, setting limits to all
creation, is not matter or mind or organism or any disembodied primordial order (Whitehead) standing in its own
right over and above events, but it is that structure which
energy must have to be creative at all. This primordial order
of creative energy, setting limits to all creation and creating
the human mind and its world, would never be acknowledged by Dewey.

At the level of man the mind can select and ignore, imagine and construct, intend and seek, but only within the
limits of the order created to date, which includes both the
structure of the human mind at that time and the structure
of the appreciable world relative to that mind. Selective
attention, organic reactions, linguistic devices, mathematical and logical formulas, the instruments of construction,
the accumulated resources of a great culture and civilization, give to man enormous scope in selecting and constructing the world that he will have. But diverse and complex as
these possibilities may be, there is an order which is
coercive, determinate, and antecedent to all that man may
do or seek or know, setting limits to knowledge, to truth,
and to all that may happen. It is the order of the existing
world as created to date, plus the order of creative energy as
it operates in the world, plus the range of relevant possi-

bility as determined by this structure of creative energy and the world with which it must work. The creative event cannot transform the world in any way other than what is conformant to its own nature.

Thus far we have been discussing truth, not knowledge. Truth may become knowledge, and nothing else can. But knowledge is a very different kind of value from truth. Truth may be sought long before it becomes knowledge. And even "when it becomes knowledge," the knowledge is only an approximation to the truth. Truth pure and perfect is an endless quest. For some it has been the passion of a lifetime. Although never captured in the rapturous perfection of purity, as dreamed by Plato, it is yet found to all degrees of that perfection.

We must now turn to that very different kind of value called "knowledge."

CHAPTER VIII
Knowledge

KNOWLEDGE is truth captured by man and domiciled in his abode; it is the specifiable structure of truth at last become specified, and, furthermore, it is this specified structure at last become descriptive of actual events. These two steps must be taken before we have knowledge: The specifiable must be specified by proper use of linguistic signs, and the specified must be rendered descriptive of actual events by proper reactions of the human organism and direction of selective attention. In knowledge the abstract forms of truth have been brought down into the flow and turmoil of this existing world of events, and these actual events have taken on the structure of truth to some degree of approximation.

These two steps by which knowledge is achieved cannot be initiated until after something else has been done. But this something else was creative and cannot be done by man. A culture and a way of living must have been developed of such sort that men have the kind of signs required to specify the structures of truth. Every human culture has had this to some minimum degree, else it would not be human. This cultural development in linguistic usage came to high fulfilment among the Greeks, whose supreme achievement, perhaps, was to specify some of the basic abstract forms of truth. However, as we have seen, in order to attain knowledge in addition to truth, the specifiable and specified forms must be rendered descriptive of actual events. To achieve this it is not enough to have acquired a language and a usage whereby the structures of truth are specified. Not only linguistic signs to specify the truth are needed but also physiological reactions and selective attention, so directed as to distinguish and shape events in a way that will render them conformable to the specified structures of truth. This last requires a technology and a civilization which shape the interests, hence the reactions and the attentive concern, of men. Only then can men act to shape events and discriminate what they have shaped according to the forms of linguistically specified structures.

The most general structures of truth must always be descriptive of some events occurring in human existence. A certain moral and logical order will necessarily characterize events wherever human beings live, because men could not exist without them. It might be stated otherwise. Human beings cannot exist without linguistic signs, and linguistic signs cannot occur without some basic logical and moral structures in existence. Hence, such structures can be known to be true as soon as they are specified and do not require the second step in cultural development mentioned above, namely, the technological. It follows that philosophical inquiry which seeks knowledge of these most general truths need only specify them correctly. It does not need to operate in any other way to find them structuring actual events, although science and common sense do require these further operations. The more special and particular truths known to common sense and science cannot be achieved to any great extent without the development of a civilization and a technology which so shape the interests, the physiological reactions, and the attentive focus of the mind that events are demarcated in a way that can be described by structures which are specifiable with the language then and there available to men. Also, there are reaches of philosophical and religious knowledge not attainable until appropriate cultural development has created the power of analysis and the fineness of discrimination required to distinguish such structures.

This interpretation of truth and knowledge in relation to each other and in relation to human cultural development, physiological reaction, and focus of attention provides a basis for solving what is called the "problem of induction." The problem is to explain how a structure descriptive of observed events can be trusted to hold true in other times and places beyond the instances already observed. According to the interpretation here defended, the structures specifiable by the human mind and linguistic usage and the order of events making up the existing world as appreciable to the human mind are both created together as one single, total, structured whole by the process of creative interaction. Consequently, so long as the world is of such a sort as to enable the human mind to exist at all, certain structures basic to all meaning whatsoever must characterize that world. Furthermore, when culture has developed to a certain form and level, certain further structures peculiar to that culture must characterize the world, else that culture with its distinctive meanings could not exist. Technology and science of a given sort could not exist if the world did not have the order permitting them to exist. Hence we can be sure that, as long as they do exist—and, therefore, as long as man could possibly seek to know or have any interest in them—certain structures inductively discovered and necessary to the existence of such human inquiry, interest, and culture will continue to characterize the actual world.

This does not guarantee that every structure which man thinks he has inductively discovered by observing special instances is truly and reliably descriptive of the actual world. But it does guarantee that those structures necessary to the existence of a particular culture, with its form of intellectual inquiry, its linguistic usage, its technology, and its focus of attention, will always be truly descriptive of the actual world as long as the human mind can have any interest in them. The human mind cannot have any interest in structures from which it has been diverted by a transformation of culture.

In summary of this point: Structures inductively discovered and necessary to the existence of any culture whatsoever will always be truly descriptive of the actual world so long as any culture exists, and hence so long as the human mind is capable of conducting any sort of intellectual inquiry. Furthermore, structures inductively discovered and necessary to the existence of a certain form and level of culture, with its technology, system of habits, and focus of selective attention, will always be truly descriptive of the actual world of events as long as that culture continues to shape human life and its appreciable world.

The human mind with its meanings and the appreciable world with its specifiable order of events are created together by creative interaction at the communicative level. Not all the meanings created in that way are true, but those which are will surely continue to be true as long as the human mind continues to have such meanings. Of course "true" here means true under specified or specifiable conditions. This interpretation of mind, meaning, and appreciable world as one single order of creation provides a basis for reliable induction.

The mind cannot be created except in intimate conjunction with the world that is knowable and appreciable to that mind; and no such world can ever come into existence unless it has a structure identifiable with certain meanings of the mind. Furthermore, no human mind could exist without knowing something about its world, because it could not otherwise be a human mind. The mind cannot develop, except as the knowable and appreciable world also develops with a structure common to both. The appreciable world and the appreciating mind are one single order of existence. The organic behavior of the human body which determines the order of events in a way that gives to that body the added character of being a mind, and these events which determine the behavior of the body in such a way that it has a mind, are reciprocally creative of one another. Therefore, when the mind discovers inductively certain structures pertaining to events and when these structures are mutually created by the minded organism and the environing world, we can be sure that such structure will always be descriptive of the actual world as long as that kind of mind continues. When such a mind ceases to exist, if ever, the question about reliability of inductive knowledge cannot be asked and will be irrelevant to whatever may then be in existence.

The ultimate determinant of truth and knowledge is not mind with its principles or reason; neither is it matter with an established structure to be imposed upon the mind, although it is matter in the sense of creative energy, progressively developing structures which are common to the mind and its environment. The ultimate determinant of truth and knowledge is the creative event generating the rational principles of the mind and the structure of matter in mutual determination of each other. Also this progressive creation rears a culture which shapes the reactions of the human body, the direction of attentive consciousness, and the technology, so that empirical findings will yield reliable knowledge inductively established within this framework of order shared in common by the mind and its appreciable world.

COMMON-SENSE KNOWLEDGE

Knowledge is correspondence between a structure specified by a system of signs and some order of events determined by reactions of the organism and distinguished by selective attention. Every human individual is born into a situation in which his reactions are guided and shaped by conditions so that his behavior breaks the continuity of ex-

istence into units (called "events") which have an order
that corresponds to the structure specified by the language
used at that time and place. As the child is given the bottle,
he hears the words: "Bottle, bottle. Mama gives baby
bottle."

Of course, at first, the child does not discriminate, much
less understand, the words; but in time he falls into a pattern of behavior automatically making distinctions in the
flow of existence, and these distinctions mark off an order of
events of such character as to correspond to linguistic specifications, such as "Bottle, bottle. Mama gives baby
bottle." His own reactions mark off the events, his attention is directed to the sequence, and the language states the
order of happenings. This is the way we all acquire the kind
of knowledge called common sense. It is easily and pain-
lessly acquired. The linguistically specified structure, on the
one hand, and the order of events as determined by perceptual reactions, on the other, have been prepared, predetermined, and put together by the culture in which we
develop. Such knowledge we can hardly miss.

When situations arise which demand action for which
this predetermined correspondence has not been prepared
and established, knowledge is a little more difficult. More
or less novel perceptual reactions must be performed, on the
one hand, and linguistically specified structures developed,
on the other, and each must be modified until they correspond. If the situation were entirely new, this might be
impossible; but it never is. The human organism would be
destroyed if it were. The organism can continue to react
only within very narrow limits of variation in the situation
which it inhabits. Revolutionary and chaotic as some
changes may seem, they never are actually so. Except for the
newborn infant, it may be said that the wide reaches of the
order of events as determined by the habitual reactions of
the organism, on the one hand, and the specified structure

of habitual linguistic usage, on the other, always correspond in great part. New knowledge is never sought except at some one point in this total system.

In every case of knowledge there is some inference concerning the order of past events and some prediction of what will happen. The propositional structure specified by the language provides for the inference and the prediction. The continued perceptual behavior of the organism will produce the order of events corresponding to this prediction and sustaining the inference if conditions permit. If the best efforts of the organism cannot produce an order of events corresponding to the specified structure, we say the knowledge is not true.

Not all common sense is knowledge. It contains much belief not determined by evidence; for belief is knowledge only when determined by evidence. Evidence is observed correspondence between specified structure and actual events when conditions are sufficiently determinate and known to justify the conclusion that the observed correspondence is relative to these conditions. Common sense also covers many habits and skills that are neither belief nor knowledge but simply ways of acting. While common sense includes all this, it also includes a kind of knowledge that is distinctive of this area, as over against that of science and philosophy.

Everything known to common sense, such as a door, a table, a tree, an automobile, is a structure of events. This may not be apparent until we analyze our experience of these things. A table as experienced is such a structure. I turn my eye in a certain direction, and there occurs the sort of event which we describe as "light rays" reflected so that I have a visual impression and my whole organism reacts in a manner habitual to such a stimulus in such a situation. Then perhaps I extend my hand, and there is a second event which we describe as "impact." It is an obstruction of the hand by an encounter with something or other having qualities variously describable. This also causes the whole organism to react in a certain definite way, which has been established by habit for such a situation. Perhaps these two complex events occur in succession or together along with others. Having in the past noted and recorded in language such an order of distinguished events, I am able to predict and biologically anticipate an order of happenings that will follow if I carry out further forms of behavior under the familiar circumstances. Also, if I am so inclined, I can specify an order of past events which must have led up to the present and can test my statement in various common ways. This total structure we call the "table," if that is the object under consideration. All facts known to common sense are of this general sort. An object is a structured plunge of process; every object is a stream rushing on in a prescribed channel.

SCIENCE AND COMMON SENSE

Science must achieve precision in order to be reliable. But, since common sense does not attempt any wide range of inference, precision is not required for certainty and reliability in the world thus known. Science and scientific knowledge have so obsessed the mind and fired the imagination of modern man that he has lost his perspective quite completely concerning the relative importance of science and common sense. Even great philosophers talk as though scientific knowledge were the most important knowledge we have, some even asserting that it alone is genuine knowledge. There is no dispute about the great value of scientific knowledge, but its value lies in supplementing the knowledge of common sense, not in supplanting it. If we had to choose which to relinquish, knowledge by way of common sense or knowledge by way of science, there should be no doubt about the wiser choice. At least a part of humanity could survive without scientific knowledge, but none could

[204]

survive without the knowledge of common sense. We put it in terms of survival, but that is not the only value of common sense. Most of the great values of life, as well as the ordinary goods, depend far more upon common sense than upon scientific knowledge. The values of family and friendship and social intercourse, of pleasant walks and most beauty, are attained and conserved by way of this sort of knowledge. The scientific supplement to this knowledge enormously magnifies its power, but still it is common sense and not science that bears the chief burden of human existence and human good; and there is no reason to think that any advance of science will change the relative importance of the two.

The temporal and spatial continuity of existence can be cut up into a great variety of different structures which yield very different kinds of worlds. This "cutting-up" of the continuity of existence is determined by a selectivity of attention, which is, in turn, determined by biological reactions, by the system of linguistic signs, by the physical instruments used, and by the cultural demands of the time and place. Every different culture and age has a different structure of events and, to that extent, a different world. In like manner, the world known to science is different from the world accessible to common sense. But one is no more real than the other, although the world of common sense is enormously richer with the qualities of concrete events.

Common sense uses the ordinary implements employed in work and play to distinguish and relate events yielding knowledge. These implements were not designed especially for cognitive purposes but to attain desired goods of various sorts. The knowledge attained by their use is incidental to the main purpose of their employment. On the other hand, science uses implements specially designed to achieve knowledge. Physical instruments and linguistic, logical devices (notably mathematics) are specially developed to achieve precision in demarcating the temporal and spatial flow of existence into units of passage (events) which can be so distinguished and related as to yield scope and precision of inference about other events and probabilities.

PHILOSOPHICAL KNOWLEDGE

Science and philosophy are both rooted in common sense, and both must come back to it to find their solid base. Scientific inquiry brings forth a structure of events inaccessible to human experience except by way of certain specially designed instruments, along with logical and other linguistic devices. As science and culture advance, the structures known to science at one time pass into oblivion with the coming of another age, except as recovered by antiquarians. Thus the world known to science is much more transitory than some of the basic ingredients vaguely known to common sense, such as "man," "world," "good," "bad."

On the other hand, philosophy seeks to know a structure much more stable and reliably present in all times and places than is even the world of common sense. It seeks to analyze perceptual events, in order to discover the structures which must be present in every instance of such events to have any human experience at all.

The dispute between the several philosophies does not appear to the present writer to be so important as it seems. Certainly, the disagreements do not invalidate—they rather support—the claim that the method of philosophy is the kind of reflective analysis which seeks knowledge of those ingredients found in all perceptual events because they are indispensable preconditions of everything else that man can experience. The human mind is such a necessary precondition. So also is matter, so also is form or structure, so also are event and quality. Since every one of these is a necessary precondition of all experience, the dispute about which of these is "ultimate" seems to be more pragmatic than metaphysical. One of these, whether mind or matter or form or event or quality, is no more ultimate than any other, since all are indispensable to every experience whatsoever. All these may be called "ultimate," not in the sense that they are outside and underlying experience but only in the sense that they are ingredients always present because no experience is possible without them.

One of these might be chosen as "the ultimate" because it is held to be creative of all the others. But when this claim is analyzed, it is generally found that the one element chosen in preference to all the others is so chosen because it better enables the philosopher to solve the kind of problems that happen to interest him. It is true that some problems can be solved more readily when they are analyzed in terms of their relation to mind. But others can be solved more readily in relation to matter, and others in relation to structure or event or quality. If this is true, then this dispute, appearing to be metaphysical in character, is really pragmatic and is a dispute hinging on the utility of one approach or another for dealing with certain problems. If a given philosopher is most interested in the kind of problem that can be treated most effectively by analyzing it in relation to mind, he will be an idealist. But, on the same basis, another will be a materialist, still another a structuralist, another a contextualist (taking the event as basic), and another a mystic, depending on what kind of problem most interests him and, consquently, the kind of approach serving best to deal with his special sort of problem.[1]

The point is not that every attempt at philosophizing is true but that a number of different elements are all equally indispensable to human experience, and if a philosophy recognizes them to be such, it is true in that respect.

We have represented metaphysics as not reaching out

[1] For this classification of philosophies, although not exactly for this interpretation and use of the classification, see S. C. Pepper, *World Hypotheses* (Berkeley, Calif.: University of California Press, 1942).

beyond events with their qualities and structure; but there is another kind of metaphysics which claims to know about a reality inferred or intuited from the world of events but not itself a part of this world. This kind of philosophy does not stop with the necessary preconditions of all experience, which are themselves events or the form or the mind or the quality in experience, but claims that these and everything else in experience can be rendered intelligible only if we postulate or infer or intuitively acknowledge something that is beyond all these. This something beyond may be God, variously interpreted; or the "Absolute," also variously interpreted; or the "Unconditioned," which cannot be interpreted at all; or some flux of energy or dance of atoms, inferred but never experienced. This Something which is not events or ingredient in events may be called "Reality," while events are "Appearance" only. In some cases all events are called "illusion," and we should strive to escape the illusory world of events to discern and live with Reality.

The transcendental kind of philosophy just mentioned we shall not discuss here. The controversial issues concerning it are too recondite and complex. Its defenders have always been exposed to attack and have developed great subtlety and elaboration of defense until the devious routes of the dispute lead on endlessly and there is no conclusion. Therefore, we shall pronounce upon this transcendental philosophy the words *Pax vobiscum*. This we can do because the kind of philosophy that we are considering, kept within the bounds of events, deals with elements inescapable to every one. Even the transcendentalist must examine and analyze events, if to no other end than to declare them to be illusion. On the other hand, the transcendental realm does not force itself upon those who refuse to take the further step leading beyond events. So we humbly keep within these bounds where all philosophers must walk,

[208]

even though the giants are able to step beyond into Super-history, the Unconditioned, the Absolute, the Hidden Deity, the Noumenon, or whatever they may call the nature of the Great Beyond.

The philosophical undertaking represented by the present writing has sought to interpret all experience in terms of the event, not because we think the event is the ultimate in any other sense than that the other necessary preconditions of all experience are ultimate. All these ingredients necessary to any experience whatsoever are for us ultimate, since we do not step beyond experience to the Great Ultimate. But we take the event as our basis, for the pragmatic reason already noted. The kind of problem which we are trying to solve seems to yield more readily when approached by way of the event than in any other way. We are trying to find some interpretation of value which will be most practically useful in dealing with the issues determining human destiny for good or for ill. Interpreting value in terms of the event seems to us to accomplish this better than other interpretations. But we do not dispute the truth of other interpretations of value. Neither do we dispute the truth of other metaphysics, which take mind or matter or form or quality as the element in terms of which all else is interpreted. We only dispute (1) the exclusive ultimacy of these other chosen ingredients of experience and (2) the pragmatic value of these other approaches to the philosophical problems of life. On this second point of pragmatic utility, we are open to persuasion. Certainly, the superior utility of one approach cannot be demonstrated unless the other approaches have been tried. So we welcome all attempts to set forth a metaphysic and a theory of value in these other ways also.

RELIGIOUS KNOWLEDGE

Man's religious faith seeks to establish and maintain vital connection with what creates and sustains all human good. Such vital connection requires that man be subject to its creative control, and this, in turn, requires that he meet certain conditions. Therefore, religious knowledge is (1) about what creates all human good and (2) the conditions which man must meet to be brought under the control of this creative source of human good and thereby become its servant and its beneficiary.

In the classification which we are following, religious knowledge is really a kind of philosophical knowledge. Not all philosophical knowledge is religious because philosophical inquiry is directed to other matters in addition to the creative source of all good and the conditions which man must meet to be brought into its keeping. But religious knowledge is one branch of philosophical knowledge.

This raises the question of the distinction between philosophical knowledge of the kind which seeks religious truth and another kind of intellectual discipline called "theology." Theology in one sense is simply philosophy directed to religious inquiry; in another sense it is a systematic formulation of religious beliefs designed to render them acceptable for religious ritual and the conduct of religious living. This latter definition does not mean that theology tries to shape them so that they will stir the emotions. That is not the task of theology. But men must be able to believe religious doctrine if they are to use it effectively in the conduct of religious living. It is the task of theology of this sort to render religious belief usable in the sense of "believable." Theology does this by removing contradictions within the accepted body of religious beliefs and between these and all other beliefs held to be true. This is not at all the same as determining the truth or error of belief by subjecting it to the tests of all available evidence. Hence theology in this sense is very different from philosophical inquiry. On the other hand, much that goes by the name of philosophy may be more truly apologetics, if not for religious belief, then for some other untrue doctrine desired or used to meet a human need.

Much confusion has arisen in religion and elsewhere from failure to distinguish cognitive belief from noncognitive, cognitive theology from noncognitive, cognitive philosophy from noncognitive. In each case a proposition is cognitive only when its acceptance is determined by evidence, evidence being correspondence between a specified structure and observed events. When belief is otherwise determined, it is not knowledge. A belief is genuine knowledge when accepted on authority, provided that the authority is a record of propositions previously tested by others and their acceptance determined by evidence. Authority in any other sense is invalid.

Any claim to truth beyond the evidence is not a mark of sanctity or virtue or humility. Rather, it displays either the arrogance of faith or an irresponsible childishness. Often these two go together. No appeal to divine revelation, the sanctity of authority, direct communion with God or any other source allegedly superior to the tests required to guard the fallible human mind from error can escape the condemnation just asserted. The false garb of humility and holiness only makes the arrogance more pernicious and the irresponsibility more dangerous. The simple fact is that the human mind is addicted to error as the sparks fly upward. Hence it must submit humbly to tests of truth; and nowhere is this more imperative than in matters high and holy, where human desire is most insistent and impatient and pride most presumptuous.

The tests of truth are three—observation, agreement between observers, and coherence. All three of these apply to every proposition alleged to be true, whether it is in the field of common sense, science, philosophy, or faith.

We have noted that observation is always a series of perceptual events in which selective attention distinguishes a structure of interrelatedness running through the series. In common sense this series of perceptual events and this selecting of a structure common to the series are determined largely by habitual and voluntary reactions of the organism, along with directed focusing of attention. In scientific observation this must be supplemented by instruments determining precisely the range and character of the observation; by disciplined study and training, which equip one to make the fine distinctions in perception; and by symbols of precision, like mathematics, with which to specify with high accuracy the structure that is distinguished. In philosophy, observation yields knowledge only when subjected to fine analysis so elaborate as to uncover within the perceptual events examined certain structures of interrelatedness that are common to all perceptual events whatsoever (metaphysics) or common to a very wide field, such as the moral, the aesthetic, the cognitive.

Agreement between observers is the second of the three tests of true knowledge. "Agreement" here means that the observers shall observe the same thing. If another cannot observe what I do, when the same conditions determining the observation are present for the two of us, then the full test of truth has not been met.

Here it is very important to emphasize "the same conditions determining the observation." These conditions will include all conditions determining the observation so far as it is relevant to the inquiry, except only the presence or absence of the object to be observed. Of course, all conditions are never the same for any two observations, but these may be quite irrelevant to the problem under consideration and irrelevant to the kind of observation to be made. The most simple and obvious of these required conditions is that the two observers look at the place where the object is to be found and focus attention in the manner required. There are many other conditions, one of which is that the two observers should have the same kind of organism. If one has keener hearing or is color blind or is less sensitive to touch, the two are not making the observation under the same determining conditions, and their agreement or disagreement is irrelevant to the issue of truth. Another required condition is the same kind of training. If one has learned to distinguish what the other has never learned to detect because he has never acquired that focus of attention and that Gestalt of apperception, the question of their agreement or disagreement in observation is irrelevant to the test of truth.

No attempt is made here to list all the conditions determining observation which must be the same when agreement or disagreement in making an observation becomes a test of truth. We wish only to guard against the erroneous claim for the "social test of truth" when this seems to mean nothing more than agreement. Agreement has nothing to do with the matter unless the same determining conditions are present for those making the observations. All the world might agree in observing the earth to be flat, and still this would be no evidence at all against one solitary observer declaring it to be round, if the lone observer had made observations under conditions which the others refused to meet or were unable to meet. Consensus is no test of truth either in the world of common sense, in philosophy, in science, or in faith. Nevertheless, agreement in observing the same thing is an important test of truth when the several observers have met the same conditions determining the observation in respect to the matter under consideration.

The third test is coherence. This means, first of all, that there shall be no contradiction between the proposition alleged to be true and other propositions held to be true. Ideally, it would mean that the new proposition under consideration would be one component in a total implicative system which included all other true propositions. Human knowledge has not yet reached that level of perfection and may never reach it. Perhaps the increase of true knowledge will demand a continuous revision of accepted systems of propositions, rendering them more inclusive but never establishing a system so basic as to be implicative of every new discovery brought forth by more extended and accurate observation. But, at any rate, within limited fields the known and the newly discovered must form one implicative system. This alone can complete the threefold test of truth: observation, agreement between observers, and coherence.

This threefold test can be elaborated into all the many parts and forms of human inquiry. But our present purpose is not to discuss the method of acquiring knowledge beyond a minimum statement sufficient to distinguish knowledge from what is not knowledge. Baffling confusion and futile controversy will continue to reign in fields of inquiry deeply concerned with the values of life until clarity is achieved concerning just what is knowledge, as compared to many other kinds of good, no less precious, perhaps, but not instances of knowledge.

It is often claimed that religious knowledge is peculiarly derived from revelation or faith or intuition or mystical experience or Bible or Jesus Christ or (more narrowly) the teachings of Jesus.

We have already examined revelation in chapter ii and have found that it provides no access to truth beyond the bounds of observation, agreement of observers, and coherence. Revelation in itself is not knowledge at all, although it may open the way to knowledge. Revelation is the lifting of the creative event to a place of domination in the devotion of a continuing fellowship to form one enduring strand of history. This lifting to a place of domination was not done by man. It was accomplished by certain events which might be listed thus: the life and teachings of Jesus;

[214]

the Crucifixion; the Resurrection; the forming of the fellowship; the disentangling of the new faith from the Hebrew
cultural perspective and from bondage to any one single
perspective or set of rules. The chief consequence of this
revelation is not knowledge but the release of creative
power to transform the world into richness of value and to
save man from self-destruction and other evils which impoverish and break him. The first consequence of revelation
for man is, therefore, faith and salvation. In time he gains
knowledge from this revelation that he never could have
gained without it. But this knowledge derived from revelation, when and if man attains it, demands the same tests of
truth as any other knowledge. When professional religious
leaders, without submitting their assertions to the tests of
truth which others must follow, claim by right of revelation to know what others cannot know, they display that
mean kind of arrogance that hides under the cloak of sanctity and pseudo-humility.

Not only revelation but also faith is sometimes alleged to
be a peculiar way of knowing that can cast off the ordinary
tests of truth. We have tried to show that faith is not
knowledge primarily but is a self-giving. This self-giving
may be guided by knowledge, although in most instances it
is guided by beliefs that are mythical rather than true.
Most of all, it is guided by the practices of the religious
group in which knowledge may play a negligible part in
directing behavior. Events, habits, and ritual may guide
faith more effectively than knowledge, although knowledge becomes increasingly important with civilization.

The Bible is a necessary part of revelation, for without a
record of the initiating events, men could not have continued to be primarily concerned with the creative power
issuing from the fellowship about Jesus and his followers,
and the commitment of faith to this power could not have
been perpetuated. But, without the perpetuation, there can

be no revelation. Hence, by a kind of metonymy, the Bible is the Word of God. More precisely, the Word of God is the living Christ, and the living Christ is the creative event in dominant control over the life of man in that strand of history which forms a Christian fellowship. We must call it *a* Christian fellowship, not *the* Christian fellowship, since the total aggregation of professing Christians is by no means identical with the group giving supreme allegiance to creative power. Creative energy controlling the fellowship is also called the "Holy Spirit" in the Christian vernacular. It is rightly called "revelation" only when it holds supremacy over created good in the lives of this fellowship. The Bible, then, is not a peculiar source of knowledge about God apart from observation. It does provide peculiar, direct, and saving access to the saving power perpetuated in this fellowship by symbol, ceremony, and ritual, because the Bible is an indispensable agent and condition for this fellowship and this commitment of faith.

So also the teachings of Jesus are no peculiar source of knowledge dispensing with observation. Indeed, to set up the teachings of Jesus as having pre-eminent importance by themselves and in their own right is to misrepresent their true significance as a part of revelation and to misrepresent Jesus as being nothing more than another wise man. The teachings of Jesus take on their chief importance only when combined with a total complex event, including prospectively the Crucifixion, the Resurrection, and the forming of the Christian community and including retrospectively the history of the Hebrews as centered about their great prophets. In a word, the teachings of Jesus have pre-eminent religious importance only when treated as a part of revelation, and revelation is a complex event of the sort stated. They who think to glorify the man Jesus by representing his teachings, or his life and personality in combination with his teachings, as having the power to shape history in the way history has been shaped under the symbol of his name misconstrue entirely the truth of the matter. They miss the whole religious import of Jesus and are blind to what is supremely important in the Christian faith. The Christian faith has saving access to God by way of Jesus Christ (not by way of Jesus alone); but this is not at all the same as saying that we have such access by way of the teachings of Jesus when lifted out of the complex wherein alone their true significance can be discerned. Not any teachings can exercise great transformative power in human life, but only certain creative events have such power. The teachings are ingredients in these events, but even then it is not the truth alone which gives power to the events. Rather, the total impact of events gives power to the teaching. The teaching may well be a necessary part of the total occurrence. But events rich in value and events transformative of human existence run deeper than ideas and doctrines and are mightier.

VALUE OF TRUE KNOWLEDGE

Knowledge can be lifted out of the rich matrix of qualitied events which give to it all the true value it can have and so can be falsely exalted as a good in its own right. This, we have tried to show, is an adolescent perversion arising in an age in which science has not yet found its proper place among the goods of life. The sudden and lusty growth of science has produced an adolescent mentality which worships knowledge as a sort of god. Knowledge is good and is increasingly important, but only in its proper place and serving its proper ends. An academic institution becomes a pesthouse when it renders people less fit to live creatively by its emphasis on scholarship (knowledge) for its own sake or for the academic rank it bestows. Institutions of learning seem to be addicted to this perversion.

The value of knowledge can best be seen if we set over

against it some of the false pretenders who have been mistakenly honored as though they were knowledge when they were not. Some of these are: an event having vivid quality and stirring deep emotion; a belief held with a strong feeling of certitude; faith which reaches sustaining and life-giving reality by noncognitive methods; great skill in doing anything that is important; a proposition that works in the sense of producing desired consequences; perception that is vivid and gives the feeling of being true; a clear and coherent implicative system of propositions; the consensus held by a group; intuition in the sense of a newly emergent and innovating idea which gives one the feeling of its being true; declarations issuing from a source commanding high social prestige; myth in the sense of a proposition stimulating conduct within the grooves of a tradition when the tradition guides to important reality but the proposition does not give a truthful account of the nature of that reality.

While the intrinsic value of truth has always stood high, its instrumental value is not always so important. When custom, tradition, coercion, myth, and noncognitive faith direct men so that they live in the keeping of what sustains and enriches life and do so under such conditions that truth then and there available could not guide them so well, they live more securely and richly than they would do if they depended on knowledge to direct their lives. Even at the highest level of civilization we are guided by noncognitive tradition and custom and faith and would be greatly impoverished if all our lives could be controlled and guided only by the knowledge that we are able to achieve. It is, then, quite possible and not uncommon to overmagnify the instrumental importance of knowledge as compared to other guides and controls of human conduct.

Yet it must not be forgotten that advancing civilization always puts a heavier and heavier burden upon knowledge. Hence the mastery of truth becomes increasingly imperative to avoid great evil and attain the greater good of human existence.

Perhaps nowhere is the need of knowledge more urgent than in the fields of religion and morals which are most directly concerned with the creative event. Here is the great lag. Throughout history to date, the amount of knowledge needed in these areas to conduct human affairs fairly well was not so great as it is today; but it is in precisely these areas that the modern world has been most negligent in its search for truth. The increasing power of man to control the course of events and direct the social process according to his will makes it necessary that he know more about what is good and what is bad—he must know more about what creates value and how to deal with it. His increasing power to control makes more dangerous his presumptuous attempts to direct and predetermine what the creative event may do.

This limitation on the predictive control of outcomes in dealing with the creative event is easily misunderstood. Prediction can be made concerning what the creative event will do but in a restricted and peculiar way. We can predict that under certain conditions creative intercommunication will be more free, more full, more frequently practiced, more efficacious in transforming the minds of the participant individuals and their appreciable world in the direction of greater scope and richness of meaning. But we cannot predict and control what the creative event will produce. We can predict that individuals will communicate more freely and creatively under certain conditions than under others. But we cannot predict the specific system of meanings that will emerge from this creative communication. This illustrates the sense in which prediction applies to creativity and the sense in which it does not.

It is highly pernicious for the human mind to try to predetermine the outcome of the creative event. Creative interaction between organisms having the required biological equipment generates linguistic symbols with logical structure. Then and then only is it possible for the organism to perform perceptual reactions which are directed to producing an order of events corresponding with the specifications of a system of signs. In this sense, truth is created by this kind of interaction. Also, wider ranges of knowledge and more precise knowledge become possible only when creative communication has developed linguistic signs and logical devices and other cultural conditions which provide for wider and more precise specification and for perceptual reactions of the organism determining an order of events corresponding to such specification. If the mentality existing prior to this creation of wider range and precision should be able to control the outcome of creative communication, it would hold the product down to what such mentality can foresee and appraise and hence would prevent this increase in range and precision of knowledge.

In this respect the creative event is unique. Every process not thus creative must be controlled by prediction to achieve foreseen consequences of value. Not otherwise can human good be conserved and increased. But no less imperative is the demand that what creates and magnifies the range and precision and qualitative richness of the human mind should not be thus controlled in respect to its specific outcome. All processes not creative should be controlled and directed in such a manner as to produce conditions releasing the full power of creative intercommunication in generating and magnifying the appreciative capacity of the human mind and in widening and enriching the world that it can appreciate. Every day that increases the power of man makes that power increasingly dangerous if it is not accompanied by a moral and religious recognition that the specific outcome of creativity must not be predetermined and controlled in this way.

[220]

Thus truth is created and knowledge achieved in the same basic way as all other good is increased. The prime requirement is commitment of faith to creative intercommunication at the linguistic level of human existence and to creative interaction that is not communicative at the sublinguistic. Faith and value precede and undergird truth and knowledge. When truth and knowledge are brought forth, they must serve faith and value, even as these serve the source of all human good.

CHAPTER IX

Morals

MORAL theories have been divided into two kinds—theories of the good and theories of the right. According to the first, moral conduct is good if it produces the best total consequence of value for all concerned. According to the second, moral conduct is good if it conforms to the right moral principle, regardless of consequences. These two ways of interpreting morality may be modified in relation to each other. For example, a moralist who declares that right moral conduct derives none of its virtue from the consequences may yet affirm the need of considering consequences as a means of discovering the right moral principle. Or, again, one who interprets morality in terms of consequences may hold that it is often difficult or impossible to know the specific outcome. He therefore advises us to follow accepted principles even when their issue is not clear.

We mention this dual classification of moral theories not to propose either but to distinguish both from the interpretation of morality arising out of the view of value that we have been developing. According to this last, moral conduct is not good because it produces more happiness or because it produces any other consequences of value, such as self-realization or harmony or some increment to the cosmic totality of good. We have already criticized the attempt to determine conduct by any such predictable outcomes and have tried to show how irrelevant are such questions in making decisions. Moral conduct is conduct guided by general principles fitted to facilitate creative interchange between people and between the individual and his material

[222]

environment. Not the moral conduct itself but the creativity released by the conduct yields the consequence of
value. This release of creative interchange is itself a consequence, to be sure, but it is not what is ordinarily meant
when moral conduct is appraised in terms of consequences.
Hence the theory here defended does not properly belong to
the ethics of the good.

On the other hand, neither does this theory represent
moral conduct as being under the guidance of intuition, the
categorical imperative, or the judgment of "the good people" as sources of moral knowledge independent of rational-
empirical inquiry. Instead, moral problems are to be solved
precisely by such inquiry: namely, inquiry to discover the
kind of relationship between human beings that is most
conducive to creative intercommunication. For example, we
must be attentive toward one another; honest and consider-
ate; not too preoccupied with ourselves and our own good;
generous, temperate, courageous, just, kind, and loving.
Examination will reveal these forms of conduct to be what
is required for interchange of interests, for integration of
these in the life of each, for expansion of the appreciable
world, and for the deepening of community.

The value of the moral order is neither intrinsic, absolute, and underived nor to be practiced merely for foreseen benefits. It is obligatory and paramount, not on its own
account or for its foreseen consequences but because the
creative event in the life of man demands a certain order of
interrelatedness among people. It demands this order in the
sense that this order releases creative transformation to produce more abundant value in human life than can be produced without it. Also it demands this order in the sense
that any impairment of this moral order prevents creativity
from operating effectively to deliver man from evils that
threaten his existence and his achieved goods. The important consequence of moral conduct is, therefore, the fuller

and more effective operation of a nonhuman power creating good and opposing evil in human life. The more power man achieves over subhuman nature and over society, the more dependent he is upon this superhuman creative power to save him from destruction. The atomic bomb and the control of atomic energy do not make man more a master of his fate than he was before, but just the opposite. They magnify the frightfulness of any human attempt to use this power except only as such attempt is held subservient to that creative interchange among men whereby each becomes more fully participant in the life of the other. Conduct thus held subservient to the demands of creative transformation is moral conduct.

The moral order is composed of those general principles prescribing what man must do in dealing with his fellow-men in order that the interests and perspectives of each may become a part of the life of the other and that the perspective derived by each from the other may be integrated with his own. Action conformant to such demand may frustrate desire and may not produce consequences which can be foreseen and appraised as satisfying. Yet such action is morally good if it provides for this creative interchange of perspectives.

It is important to note the difference between utilitarianism and this moral theory. Utilitarian morality is the practice of general principles which issue in satisfaction of human desire. Morality as here understood is the practice of general principles which may issue in frustration and transformation of desire. When the moral act provides conditions permitting creativity to generate wider perspective and finer discrimination, the consequence of value thus produced cannot be foreseen and appreciated at the time that the moral act is performed. The wider perspective and finer discrimination yet to be created must be possessed before one can appreciate the resulting value. But this wider perspective and finer discrimination are inaccessible when the moral act is first initiated, because the moral act is precisely what opens the way for creative interchange to generate in human life this more ample perspective and more just discrimination. Hence the motive and the guide of moral conduct cannot be the foreseen good that will result from the moral act. The motive and the guide must be to provide in human life that kind of relationship among men which releases the creative event, doing this in the assurance that this nonhuman power will always produce the best possible context of meaning under the conditions prevailing at that time and place.

With this analysis and interpretation it should be apparent that the theory of morality here proposed is neither utilitarian nor categorical, determined neither by foreseen consequences of satisfaction nor by intuition.[1]

BASIS OF MORAL OBLIGATION AND SANCTION

The obligatory nature of moral practice is its most distinctive feature. This obligation is not derived from the moral code itself, since moral obligation is not intrinsic to the moral law but is derived from the creative event which demands the moral law.

The imperative of moral obligation is not the "voice of conscience." A sensitive and well-developed conscience will transmit to human awareness some sense of the obligation issuing from the demands of creative good. Hence the hu-

---

[1] In the classification of W. D. Ross and the school of English ethicists, the moral theory here presented is neither naturalistic nor nonnaturalistic. It is naturalistic as we ourselves interpret naturalism. But Ross and his group mean by a naturalistic theory of ethics one in which moral conduct is practiced for the sake of foreseen consequences of happiness. Nonnaturalistic, according to them, is a theory asserting moral conduct to be determined by principles obligatory without regard to consequences. Since moral conduct as here interpreted is determined by neither of these two, but by demands of the creative event, the theory we defend does not fall into either classification.

man mind is likely to mistake the messenger for the origina-
tor and assume that moral law or conscience is the ultimate
ground of moral obligation, when, in fact, this ground is
the creative source of all good. This true source of moral
obligation is revealed in case of a dulled or perverted conscience. Then the moral obligation is to correct the misleading of conscience by inquiry into the demands of creative
transformation and exposure to its working.

The imperative of moral obligation is not derived from
enlightened self-interest or altruism or the authority of tradition and custom or social approval and disapproval.
Again, any of these may transmit the sense of moral obligation to the individual; but, when valid, it is derived origi-
nally from the demands of that event which creates and re-
creates the personality and the social group. This conten-
tion is supported by the observation that right moral standards may not be the accepted formulations of the social
group. They may not be correctly specified by the greatest
thinker. Perhaps we never verbalize these moral imperatives with absolute correctness. But all this only shows that
the moral order is not determined by any human purpose.
Not human desire or habit or compact or tradition, not human reflection or legislation or decree of any kind, can determine the moral law, but only the demands of the creative
event.

The sanction of moral conduct comes from the same
source as moral obligation. The sanction of the moral demand laid upon us by creativity is closely analogous to the
sanction put upon the living organism when it fails to meet
the biological requirements. At a lower level a like sanction
is laid upon the chemical compound. The atom must act in
prescribed ways if it continues to be the same kind of compound, and so must any living thing if it continues to live.
Variation in behavior of the biological organism is required
to meet the demands of life when dealing with a novel situa-

tion; but if the organism does not behave in a way to meet the requirements of its biological system, it ceases to be organic. It first disintegrates into putrid flesh, ceasing to live, and then dissolves into more elementary compounds. So, also, we cannot continue to be human if we do not act morally, any more than the living organism can continue to live or the chemical compound to persist in its present form, if the required sort of behavior is not upheld. Greater freedom is found at the level of morality and human conduct. The human being has access to a wider range of conceivable possibility and imaginative construction. But the sanction at all these levels is the same. Man sinks to the subhuman when he fails to maintain the required moral standards.

What creative interchange may require may be different at various levels of culture or in different kinds of situations; but, once we know the general nature of creativity, we can seek out its requirements. Habit, tradition, intuition, human adjudication, and legislation are not irrelevant. They may be exceedingly important factors in determining what should be done. They are in part shaped by prior creation to the ends of renewed creation; but, since they are also shaped by many other conditions, they are not in themselves reliable guides to moral conduct. They cannot be ignored, but neither are they the final determinants of moral action.

WHEN IS MORALITY RELIGIOUS?

Morality is not religious when practiced as though the moral order were an end in itself. Neither is it religious when practiced as a means of producing desired consequences of value foreseeable in their specific nature. It is not religious when the sense of obligation is derived from any of the sources noted above except only creative power (will of God).

When moral practice takes on religious character, the

moral law is changed from being sovereign to being a
servant. It is not primarily a servant to man, but primarily a
servant to the creative event and then, derivatively, a
servant to anyone who is supremely devoted to creativity.
Hence religious morality enables the individual to defend
the moral law to any limit but without bondage to it, so
that he is able to criticize and revise it in conjunction with
others, as the demands of creative good may require. This
basis for revising the moral law must not be confused with
criticizing and revising it to suit human desire or to serve
the anticipated consequences of a utilitarian morality.

When morality is religious in the sense indicated, it is
possible to conduct moral education without producing
either an egoist, subjecting the world to human desire, or a
moral prig, always concerned about his own moral perfection. With commitment of faith to creative transformation,
moral education becomes not merely the transmitting of an
accepted code or set of standards but co-operative inquiry to
discover the guiding principles of conduct best fitted to
release creative interchange for producing values beyond the
direct consequences of moral endeavor. All the human resources of criticism and inquiry, experimentation and moral
revision, can then play upon the accepted formulations of
the moral order but always under the sovereign control of
the source of all value and what it may demand.

Since this faith delivers the moral law from being either a
servant of human desire or a pattern of human perfection
self-consciously achieved, it provides a resource for developing a new moral order when old forms have become inadequate to a novel cultural situation. When higher levels of
fulfilment require moral discriminations not previously relevant to human conduct, the demands of creativity become
the guides to formulating improved standards. These then
point out the discriminations now become necessary in the
conduct of our lives. Consequently, this faith opens the way

for progressive advancement of the moral order, keeping it moving along with emerging levels of value produced by new creations.

No man is a pure exemplification of religious morality in its perfection, and no man is a pure exemplification of non-religious morality in perfect form. All men fall far short of high morality, whether religious or nonreligious. In actuality the man who represents religious morality may be worse than the man who is highly moral without religion, because the first may not have enough either of morality or of religion to be a worthy man. What little positive morality he has may be religious, but it may be so mixed with immorality that we may prefer the moral man who is not religious. While all this is true, we believe that the distinctions in type do hold as traced above and that the potentialities of religious morality are far more abundant, however imperfectly these may be exemplified in actual instances.

MORAL RULES VERSUS MORAL CONDITIONS

Morality is not achieved by trying to practice moral rules in disregard of actual conditions which shape the existence of men. Moral principles are truly moral only when we follow them as guides in so ordering this actual world that men can live together creatively. They are immoral when they lead us to "defy" the actual world or to strive to extricate ourselves from it in order to live for some other realm.

Moral principles may be presented, however, as incursions breaking into this mundane sphere from some other realm; and yet, under the prevailing psychological and social conditions, this myth may render them efficacious in guiding human conduct. Even though the myth does not give a true interpretation of their nature, the principles may retain their moral character. But when they lead men to strive by sheer "will-power," in pseudo-moral heroism, to

[229]

exemplify in their own persons the character of morality, treating this evil world as an arena provided for discipline and self-display of personal virtue, we do not have genuine morality. Conformity to moral principles in the abstract, "personal exemplification of moral principle" in opposition to actual conditions, is moralism. Genuine morality is the struggle to reshape the actual physical, biological, and social conditions of this world so that individuals shall be impelled to live sensitively and responsively to each other, undergoing creative transformation of individual personality and social structure.

If the required physical, biological, and social conditions of human life should ever be so completely achieved that all things constrained conduct into conformity with the moral demands at that level of attainment, the sense of moral obligation would disappear from human life in that particular form. Morality at that level would become spontaneous, easy, common, almost universal. Yet the task of moral reconstruction of the world, with its sense of duty, its struggle, and its heroism, would still remain. It would simply move on, to undertake reconstruction at levels outside the concern of the older morality. Whether or not such progression ever occurs in human history, moral obligation, moral responsibility, and moral struggle do not lessen.

BASIS OF MORAL APPRAISAL

What we have said about moral struggle and actual achievement may be misinterpreted. A man's morality is not measured by his success in changing actual conditions. His morality is the struggle to change conditions and not merely to exemplify in his own person the so-called "moral" characteristics. It is measured by the degree to which he employs every resource accessible to him to the end of providing conditions releasing the full power of creative good in human life. If a man fails to do this, having employed every resource, he is no less moral. Nor is he unmoral if, in a world of specialization, the work he does to shape conditions for growth of value isolates him from areas open to others and prevents his rich and free communication in ordinary contacts. An individual might fail to fulfil certain moral requirements, even while living to his utmost in obedience to other special moral demands. This situation is perhaps not uncommon. Men are not uniformly moral: in the meeting of some situations they may live with high moral effectiveness but in other respects be delinquent. When the moral effectiveness happens to be along lines observed and praised by society, while the delinquency is of an order ignored by society, the moral one-sidedness may not be apparent. But when high moral excellence and delinquency are reversed in respect to social recognition, the world may see only immorality.

Specialization, immoral or moral conditioning, and other such complexities enter into the problems of moral personality. But, through them all, the general principle holds that a man's morality is his effort to change conditions in such a way as to facilitate the transformations creative of value in human existence.

THE MORALS OF COMMUNICATION

Our emphasis upon communication as the one thing to be conserved and promoted by all moral codes does not signify that all communication is good. Not mere communication, but creative communication, is required. The genial and uninhibited transmission of everything entering the mind may be very pernicious. Moral practice must sustain communication of such content and under such conditions that new meanings emerge, integrate, expand the appreciable world, and deepen community. Even then improvement does not necessarily follow, for loss of meaning may be more rapid than its creation.

[231]

In some cases the moral requirement may involve retiring from communication for periods of solitude. This might be a time of study and contemplation of art, of books, of religious symbolism—these all being a type of communication. Or it might be a time of quiet relaxation under conditions that favor the integrating of many diverse meanings previously acquired. The period of seclusion might be devoted to the labor of putting into communicable form what one has to communicate. How much solitude there should be, protected from every visible form of communication, varies with different individuals. Doubtless there are some who degenerate very quickly with solitude and should not attempt it but should spend almost all their waking life in continuous interchange with others. But this is not true of all. Ordinarily, creativity requires alternation between association and solitude, communication and integration.

It is an error to appraise people as better or worse according to their "sociability," meaning the ease, grace, and enjoyment which they display in every sort of situation. A very shy person, who finds it painful to associate with others, is not necessarily less fit to participate creatively in communication under proper conditions than is the very aggressive and bumptious or one who has mastered all the arts of "making friends and influencing people." The blandly suave, the complacent and artful, the one who always strives to be the center of attraction, the one who enthrals with charm—these are not necessarily living more faithfully to the demands of creative interchange than the one who is awkward and self-conscious. To be sure, a man would not be self-conscious if he were completely given to creative transformation in that time and place, but neither would he display any of the other more graceful and attractive characteristics noted above. Gaiety, complacency, adaptability are not necessarily creative. Indeed, it is so easy to move down the noncreative grooves of social acceptability that a man can scarcely be saved from this fate if he does not have some difficulties to overcome in dealing with people. Of course, it would be better not to have difficulties if the other evils could be avoided.

Increasing closeness of interdependence between diverse cultures and increasing specialization within each culture has forced to the front the acute problem of communication between these diversifications. Anthropologists have demonstrated that distinct cultures are integrated wholes. Therefore, communication of parts of a culture from one integrated whole to another does not achieve any basic understanding of the one by members of the other. Anyway, the great number and diversity of cultures on this planet now bound together by modern technology render impossible any appreciative apprehension of them all by any ordinary mortal.

Analogous difficulty applies to the specializations within a culture. The several sciences, the fine arts, and the practical arts are all so highly specialized in modern civilization that bridges cannot be built between them of such sort that a person can pass from one to another with understanding of each. This presents a serious problem of communication which is basic to the welfare of society and to education.

Many alleged solutions of this problem of communication between the cultures and the specialties have been proposed. Some urge a comprehensive synthesis, others reduction of the diverse cultures and specializations to a simplified language made common to them all and so providing intercommunication from each to the others. Again it is asserted that certain basic principles undergird all these diversifications, and the hope is held that mastery of these general principles will be sufficient to integrate the cultures and specializations. Some suggest study of the great books supposedly basic to them all. These proposals have all been critically examined and found to be inadequate.[2] We shall not here take space to demonstrate their futility and shall only state the conclusion that the several diverse and unique cultures, on the one hand, and the highly developed specializations of the arts and sciences, on the other, cannot communicate to outsiders the depth and intricacy in each which make it important and vital. What, then, shall we do?

While these many unique cultures and specialties cannot communicate directly across their boundaries, they are all rooted in the creativity of life, and they contribute to human good only as they serve this basic source of value common to all. If this is true, the problem of their integration and the basis of communication between them should be sought not directly across their boundaries but indirectly by way of the common good which they all must serve. While their intricacy and distinctive content cannot be communicated, their relation to the source-good common to all men and their service to this source might be communicated to all. If this were done, it would not be necessary or even desirable (as it is also impossible) to communicate across the boundaries of the diverse divisions which multiply and deepen in human life with advance of civilization. It would be quite sufficient if we communicated (and so had understanding and agreement) concerning the basic moral and religious demands made upon human life by the creative event, whence all these divisions emerge and to which their several diverse contributions must return. This would solve the problem of communication in the modern world without the effort to overcome the insuperable barriers that block communication between the specializations, whether they be technical or cultural.

[2] See especially *Approaches to National Unity*, ed. Louis Finkelstein, chap. xxxiv by Philipp Frank and chap. xxxvii by Lincoln Reis (New York: Harper & Bros., 1945).

If the approach just outlined is to be followed, the specialists in their several fields should be led to acknowledge their relation to the root value of human existence and should accept contribution to it as their main concern. They could then understand one another and co-operate effectively, not, so to speak, by weaving a web of understanding from branch to branch and twig to twig of the tree of life, but by recognizing and pre-eminently serving the root and trunk which they have in common. Also, the layman in respect to all the specialties and the common man who cannot transcend his native culture might understand and appreciate in this way these various specialties and alien cultures in terms of their relation and contribution to the source of all value. To the measure that this creative source is acknowledged as supremely important for all, a language of communication between these diversifications of culture and specialization might be developed in terms of this common source of human good and the service rendered to it by each specialty. This would give us the kind of communication and integration required without the futile attempt to make accessible to every man the uniqueness and depth of each culture and each specialization.

If this analysis is correct, the moral problem of communication, rendered desperately acute in our time, finds its solution in religious commitment of faith to creative value.

MORALS OF SEX

The bond of sex is not necessarily the bond of love, and love is by no means always sexual. Nevertheless, love and sexual response in union can lift to such heights of happiness as are scarcely attainable elsewhere. Some will deny this because they have not found such love; for, although sexual love in some form is very common, the supreme fulfilments of it are very rare. Sexual love in its high glory is more a promise and a hope than a stable achievement in human life. When interresponsiveness is quickened to the maximum by the full release of sexuality, when the environing group provides every favoring condition and all the resources of a rich culture make their contribution to this end, sexual love can spread a glowing quality throughout the whole fabric of human existence and into every area of life, giving to all the world a joy underivable from any other source. But the world to date does not provide for this except in rare and fleeting conjunction of favorable circumstance.

Perhaps human sexuality, more than anything else, is what renders man capable of undergoing great creative transformations in the direction of an indefinite increase of qualitative meaning. Of course, all the resources of culture must be added—art, religious devotion, intellectual search and knowledge, social order. But, given these resources, human sexuality provides the psychobiological condition and profound responsiveness that are indispensable to supreme fulfilment. Demonstration of this claim would require far more space than is permitted here, but a few pertinent facts can be noted.

Birth, adolescence, finding a mate in love, marriage, the coming of children, are the occasions when men most commonly undergo the major transformations leading to richness of meaning. But these all are the direct expressions of sexuality and could not occur without it. Of course, all animals have these expressions of sexuality, but certain further characteristics of sexuality peculiar to man are what render these occasions creatively transformative.

The sexual life of man is not confined to any fixed pattern of behavior or order of life. Neither is it directed to any limited ends, such as biological reproduction and survival of the species. It undergoes indeterminate variation and takes on innumerable forms. There is no known limit to this transformability and the richness and variety of qualitative meaning that it may yield. This gives to human sexuality enormous potentialities for good and for evil. This release from the primary demands of biological reproduction renders it second to nothing in bringing human life to cultural attainment far beyond any other animal. Also, it enables man to become more self-destructive and self-impoverishing than any other creature.

Another remarkable characteristic of human sexuality should be noted. The bisexuality of man, with all its social consequences, produces a social unit which is not the biological individual but the intimate group.[3] Western culture has made a tragic blunder in conducting society upon the theory that the minimal social unit is the individual human being. Perhaps this more than anything else has brought modern democracy to the verge of disaster. The human being simply is not human except in relation to the intimate group. Human sexuality rising to heights of love; its pervasive character, weaving webs of meaning throughout an entire neighborhood; its reaching-out into all the resources of culture to find nourishment and enrichment; its need of wide and deep association with others beyond the two—all these, combined with the prolonged dependency of the human infant and the need of the parents to draw upon the whole of the resources of culture and social institutions for the care of the child, reveal the socializing potency of human sexuality.

Creative power cannot transform a human being at the depth and with the scope required to produce the great values of life unless he passes through that transformation of maturing human sexuality called "adolescence." Prior to this transformation the human individual lacks the capacity for the revolutionary changes produced by interresponsive-

[3] See *The Peckham Experiment: A Study of the Living Structure of Society*, by Innes H. Pearse and Lucy H. Crocker (New Haven: Yale University Press, 1946), for an excellent statement of the significance of sex in relation to the social nature of man.

ness to others. He simply cannot respond with the required depth and fulness. Sexuality breaks down the egoism which otherwise confines the individual and makes him profoundly responsive not only to one other person but to all persons and interests and causes associated with the loved one. Human sexuality does not necessarily undergo all this, but it provides the biopsychological condition without which it could not happen. This responsiveness to another person of the opposite sex, reaching down and out into all the interests and issues of life involved in that other, leads on into all the supreme goods of human life. When carried far enough, it brings into its concern the whole of human history and society. This is true even though ordinary instances of human sexuality never develop this far. This is a capacity open to man because of his sexuality, however far from full realization it may be in most cases.

The great disaster of human life is not failure to attain biological fulfilment of sex, grievous as that may be, but it is failure to love under the impetus of sex to the height and depth that love can reach in this way. Nothing can take the place of sexual love, even though there be many other kinds. Perhaps it is fair to say that none of the other kinds of love could develop very far if the protective resistances to human responsiveness in the individual were not first broken down by the coercive outreaches of sexuality, even when these are unfulfilled by union with any one other individual. A great love unrequited or otherwise unfulfilled, provided that it does not produce bitterness and protective regression, will be effective in opening the way for the work of creative transformation. Perhaps nothing is more effective. Religious commitment is, no doubt, necessary; but if it is to be truly effective in delivering the individual over into the power of creative transformation, it must build on that profound and revolutionary responsiveness derived from sexuality.

[238]

Some such understanding of human sexuality is necessary to provide a basis for any adequate moral standards pertaining to it. Moral standards can be and often have been monstrously evil in restricting and misdirecting sexuality. They have often cut off the indispensable and enormous potentialities of sex for human fulfilment. They have produced a crabbed and crippled creature, unable to respond to others with sufficient depth of emotional appreciation to permit that creative interchange of perspectives which elevates the good of life to heights of value.

Moral standards pertaining to sex should guide man away from failure to love and into the ways of abundant love. Moral standards by themselves are not sufficient to awaken and direct sexual love to its precious and far-reaching fulfilments; but moral standards are indispensable to this end. The pity is that they have often been obstructive because so poorly designed and have been even worse in the manner of their enforcement, interpretation, and appreciative apprehension. The morals of sex should not be administered and interpreted negatively, as though the chief concern were to protect individuals and the social order from the destructive and impoverishing power of sexuality run wild. The real purpose of morals in sex is constructive. It is, or it should be, to guide the sexual impulse into a love so powerful that it shatters and transforms a man's life and brings him into social relations which enrich not only himself and those in his intimate group but also society in its wider ranges. Moral standards are effective not primarily by establishing prohibitions but by directing interest, impulse, and behavior into channels which open the way for creative transformation in the direction of richer meaning.

One of the dangers which moral standards should be set up to prevent is the narrow obsessive interest which sex may come to possess. Comparing this with interest in tennis may seem ridiculous because sex is so much more compulsive. But tennis becomes absorbing as one perfects one's skill and has the proper physiological equipment, psychological organization, and social conditions. Ultimately, it can produce what is called "the tennis bum," who dreams and sleeps and lives supremely for tennis and becomes so obsessed with it as to be useless for almost everything else. The same can happen with sex, only it can become even more obsessive and can enthral more people. As life becomes more easy, even luxurious, as other imperative needs of human existence are more readily satisfied, as techniques and attitudes required for erotic delight are developed and widely known, this enthralment by sex so as to incapacitate for other major concerns of life may become a serious danger.

The context of value developed by love between the sexes is a delicate web, binding together into a single net of meaningful connection a wide range of many things and persons and acts and memories, hopes, and dreams. Therefore, when love is possessive or furtive or in any other way walls in the little group of lovers and shuts out the responsibilities and demands of life in full circle and wide range, it cuts off the growth of love and, in time, is likely to kill it altogether. Perhaps this is a common fate under conditions now prevailing. Certainly, it is the fate of all attempts to love in transgression of the established social order and institutions.

Our social order as it now stands does not ordinarily provide opportunity for the weaving of that gorgeous tapestry of life out of the vitalities of sex which might be ours if we had an education, a religion, an art, moral standards, and social relations fitted to this attainment. On the other hand, the institutional structure and conventions of society cannot be repudiated by love. The context of love cannot be had without the social order. As we have seen, love between the sexes requires intricate and wide connections freely and openly established with all the rest of society, giving access to the human heritage of beauty, truth, and devotion. The social order, with its great body of institution and convention, is indispensable for this fulfilment of love. Therefore, solution of the problem is found not by repudiating the established order or by transgressing its demands but by changing it slowly so that it will permit the creation of contexts of value more widely and freely. When the nature of value and its source is understood, it should be possible in time to develop standards and a religion and social practices more hospitable to love's fulfilment. Perhaps the world of sexual love is in the making. Sometime a social order and a personal discipline may be reared that will be fitted to bring forth the unexplored possibilities of value resident in love but now hidden.

There is evidence of these undeveloped potentialities of great value in sexual love. Sometimes a magic union of favorable conditions enables love between a man and a woman to transfigure the whole appreciable world, revealing what life might be if this transfiguration could be more commonly attained and stably conserved. The magic union of sustaining conditions is swiftly swept away by the fatalities of existence. Yet not in vain. These rare occasions carry a promise—they tell us of what might be and whisper of a wonder that is hidden. Sometime, somewhere, to some degree, it may be revealed. A social order and a personal discipline, a culture and a sustaining group, a tradition and an art, abounding vitality and tender grace, may all be so developed and combined that the great transfiguration will be attainable. Meanwhile, on rare occasions of love between the sexes, heaven has touched our earth timidly and fleetingly. The sweetness and the magic of that touch may keep us faithful to a high devotion. We know wherefor we labor, having had that visitation. The hope and the dream of a world more fit for love shall henceforth be the goal of our endeavor.

If love is to be fulfilled, development and discipline of responses capable of the great transformation must begin in childhood. This does not mean mere information about sex or erotic play. It means developing the capacity to be lured, transformed, and glorified by the depth and richness of creative interchange between people. Then, when sexuality matures, it can expand and enrich this responsiveness to that height and depth and breadth of human good attained only when the full release of sexuality in its passionate power delivers to creative transformation all the resources of human nature and human culture to make of life what it can.

When any man and any woman meet in love, the world trembles with the beginning of a new creation. It may fail. The new emergent may die in the bud. The failure may even cause their world to lapse into evils too drab or too terrible to endure. But the undreamed transfiguration of a world hovers over every union of man and woman where love breaks the constraints of self-protective concern, opening the way to deepest appreciative interchange.

CHRISTIAN LOVE

Another kind of love, very different from the sexual, is part of our moral heritage. It is called distinctively Christian, although it can be found outside the bounds of professing Christians. It has been called *agape*, but we shall not use that term for several reasons. For one thing, this Greek word has been given a peculiar interpretation by Nygren and Buber, whose analysis dominates theological thinking on the subject, and so might confuse what we have to say about Christian love if we used the term associated with their treatment. Our own interpretation differs from theirs.

Perhaps the nature of Christian love will stand forth most clearly if we contrast it with community. This will be all the more clarifying because Christian love and community are very different, even though the two are often confused both in theory and in practice.

In community two or more persons not only share the same interests but the shared interests enter into the distinctive organization of personality peculiar to each. The persons in community will, of course, always have some interests not shared with others. Some of these may be shared with other persons forming another group. Thus each may belong to many different communities. But, in each case, what I share with others in community must not conflict with the organization of my own mind and person but must be or become elements more or less essential to the makeup of my own self.

When interests derived from association with others do conflict with my own personal organization, this conflict must lead to some reorganization so that I can integrate these alien interests either positively or negatively into some new organization of myself. If not, we say the community fails or breaks at that point. Community provides reinforcement, harmony, and mutual support in respect to the interests comprising that community.

Christian love stands in sharp contrast to community. To be sure, Christian love includes reinforcement, harmony, and mutual support between the interests of participant individuals in community. Hence it can and does occur in community. But it ranges beyond community, and in this wider range it is unique. We wish particularly to examine this distinctive character of Christian love revealed beyond community; for it is here that Christian love opens a new dimension for the creative transformation of human existence.

When Christian love extends beyond community, it enables the individual to feel in himself the interests of the others, even when these interests are so alien and disruptive to the organization of his own personality and community that they would be unendurable were he not sustained by something other than his own personal organization. Only when man is sustained by faith in the creative source and creative power of life, and not by any power or organization within himself or his community, can he allow these alien and hostile interests to enter his sympathetic awareness. In Christian love one can allow the interests of the enemy and the alien to enter appreciative apprehension. In such case the interests of the other may become my own even when I must repudiate them as evil and fight them as degrading and destructive to him and to me.

In Christian love I can disapprove what I receive into myself and condemn as monstrously evil what I share. I condemn without limit even when I feel sympathetically. Hence I am on the inside of that other person even when he is hostile, degraded, or perverted. This, we repeat, is disruptive and evil, if not impossible, for any save a person whose center of organization is not his own personality or any sustaining community, not even the Christian community, but is only the sustaining power of God, creatively ordering the most diverse interests and ways of life into a more meaningful world.

This intuitive awareness and sympathetic understanding of the concerns of the other, across the barrier of hate, alienation, foreign culture, and racial difference, is a gift of God's grace. It cannot be acquired by willing or by any sort of training or education. It is excluded by automatic, self-protective reactions of the biopsychological organism, reactions built up through ages of struggle to survive in a dangerous world. Only when the demands of creativity are sovereign over all other demands in one's life can one be sufficiently open, receptive, and responsive to permit this kind of love.

With this interpretation, not only is Christian love unendurable, it is destructive and evil to anyone who does not first love God with heart and soul and mind and strength. Only then can he love his neighbor as himself, however alien the interests of the neighbor may be. The distinctive mark of Christian love is precisely this duality and conflict of interests which it alone can tolerate. It alone can bridge the chasm between the good and the bad, between friend and foe. If others than Christians display this kind of love, we can only rejoice and say that this is what we mean by "Christian love," even though the label is not always accurate. Certainly, this kind of love is rarely found among professing Christians. Nevertheless, there seems to be no other term available for designating this remarkable kind of love.

Only by loving persons who stand in radical contrast to all that I have ever been can I gain access to the wide area of value yielded by this diversity of interests added to my own. In time, if I am sufficiently committed to the creative power in life, these alien interests may be integrated positively or negatively into the scope of my personality and its world. If integrated positively, I and my world are so transformed that these interests and persons previously so destructive to my personal organization become in some way sustaining. If integrated negatively, I and my world are so transformed that these interests and persons are deeply imbedded in my concern but are forever opposed to me and all that I would support. In case of negative integration my good will goes forth to them without reciprocating good will from them, because my good will must express itself in seeking to take away what they want. Negative integration means that my love goes forth to the other without hope of reconciliation or reciprocity.

One may ask: What good is Christian love under such circumstances? To be sure, it yields suffering and struggle and can never bring harmony under the *circumstances mentioned*. But it is not nonsensical on that account, and it is not without its own glorious good, tragic to the uttermost though it be. The good it yields is that magnificent spread and vividness of qualitative meaning, only possible with such love, connecting persons and strivings into a single glowing web of mutual reference, where cold indifference or instrumental connection alone could otherwise prevail. This suffering glory yields a vividness of contrast between extremes beyond the compass of any other outreach of the human spirit. Such suffering love provides forgiveness in the sense that the alien, the enemy, and the despised can find a love waiting for them whenever they are willing to receive it (even though they never become willing). They can enter into creative responsiveness with the other without a barrier to repel them, if only they accept his love. Some theological interpretations of Christ's taking our sins with him to the Cross seem to be saying in mythical form something like this. In any case such love is possible not by human effort but only by the gift of God in Christ if one means by such an expression that domination of creative power over the lives of men in a continuing fellowship issuing from the Cross after the manner described in chapters ii and x. It is possible only when one can truly say: "It is not I that live but Christ liveth in me."

The more abysmal the difference between persons, generating hate or contempt or indifference without this kind of love to bridge the chasm, the greater is the scope and variety for creative increase of value. In this way Christian love adds a new dimension to what the creative event can do with human existence and with this world, in magnifying the meaning of it. Christian love enables the individual and the community to apprehend and participate in values remote from, contradictory to, and destructive of their own order of value. Yet this opens the way for a creative transformation which will vastly magnify the good of life beyond anything else. Without Christian love between men, this most ample fulfilment of creative power is impossible.

The self-sacrifice attributed to Christian love is genuine, but it is sacrifice of that organization of interests which is the self or, in the case of a community, the community. It is not the sacrifice of those wide and varied values found in others and brought within the scope of appreciative apprehension by way of this kind of love. Hence, to say that Christian love goes beyond mutuality, meaning that he who loves in this way gains no great good through enjoying the goods of others, is to misinterpret the nature of love. Christian love that did not expand the good of life for the lover by giving him access to a new world of value would simply not be love.

JUSTICE

Justice is the distribution of goods and services; the adjudication of claims, rewards, and punishments; the adjustment of the consequences of public action affecting the interests of different people—all these according to a guiding principle. The great problem has been to find the guiding principle. Plainly, the distribution, adjudication, and adjustment cannot be equal in quantity; for, in many cases, that would be the rankest injustice. To say that it should be according to what is due to each or according to some golden mean is to state the problem again without solving it; for these propositions give no guidance at all unless one means to refer in a subtle way to established practice or to the practice of sensitive, noble, and just men. If one means that, one still is at a loss to know what are the established, just practices as over against the unjust, or the men who can truly be called "just," in opposition to the many who are not. If one says that the guiding principle is natural law, imbedded somehow in the nature of things, still one has pointed to nothing open to inquiry and so has given no answer. If one says that this natural law is revealed to intuitive apprehension, then which intuitive apprehension is correct, since different men can have diametrically opposed intuitions concerning this law?

We have not space to list and criticize the many interpretations of justice. For brevity we must state very bluntly the principle derived from the interpretation of value here developed. Distribution, adjudication, and adjustment are just only when they dispense to each individual what will enable him in association with others to enter most fully into creative interaction with them. For the most part this cannot be determined by judgments handed down by man. Rather, we achieve a just society only when it is so regulated that each is free to seek and find for himself what he most needs for the creativity of life.

Freedom and justice are complementary, and neither can be had without the other. Justice can occur only where there is freedom, and freedom can be had only where justice reigns. Discussion of the nature of freedom must be postponed to a later work. But it is obvious that a society both free and just requires appropriate judiciary and administrators.

A society both free and just must have an impersonal regulative system of laws and customs to serve as a frame of reference to guide the sensitivities and intelligence of men in making whatever distributions, adjudications, and adjustments are required of them. Without such a regulative system, the individual, with his limited apprehensions, does not know where to begin or what to interpret and apply. Such a system must be revised from time to time—or, perhaps we should say, continuously revised—to meet changing conditions. But for the individual in a particular situation it is largely fixed.

A society both free and just must have an art, a religion, and an education equipping the human spirit for freedom and justice. The kind of education needed for this will be treated in another book to be published in the future. An attempt to sketch the kind of art and religion required appears in chapters vi and x, respectively.

We have mentioned three conditions of freedom and justice, which apply to any society whatsoever. There is a fourth which applies peculiarly to our own. Most societies have some one institution and practice which is more basically determinative of their character than any other. For Western culture in the recent past this was buying and selling at a profit and the whole machinery of finance, all of which was put together under the head of "the market." So long as this condition prevailed, the basic requirement for a free society was a free market. Art, religion, home, neighborhood, industry, and scientific inquiry were all required and could make society more or less free, according to the way they were conducted. But the key was the market. These other agencies could produce a free society only if they carried with them a free market.

A great transformation is occurring in our culture. It is basically a shift from the market to industry as the determinative factor in society. Not profit but production, not finance but the unrestrained application of technology to the industrial process, are the keys to a free and just society. Of course, profit and finance may continue, as art and religion, home and science, must continue. It is not a question of what continues but of what basically determines the others. Without science there can be no technology; without morals, education, and religion, there can be no men competent to conduct industry. All that is taken for granted. But the point of strategic concern, demanding first consideration from government and all other agencies that seek to promote a free and just society, is no longer business and profit. It has become the free and abundant flow of industrial production, providing employment and goods for all. The question here is not how this is to be done. It is asserted only that this is the first imperative for a free and just society under present conditions.

Even if a free market should continue to be a necessary part of a free society, in any case we cannot have it by working directly for it. We can have it (if we have it at all) only on condition that, first of all and basically, we have industry producing at full volume. In that sense the industrial plant takes the place of the market as the fundamental determiner of society.

If the above claims are true, we see the fourth necessary condition of a society both free and just in our time. It is the industrial plant so organized and conducted that the workers will be stimulated to exercise their initiative and assume responsibility within the bounds of their competence for the production of goods. Such a plant stands over against one in which the workers follow authoritative regulations without exercising initiative, without sense of responsibility for the quality and quantity of production, and without co-operative planning and creative interchange among themselves and between themselves and their overseers. In a free industrial plant the common worker cannot be discharged until his case has been reviewed by his fellow-workers. In such a plant the workers will think and plan and, within their competence, determine some of the immediate conditions and procedures of their labor.

In the age which we are entering, the slogan of the free society must be the free industrial plant, which takes the place of the free market as basic to all else. Religion, education, art, science, home, and neighborhood cannot create a free and just society if we do not have freedom and justice in the industrial plant, because the unrestrained release of technology for industrial production is the instrument of supreme power in our society. The way in which supreme power is exercised in a society determines the freedom and justice of that society. Therefore, if the application of tech-

[250]

nology to industrial production is not made in such a way as to quicken the intelligence and discrimination of the workers, their sense of responsibility, and their capacity to appreciate, we cannot have a society both free and just. No matter what other agencies may do in the name of freedom and justice, if they neglect to establish these in industry they have neglected the one thing needful, and their efforts will be only those of salvage, not of constructive achievement.

The claim that the road to a free and just society is by way of full production and full employment is not based on the belief that men will be just and provide for freedom only when they have economic abundance. That misses the point entirely. The point is that every impulse and social development inimical to justice and freedom is magnified enormously when unemployment spreads in a society highly industrialized. This is not a universal fact of all history but springs from present social conditions. When unemployment deepens, racial hatred becomes a mania, with Jews and Negroes the chief victims in our country. Between employers and employees and between the wealthy and the impoverished bitterness and suspicion get beyond control. Sources of information indispensable to a free and just society become unreliable and deceitful because they become more intensely partisan. Fanatical or cynical demagogues whip up a frenzied following. Agencies striving to control the masses employ spies and use the courts, the police, and the militia to restrain outbursts of fear and hate and mass movements which are blindly seeking some escape from their troubles. Men unemployed in a highly industrialized society lose the sense of belonging, of social function, and of responsibility and so are less subject to regulation by that subconscious structure of life which directs the interests of a man when he has some responsible part in the social order. Hostility between national states becomes more intense;

war threatens and surely comes if there is no other escape from the down-spiral of economic depression and unemployment.

These are the conditions that arise in our society when unemployment spreads and production lags. Plainly, these conditions render impossible the attainment of a free and just society. Therefore, full employment and full production in a society as highly industrialized as ours becomes an imperative for all who seek freedom and justice with any intelligence at all. This may not always be true; a time may come when economic abundance is so easily achieved that the serious work of human life will shift to other concerns. But today this is the situation; hence, he who talks about freedom and justice without giving first place to this prime condition is talking folly. Full production and full employment will not automatically of themselves alone bring justice and freedom; other things are also required. But these other requirements become ineffectual as means to a free and just society when the first necessary prerequisite has not been met.

Full production and full employment will come sooner or later in any case because they are a modern imperative; but they can come either destructively or constructively. They can come by way of a dictator combined with the threat of war; or they can come under the leadership of organized labor demanding high wages and low prices, with initiative and responsibility granted to them in the conduct of industry. Full production must come because modern technology applied to industry has become the supreme instrument of power and it is impossible to prevent the use of the supreme instrument of power. It must be used to stop anyone who attempts to use it; and someone will always attempt it in a power-hungry world. If we do not use it, Russia will; and then we shall be compelled to do likewise in order to protect ourselves in war or hold our own in peace. If Russia has full production and full employment with economic abundance and with a sense of social function and belonging among her workers and if we are suffering from unemployment and underproduction, then it is very certain that the mass of the American people will insist on having what Russia has. Either we shall be compelled to attain full production and full employment because we succumb to the domination of Russia and her ways; or else we do not succumb but in that case must have full production and full employment in order not to come under her domination. However you take it, full use of modern technology in industry must be achieved, even though we lag for a time and refuse to make the institutional reconstruction necessary to that end.

So, we repeat, two ways are open to this predestined end of every highly industrialized society. One is under a dictator combined with the coercion of war or the threat of war; the other is under the direction of organized labor. The query immediately arises in the minds of many: Is not organized labor just as fascistically inclined as any other powerful group in the industrial world? The issue raised by this question points to the basic problem of our society and must be carefully analyzed.

The claim that more power in the hands of organized labor will bring a better society does not rest on the assumption that organized labor alone is seeking a free and just society. It is very doubtful that organized labor either as a body or in the person of its leaders is seeking freedom and justice any more earnestly than are many others. It is not a matter of intention or purpose but a matter of using the means and following the road that will issue in the consequence desired. The following analysis will attempt to demonstrate that organized labor, given power and responsibility for the conduct of industry within the bounds of its competence, will bring forth a just and free society and that

[253]

no other means now available will produce this result without an interval of fearful injustice and terror.

People become a mass that must be herded and coerced by spies, by violence and torture, and by a tyrannical government unless there is a structure of habit and desire and a subrational organization of personality whereby interests and strivings of individuals and groups are so co-ordinated that each finds his associates sustaining him when they seek their own ends. In such manner this sort of structure, when established in society, gives to each a sense of belonging and self-respect, a sense of function and social responsibility, a sense of importance and of being needed, because his activities sustain and give social and historic meaning to others and theirs sustain and give like meaning to his efforts. Such a structure gives to each a sense of importance in life because his strivings and the fulfilment of his needs are caught up into a whole system of mutually sustaining parts and become contributory to the movement of society and history within the bounds of his concern and vision.[4]

There can be no freedom and no justice in a society where such a structure is lacking or where it disintegrates; or where the government does not sustain it and find support in it; or where the demands of industry and the prevalent technology are in conflict with it. The trouble with our society is precisely here. Our basic, regulative social structure, too deep and pervasive for intellectual formulation, beyond the reach of human manipulation—a structure giv-

[4] What we here describe as a subrational structure is what we believe Charles Howard McIlwain means when he speaks of the intrinsic constitution of a society underlying its legislation and its government and any written constitution which it may have. According to him, government, statute law, and the written constitution are good only so long, and to the degree that, they sustain and enforce this basic constitution, which is the structure intrinsic to that society and makes it a society as over against an aggregate or mere mass of people. Only when this constitution exists and is sustained can we have a free and just society (see *Constitutionalism, Ancient and Modern*, by C. H. McIlwain [Ithaca, N.Y.: Cornell University Press, 1940]).

ing shape and character to habit, impulse, and the whole psychosomatic functioning of individuals in relation to one another—was developed before the time of modern technology and the present demands and ways of industrial production. Consequently, this structure has begun to disintegrate by reason of its unfitness under the ruling industrial imperative; it does not find support in, nor is it supported by, the full use of our technology. Society tends to lose its character and become a mass or aggregate without internal, intrinsic self-regulation when this structure loses its control through conflict with some imperative social demand like full production with new technology. To the degree that this occurs, coercive government and other artificial devices must be used to co-ordinate the activities and interests of men sufficiently to sustain a tolerable social order.

This structure of habit and impulse automatically adjusting the lives of individuals to one another must be recovered in our society; but it must be developed around the demands of supertechnology applied to full production, because this is the ruling imperative of our time. Such a structure fitted to this imperative can give to industry all the nobility and beauty which corresponding structures in other ages gave to the ruling imperatives of their time, as, for example, to knighthood and Holy Church in the twelfth century. Industry organized to give the workers a sense of function and responsibility, a sense of belonging and self-respect in the production of goods, is precisely the kind of structure which we are talking about. How such a self-regulating structure actually developed in certain industries in which labor was given initiative and responsibility has been described by Golden and Ruttenberg in their book *The Dynamics of Industrial Democracy*.[5]

Once established in industry, such a sustaining and regu-

[5] New York: Harpers & Bros., 1942.

[255]

lative structure will spread throughout the rest of society for two reasons. First, when the masses of men are awakened to think and plan and order their lives co-operatively in industry, they become aware and alert to other areas, such as legislation, neighborhood, education, art, and religion when these bear upon the field of their initiative and planning. This consequence has been demonstrated. Hence men will develop the regulative and mutually sustaining habits and desires in these other areas along with the industrial. Second, when this structure has been established in industry, it has become the structure of the one supremely dominant concern in our society about which all else must be organized and to which all else must give way when obstructive to it. Hence the automatically regulating structure of mutually sustaining personalities in industry will spread to other areas, when the reverse cannot happen. The structure developing in these other areas will not be the same as that of industry, except in respect to releasing the initiative of individuals and creating among them a sense of co-operative meaning and mutual support.

If our civilization of supertechnology survives at all, we shall sooner or later in any case have a structure such as we have described pervading our society and fitted to the demands of industry, because these two are both indispensable to our civilization, namely, the full use of technology for abundant production and a self-regulating structure giving meaning and richness to our lives. But will such a structure arise only after a period of breakdown so great that the horrors of tyranny must prevail until needed habits and impulses and psychosomatic organization of personality have developed to the point where such tyranny is unnecessary? Or can such a structure develop without such an interval of terror and destruction, seriously endangering the continued existence of our civilization? We cannot erect such a structure by deliberate intent in the sense of putting its several parts together. But we can have it if we allow labor to take the lead with power and responsibility in the way described.

If this analysis is correct, there is just one road leading from where we are to a just and free society without passing through a period of horror which may destroy our civilization. This one road leads to a society endowing the individual with cultural as well as with economic abundance. When we say that labor must have more responsibility if we follow this road, we are not "siding with labor." It is not a question of taking sides; it is a question of following the only road and using the only means for achieving a good society in our time.

In every industry there must be a few managers who exercise supreme authority, but this control may be thoroughly democratic. No kind of social organization is possible without this apex of authority. The need is not to abolish the apex but to distribute as widely as competence permits throughout the ranks of labor the initiative and responsibility for the conduct of industrial production and for ordering their own relations to one another and the conditions under which they work. At present the majority of workers in the United States may not want to assume responsibility and may not be able to exercise it at once, but this is due to conditions that can be changed.

Whether we follow the road to freedom and peace or to war and tyranny will depend in great part on the policy followed by management now in control of industry. If the management opposes any advance of power and responsibility on the part of labor, it will be dragging us toward a fate which no men in our society really want, least of all the managers. On the other hand, if management will help to extend responsibility and power as widely as possible to industrial workers and their organizations, it will lead us into a world which will be best for the managers, best for the workers, and best for us all. It will be a world more just than ours today can be.

There is much confusion concerning the relation between love and justice, particularly of Christian love in relation to justice. Increase of love does not diminish the demands of justice. Instead, the more love, the more rigorously must justice be enforced to avoid chaos in a society rendered more dynamic and creative by such an increase of love. There are four grounds for making this claim.

A legal order is indispensable, no matter how much love there may be, to establish and coerce a uniform pattern of behavior. Without it we could not know what to expect in human conduct beyond the bounds of the intimate group. Even within the intimate group, and certainly in all relations beyond it, any great increase in love, accelerating creative transformation, produces social confusion if the legal order does not impose restraint and uniformity. If the law prescribes certain forms of behavior and enforces the prescription with maximum power, I can be fairly sure that people will turn to the right in America, no matter how eager love may be on special occasions to turn to the left to meet the need of a particular person in a peculiar situation. So also I can know that contracts will be fulfilled, even though love at times might desire to do otherwise; that interest will be at a certain rate, regardless of the desire of love to pay more; and on through an endless maze of interdependent conduct requiring prediction and fulfilment of expectation regardless of personal feelings. The personal sense of justice gives some social stability, but not nearly enough to bear the weight of a highly advanced civilization. Nothing except the legal order, self-enforced by reserving to itself the use of organized violence, is sufficient to provide the stability required for a complex society.

[258]

This enforcement of legal order by the threat of organized violence would be required even in a community of perfect love. In such a community, all people would be restive under any injustice. Hence the social order would always be threatened with confusion by the zeal of love to correct real or fancied injustice. Since the legal order cannot adapt itself to the unique demands of each individual as love will do, the legal order will often appear unjust to the eyes of love, even when it is the best that is possible. The zeal of love might be more restive under the legal order than thieves and murderers would be, because perfect love in a perfect community would be more energetic to deliver the beloved from apparent injustice than the murderer would be to get his victim or to save himself.

Another consideration reveals the need of justice in a community of love, with its legal order, its threat of violence, and its actual use of violence at times. Christian love can never apprehend appreciatively *all* the interests of the other person. The greater the number of other people concerned, the more remote in time and space, and the more diverse their character, the less can be that proportion of their interests which one can truly apprehend. Inevitably, one misinterprets many of their interests and attributes to them needs and goods not truly theirs, or even truly good for them. The greater the number of people associated, the larger will be the area of their interests ignored, not for lack of love but for lack of any possible way of gaining appreciative awareness of them.

Finally, a man with Christian love, as much as any other, must have an impersonal regulative system to serve as a frame of reference and a starting-point in developing a way of life that will meet justly the claims of others when millions of people are interdependent.

In sum, Christian love must be regulated and guided by impersonal law and rules of equity in meeting justly the claims of others because of the many interests which love cannot apprehend or which love misinterprets. No increase of virtue can ever be sufficient to regulate human conduct without legal order in its character of justice. The more Christian love there is, the greater will be the diversity of conflicting interests, made more numerous, powerful, and energetic by the fostering care of love. Whatever other excellence the Kingdom of God may have, it will not have a stability independent of the threat of legal violence. Since perfect love is so ready to sacrifice itself, even such a legal order might not be sufficient to maintain stability, except as the saints periodically discovered that their efforts were producing social confusion. On this account they might tolerate apparent injustice to avoid the evil of social chaos. But their love would make them restive under this compromise. It is probable that social confusion will always be breaking out in the Kingdom of God because people there will love with so great and perfect a love.

It can be demonstrated that social instability increases instead of diminishes as justice and love increase. Not every form of social instability increases, but many forms of it do, and these may require more legal control under coercion of the government. To demonstrate this let us note what happens as social welfare increases along with the growth of love and justice.

When a people are ground down to the level of brutes so that they have no sense of the injustice done to them; when they have little information and imagination with which to think of a better order; when there is no adequate means of communication with which to build up an ideology in opposition to the established order; when no education and other opportunity develops in them the ability to plan and organize action against the prevailing system; when they have not enough food, health, and leisure to generate the surplus energy required for strong opposition, then they will not try to change the social order unless driven to desperation. Hence there will be social stability.

On the other hand, the more power, wealth, opportunity, leisure, education, communication, and ideology any group has, the more it will demand for itself and for others. Therefore, it will seek social change and will often have the power to produce it. The more highly endowed a group becomes, the less will it tolerate disparity or even imagined disparity in the allocation of goods. For these reasons a social order is likely to become less stable with rising prosperity and culture. People who have every opportunity to imagine something better according to their own desires, and with desires enormously magnified through opulence, dreams, and suggestion, will demand some change and will often have the power to get it.

CONCLUSION

Moral problems are innumerable, and it was necessary to select from the host of them. We have treated the morals of communication, of sex, of Christian love, and of justice because these seem to be among the most important and the most difficult. They serve as well as any to exemplify the nature of morality as derived from the interpretation of value here under consideration. Also they are basic to the fulfilment of human good. Life staggers and falls or recovers and marches according as men practice the moral principles intrinsic to these concerns of human life. But morality is not by itself sufficient. It requires the addition of religion. It may or may not be religious, as we have seen; but even religious morality is not religion in its fulness. So we turn to religion as one further condition which man must meet to open wide the source of human good for life's fulfilment.

Morality is sometimes like a knife, gashing deep and leaving wounds that never heal. Sometimes a precious possession must be cut away with lacerations worse than death.

Scarcely then can life go on without some balm in faith and worship. We must have a religion with this restorative power. We must have an expectation and a hope that can survive the terrible incisions of moral sacrifice.

There is still a deeper need arising out of the moral struggle of man. One will find one's self caught at times in a net of immorality, partly his own doing and partly the doing of others, from which he cannot extricate himself. Every effort is frustrated, every outreach perverted. Such a one will give up in despair and sink into the depths of immorality unless he can know and trust a creative power that works in ways beyond the plans of man. In faith and penitence and self-giving to this creative power one may hope that good can grow like a miracle, though his utmost efforts seem to fail.

He who despairs of his own righteousness is lost if there be not such a faith and a reality rising in might to meet such faith.

Is there redemption for the life that is morally ruined? Can despair of one's own righteousness remove resistance to creative remaking and fit one to endure the suffering of radical moral reconstruction issuing in the supreme attainment of moral personality? Can the morally lost and hopeless, if they have faith and penitence, enter the Kingdom of God more readily than the righteous, who are overconfident of their own virtue? Can the outcast and the damned be redeemed by self-giving to the sovereignty of a power that works as man cannot work? These questions drive us beyond the bounds of morality into the ways of religion.

CHAPTER X

Religion

THE religion of Western culture is an inheritance from Christianity and Judaism; hence we have no vital access to the depth of any other living faith. Some few experts may achieve erudition about Buddhism, Confucianism, or the religion of the Australian aborigines; but even they learn only the observable facts. They cannot acquire the personal intimacies and vital resources of these other fellowships. Western man must find his strength in his own tradition—we have to accept this inescapable fact. The endeavor to understand and appreciate the quality and vigor of other religions is a virtue; but the failure to search the depths of one's own in order to possess them with equal solidity of impact impoverishes the human spirit. One must be nurtured in wisdom in one's own home before one can acquire riches from other sources. An eclectic cosmopolitanism is deadly. Man must drink deep from the well of his own vitality before he has the strength and insight to receive what others would give him. Otherwise, he picks a little here and there, utterly unable to absorb the power which these selections have for natives of the cultures from which they are taken. For these and other reasons we shall here confine our study of religion to our own heritage.

Christianity has come to be identified with a faith directed to a transcendental reality. This "ultimate ground" and "supreme goal" is said to be the only absolute good. It alone can rightly command the all-engulfing commitment of faith. All else is relative in value and becomes demonic when treated as though it were final and supreme. God thus interpreted is beyond history, hence beyond time, space, matter, and society, although reaching down into these with power to transform and save. Such is the traditional Christian way of thinking.

We here propose to interpret Christianity in terms of the source of human good as analyzed in preceding chapters. This source is not metaphysically transcendental, but it is functionally transcendental. It serves everyone of the vital and saving functions performed by the myth of a meta-physically transcendental reality. Therefore, we claim, it is, in truth, the very same reality to which faith was directed by the myth of the metaphysically transcendental, even though it could not be known in its true character until cer-tain philosophical and social discoveries had been made. To demonstrate the functional identity of this source with the reality alleged in the Christian tradition to be meta-physically transcendental, we must briefly summarize the six saving functions of this metaphysical myth of super-naturalism.

The Christian myth has directed the absolute commit-ment of faith away from all created good and thus delivered man from bondage to any relative value and has thus saved him from good become demonic. It has established a de-mand for righteousness far beyond the socially accepted standards of a given time and place and so has broken down the arrogance of the "good people" and opened the gates of forgiveness to each and all, since the difference between better men and worse men is slight compared to the extent that all have fallen short of the transcendental demand. It has established a bond between men vastly deeper and more important than personal affection or kinship, mutual inter-est or shared ideal, institution or race. Moreover, it has shown evil to be deeper and darker than any wrong done to society, to any group, or to any person, because in the last analysis evil is against the transcendental reality. It has re-vealed an obligation laid upon man which overrides any obligation derived from society, tradition, ideal, or loyalty to persons. Finally, it has opened possibilities of creative transformation beyond anything that could be expected from human effort, idealism, or any other such power.

These are the six services rendered by the Christian myth, and no greater service can be imagined. But a myth known to be a myth loses its power unless some actual reality is seen to do the work which is symbolically portrayed in the myth. We shall try to show that creative good, as set forth in previous pages, is, in fact, the actual reality which has done the work and played the part fictitiously attributed in the Christian tradition to something eternal (nontemporal), immaterial, and superhistorical.

The creative event fulfils every one of the six saving services mythically attributed in traditional Christianity to the transcendental. But it can accomplish these services only when men by faith give themselves to its control and transforming power. They may do this under guidance of the Christian myth without truly knowing the natural process that actually saves them. But this generative source of value is equally efficacious in accomplishing the six saving services when men truly know its nature, provided, however, that they give themselves to it in religious commitment of faith, for mere knowing it will not save them. On these grounds we claim that creative good is the actual reality mythically represented by the transcendental metaphysics of traditional Christianity.

There is another important distinction that must be recognized between the traditional Christian representation of God and this creative event. God has generally been represented as a person. It is true that many theologians, when pressed, will admit that personality is only a symbol directing men to a reality which the concept of person cannot compass. Others, however, will insist that God is truly a person—in fact, the only true and complete person, human persons being only remote approximations to what God is in perfection. While this sounds very different from the first admission, it really comes to the same thing. The substance of this second concession is that God is very different from what we know as human persons—which grants all that is here contended. Another device to avoid the difficulty of attributing personality to God, while at the same time insisting that he is in some sense a person, is the Trinity. All these and other theological contrivances for upholding the popular demand for a personal God, while being forced to admit the inadequacy of the concept of personality as applied to the creative source of all value, need not detain us longer. They all testify to an inner contradiction which always emerges when rigorous thought undertakes to interpret the source of human good, while at the same time compromising with this demand of practical religious living.

An examination of creative good will reveal the reason for this insistent need of religious devotion to think of God as a person, while at the same time demonstrating that the source of human good cannot be a person but is much more. The creative event at the level most important for human living always operates between persons. Without interaction between persons it cannot work at the level where it creates human personality with all its values and saves human life from goods become demonic. This necessity for interaction does not necessarily mean the physical presence of the persons concerned. There is always an interval of time between the expression of thought and feeling by one person and its apprehension and assimilation by another. This interval may be extended indefinitely and become so long that the most important participating persons may have died centuries before the present recipient of their communication was born. Perhaps this is always the case when the creative transformation of the present person or culture is most profound and enriching.

All this shows that, while the generator of value at the level where it brings salvation to man cannot work apart from interaction of persons, the chief persons involved may not be in physical presence. The conclusion is obvious. The religious man who commits himself in worship to the source of human good will most naturally think of this reality as an invisible, transcendental person who somehow pervades the universe or, if not that, at any rate pervades some long segment of history. This is, in fact, precisely the way the ordinary Christian thinks.

The point of all this is to demonstrate the psychological need that most people have all the time, and that all people have some of the time, to think of God (creative source of human good) as a person. Since creative good at the level where it saves and transforms human personality always works in the form of interaction between persons, we must deal with persons to deal with it. Furthermore, the persons are much more easily apprehended than the deep and subtle and mighty working of this creative event. Therefore, what more natural than to represent the reality commanding religious commitment as a person, if, in truth, it is the creative good which we have described? As previously noted, the persons with whom we deal when creative transformation is most profound and regenerative are, for the most part, not visible and not even known, having died long since. Naturally, then, the "person" that comes to mind when we commit ourselves to the source of good will be an invisible person, eternal in character, either in the sense of being "beyond time" or in the sense of running through all time. But all this is mythical, wholesome and useful though it may be.

From all this we conclude that the mythical symbol of person or personality may be indispensable for the practice of worship and personal devotion to the creative power, this need arising out of the very nature of creative inter-

[267]

action and so demonstrating that the creative event is the actual reality when this symbol is used most effectively in personal commitment of faith. This symbol may be required even by those who know through intellectual analysis that a person is always a creature and that therefore personality cannot characterize the nature of the creator.

This human need to guide practical action and disposition of personality by mythical representation of certain realities, even when the myth gives a false description of the reality in question, is quite common and by no means limited to God and matters religious. One of the most simple examples of it is a singer thinking of her voice as emanating from between her eyes, in order to "place" the voice correctly.

We have tried to show the mythical nature of two deep-laid Christian teachings—the transcendental status and the personal character of God. We shall now try to demonstrate that the creative event is the actual reality doing the work in history which has been mythically attributed in the Christian tradition to a transcendental person, even though the real source of human good is neither transcendental nor a person.

THE BEST IN CHRISTIANITY

Like every great historical religion, Christianity includes all degrees of good and bad, with the bad predominating. Neither the "essence" nor the "substance" of this religion will here concern us but only the best to be found in it, as far as we can find this best with our criteria of evaluation. For the sake of brevity we shall call it "Christianity," but we shall mean only one small thread in the complex historical fabric which bears that name.

The best in Christianity, put into the form of ancient doctrine, is revelation of God, forgiveness of sin, and salvation of man—these all by way of Jesus Christ. These three are different strands woven together into a single complex

[268]

event, the character of which can be simply stated: the reversing of the order of domination in the life of man *from* domination of human concern by created good *over to* domination by creative good. This event saves the world when it includes the establishment of a community which carries the new order down through subsequent history. The event derives its importance not only from the initiation of the new order in the lives of a few but from making this accepted domination of creator over creature a continuous part of history.

This new order of domination may have appeared many times outside Christianity in individuals and groups but without transmission throughout subsequent history by way of a continuing community. Such sporadic instances of the new order might be compared to the discovery of America by individuals and groups prior to Columbus. Doubtless, they were great achievements, but only the discovery of Columbus had historic consequences which transformed human life throughout the world and in all later times. So in Christ the new order appears with world-transforming efficacy.

Christ, as here understood, is not merely the man Jesus. Christ is the domination by the creative event over the life of man in a fellowship made continuous in history. How it was achieved we described in chapter ii. Through this domination Christ is the revelation of God to man, the forgiveness of sin extended to all men, and the salvation of the world. This historic consequence of events centering in the life of the man Jesus, and not merely the deeds, teachings, and person of the man, is the hope of the world and the gospel of Christ. God incarnate in these creative events, and not the human nature of the man, is the Christ revealing God, forgiving sin, and saving the world.

These terms—revelation, forgiveness, salvation—along with the conditions demanded for their fulfilment (faith and repentance) and the evils from which they deliver us (sin death, the devil, the law, and the curse), call for interpretation. These names refer primarily to actual events and only secondarily to doctrines about these events. Our leading concern is with the actual events, but, after sketching them, we shall examine the doctrines. The events designated by the names just listed occur not in sheltered cloisters but in industry, business, government, education, city, family, neighborhood, and rural community. Not the doctrines but these actual happenings in daily life are the important matters. Doctrines take on importance only as pointers to direct attention and commitment to the new order of events, namely, creative good dominant over created good in the devotion of man.

Salvation through Christ Jesus is this transformation in the life of man, which is accomplished not by human intelligence and purpose but by certain happenings in history centering in the man Jesus. The transformation occurred, first, in the lives of certain individuals; second, in a continuing fellowship; and, third, in the outcome of history. The consequence of this transformation is a new kind of existence with enormous and revolutionary potentialities. It opens the gates of history so that creative good can transform the world into a living responsiveness of part to part.

The sequence of events issuing in this salvation has no definite beginning. In that respect it resembles everything else in history. One might begin far back in the Hebrew story, in which the pattern is one of recurrent catastrophe, with a prophet appearing in the midst of each breakdown, declaring that all created good is destroyed when not held subject to the will of God. The flight from Egypt under Moses was one of these turning-points. Wandering through the wilderness, almost destroyed by the Amalekites, the children of Israel "met God at the Mount." In the Ten

[270]

Commandments the covenant-relation with God was established, which meant that God was not the servant of Israel in the sense of being bound to protect and uphold this people by right of their native claim upon him but, rather, that God was master and they were servants, and they were to give first place to the will of God if they would receive the good of life. This is another way of asserting that creative good must be dominant over all created good in the devotion of man.

Another catastrophe leading to the culminating event of creativity's winning supremacy over all created good in the lives of a continuing fellowship was in the time of Hosea, when he cried: "I am thy destruction, O Israel." This meant that God in commanding commitment of faith from Israel was not the protector of created good but the creator of good and must have first place, else destruction would come. The source of human good cannot sustain and produce the good of life with freedom and power unless it has supreme control. Jeremiah, Second Isaiah, Jesus, Paul, Augustine, Luther, all arose in a time of historic transformation; and each cried aloud the same message, however different the form of expression: "I am thy God, O my people, and none other must thou serve."

The most important thing in Judaism and Christianity is the historical development of a fellowship of faith by way of a series of catastrophic events culminating in the Crucifixion and the Resurrection of Jesus. Through this progressive sequence of transformative events, the source of good won supremacy in man's devotion over all created good and formed a tradition continuing as one strand in history. The winning of this supremacy by the creative event was a difficult struggle, conducted not by man but by God, and scarcely yet won. But it is won in the sense that World War II was won at Stalingrad. The strategic victory determining the outcome of history occurred not on the Volga but on the

Jordan, and the most critical turning-points in this battle were the life of Jesus, his death, and the Resurrection.

The struggle was, and the struggle still is, to save man from self-destruction and from internal, disruptive conflict within the individual and within society and, finally, to establish the Kingdom of God. The Kingdom of God is a world so transformed that every part responds with rich delivery of meaning to every other part and supremely to the spirit of man.

All this can be done only by transformation of man, his individual personality, his society, and his history. But man cannot be transformed in the manner required, and the way to a transformed world is insuperably blocked as long as man serves created good first and the creative event second. Hence the creative event had to win domination in man's devotion before it could create that richness of value and greatness of personality for which it works. The winning of this control in a continuing fellowship was the supreme accomplishment initiated at the point in history at which Judaism gave birth to Christianity. When this reversal and transformation are accomplished in a fellowship of faith running continuously through history, the gates of hell cannot prevail against creative power released in the life of man. Hell still continues, but it cannot prevail. The victory is won in the sense of winning the strategic battle which determines the outcome. This battle and this victory are the salvation of man, achieved not by human power but by the power of God reconciling the world unto himself.

This victory is won over sin first, then over death, the devil, the curse, and the law. Man is saved from these and is saved unto everlasting life. Let us again briefly characterize each of these.

Sin is the domination of created good over creative power in the concern of man. Death is the atrophy and destruction of personality, of human capacity for appreciation of val-

[272]

ues. This atrophy and this destruction always occur sooner or later when created goods are sought first and creative good served second. Man must give priority to creative intercommunication if he is to solve his problems, maintain a wholesome personality and a stable and rewarding society, and be saved from psychopathic personality and social disruption.

The devil is the pride and rebellion of man arising from power and prosperity when these are sought or held in opposition to that interchange between each and all whereby each sees through the eyes of the other, hears through his ears, feels through his sensitivities. The devil is man's arrogant or desperate rebellion against God, this rebellion being the outcome of seeking first the goods of life and serving second, if at all, the demands of that intercommunication by which we participate most deeply in the lives of one another.

The curse of the law is the frustration and corruption accompanying all human effort to attain the greater good when any set of abstract principles rather than the creative event is dominant in man's concern. The moral law becomes a curse when it dominates rather than serves the concrete source of human good.

The victory over sin, death, the devil, the curse, and the law and the gift of eternal life are all included in the complex event called "salvation." This victory, this salvation, this opening of the gates of history to the conquering advance of creative good (life everlasting or "eternal" or victorious) has been, perhaps, the most important happening on this planet since the creation of man. Creative power won a comparable victory over obstacles to its advance when certain limitations of the biological organism were surmounted by the creation of man. With man's ability to get the interests of the other through creative intercommunication, the single organism was no longer limited to its own perspective. Another comparable victory was won, still earlier, with the creation of the living cell. Within the living cell, and within living organisms generally, the creative activities of atom and molecule ceased to cancel out in a way to produce the average impact called "brute matter." Within the cell and in all forms of developing life, these activities are so organized as to produce progressively more vividness of quality and richness of meaning. In living forms what would otherwise be lumps of matter become creatively responsive to one another, and the world grows richer with quality and meaning through this responsiveness.

So far as our knowledge reaches, no other events outrank these three victories of creative activity in overcoming the obstacles to transformation of the world into richness and fullness of meaning, namely, creation of the living cell, creation of man, creation of the living Christ in history. If any other victory of comparable importance is ever to occur in the future, it will have to be the transformation of man himself into an animal capable of more radical creative transformation. Perhaps human nature as it now exists is incapable of moving with creative advance up the heights to be ascended. If so, another creative crisis awaits us in the future, foretold in Christian myth and symbolism as "the end of history," "the Judgment Day," "the Second Coming of Christ."

In chapter ii we have already analyzed and interpreted the events of salvation clustering about the man Jesus: his life, the Crucifixion, the Resurrection, the fellowship of faith in Christ. Added to these was the disentangling of this faith from bondage to any one cultural perspective, such as Judaism. Creative compounding of perspectives is not dominant over created good so long as it is bound to any one culture or form of life. The achievement of a fellowship of faith not so bound and the disentangling of its faith from bondage to any one single cultural perspective constitute the story told in the Acts of the Apostles and in the writings of Paul. The particular cultural perspective from which it had to be delivered at that time was traditional Judaism.

We shall not further discuss the man Jesus except to note again that the reversal in the order of domination which gives victory to the source of good was not the work of the man Jesus. Jesus had to be the kind of man he was, and, so far as we know, the reversal would not have occurred without him; but he did not plan it by his own intelligence. He did not understand the conditions releasing creative power in the fellowship of his disciples, nor did he understand the nature of creativity itself. He simply walked and talked and did what he did, quite unconscious of the exact nature of the world-transforming event under way. Perhaps he thought he was destined to save the world. But what he thought and planned and hoped could not be what occurred. Otherwise, he would not have been a man at all. Outcomes produced through basic creative transformations can never be foreseen by the human mind involved in them, for reasons already made plain. The human mind can foresee only what it can learn from the past. Therefore, if Jesus had been able to understand what was taking place, his mind would not have been human, and, hence, he would not have been a human being.

Salvation through Christ is not the work of man, not even of the man Jesus. It is the work of God, the creative event, working through history to win dominance in the life of man, this dominance culminating in the life of Jesus, his death, and the Resurrection, with the consequent forming of a fellowship of faith to carry the new way of living through subsequent ages.

Let us summarize the most important thing in Christianity as we have sketched it: the historic development of a fellowship of faith by a series of catastrophic events (1) breaking the bondage of faith to every achieved perspective and created good, (2) directing faith to the creative source of all good, (3) thus enabling men to relinquish all created good when creative moments so require and to apply all their intelligence and effort at any cost to providing the conditions demanded by creative transformation in achieving the Kingdom of God.

Men under this control of Christ may have no understanding of what is happening to them or to the world. Certainly, they need not use the language we have used in describing their faith. They may not even be very good men, and certainly many of them are simple people. But they are repentant when they cling to created good in opposition to creative power, and their sins are forgiven in the sense that they are deep-held in the power of God, no matter how great the evil they do or how completely destroyed may be all their plans and hopes except their trust in God. Without understanding and without power, in the midst of evil done to them and by them, they give right-of-way in their lives to the creative power which transforms the world in ways they cannot understand. This is their greatness, and to continue in the keeping of this power, despite their sin, by reason of their repentance is their forgiveness and their salvation.

The deeper significance of this victory of creative transformation achieved in Christ and his fellowship cannot be seen until we look again at the relation of Christian faith to moral law as interpreted through divine forgiveness of sin.

FORGIVENESS OF SIN

When commitment to the creative power transforming the world displaces the moral law as the last stand and ultimate hope of man, the way is opened to forgiveness of sin and salvation. In this sense we are saved by faith and not by righteousness. The man who has only the moral law has no resource when he has failed morally and become hope-lessly delinquent in terms of the moral order. He has no redeemer. But if he puts his trust in Christ (creative power made dominant in the life of man by the faith of a continu-ing fellowship), he can be redeemed, his sin forgiven, and his life saved, despite his failure. He who lives for the source of good first and the moral law second in this strand of his-tory can make his appeal to something deeper than the moral order. He can cast himself into the power and keeping of creative transformation to be remade and lifted anew. He can find forgiveness, not from men alone and possibly not from men at all. But he can find forgiveness in the sense that this power creatively transforming the life of man will take him, pick him up at any level of degradation, and sustain him with unlimited patience if he has faith and is repentant. Again and again he may fail—and he may al-ways fail—but with this faith and repentance there can grow even through his direst failures a good that he does not create, a good of God and not his own. Yet it will be a good that never would have grown had he not lived and in his failure given himself in faith and repentance everlast-ingly to this deepest enfoldment of creative power.

How forgiveness of sin was accomplished by the Cross of Christ has already been noted in chapter ii, but we must glance at it again. The Cross removed sin in the lives of the disciples, first by wiping out the created good (Hebrew perspective of value) which had been dominant over their lives prior to the Crucifixion. This wiping-out left only despair, but it opened the way to the next step. This was the Resurrection. The creative power of God worked mightily in their midst when Jesus was with them, but it could not break through the domination of their established cultural perspective. The Crucifixion broke this dominant perspec-tive and left despair.

Despair is the state of mind ensuing when the good to

which one clings as source and sustainer of all other good has been taken away. When that to which one clings is not truly the source and sustainer, its removal and the consequent despair open the way for the real source to enter. The real source, however, does not always enter when despair opens the way. But in the case of the disciples it did with the Resurrection, because at that time the creative interchange, held subject to the Hebrew hope while Jesus lived and seeming to disappear with the Hebrew hope when Jesus was crucified, rose from the dead. This creative power could now dominate over all else as it could not before and could penetrate beneath every obstruction raised against it in the persons of the disciples, because there was nothing else to which they clung for security that was more important than it.

This domination over and penetration beneath every obstruction in the life of a man constitute forgiveness of sin. Sin is anything and everything in one's personality which is obstructive to creative transformation, so far as one is responsible for the obstruction. Forgiveness of sin is accomplished by the creative power itself when it dominates over and penetrates beneath the obstructions to its own working within the personality concerned. The life, death, and Resurrection of Jesus Christ enabled this creative power to dominate in the lives of the disciples. The same thing may be accomplished today through the efficacy of symbol, myth, and fellowship arousing in us repentance and commitment to that creative power which rose to dominance through the life, death, and Resurrection of Jesus Christ. In such a case our sins are forgiven through Christ.

But this forgiveness and consequent radical transformation cannot occur without despair if by despair is meant the removal of every other good to which one clings as ultimate source and sustainer. If one clings to something as though it were the source of all good when it is not, then the true source cannot dominate and penetrate and so cannot do what is called the "forgiving of sin." But when one finds no other source of strength save this source of all good, no other hope and no other courage save what he finds in this, he is forgiven, although he still will sin. He may sin very grievously and repeatedly in that he continues to do, think, and feel in ways obstructive to the creative transformation of human existence. But his sins are forgiven in the sense that the creative power continues to rule in his life despite the obstructions he raises against it. This forgiveness is accomplished not by himself or by any human power but only by the creative event itself as it takes supreme control over the individual, despite the resistances within him which still continue.

Without difficulty, danger, and loss a man will scarcely seek his security in the true source of human good. Always he will seek it in some created good, if not the Hebrew Law, then American democracy or scientific method or his health and popularity or his past record or whatever else it may be. These other grounds of security must be seriously threatened or taken away before any man will seek and find his strength, his hope, and his courage in the creative power which generates all value. In this sense, perhaps, despair and recurrent despair alone can open the passage into the ways of forgiveness and salvation.

DEATH

No one knows what happens to the individual after death. But this we do know: Whenever life has met an impassable barrier or destroyer, creative transformation alone has been able to circumvent it by reconstructing the order of life, sometimes lifting it to a higher level of abundance. Whenever in his history man has encountered what seemed to be the blank end of all, and yet has been led around it or through it, the miracle happened by the emerging of some new perspective previously beyond his imagination or the creation of some new power of mind and personality by the integrating of meanings or the looming of wider horizons revealing an appreciable world more ample than he had known or the increase of fellowship folding him more securely in the depths of community and mutual aid, or a combination of all of these. These are the working of the creative event.

With faith in this creator and sustainer, we know all we need to know to face triumphantly the great destroyer. We know what we must do. It is simply this: Commit ourselves absolutely into the keeping of this creative power. We could not do more than this if we knew with complete certainty everything that might happen to the individual after death. We should not do less than this, no matter how ignorant we may be. If death is conquered beyond our reach of knowledge, it must be done by creative transformation released to the utmost scope of its power by giving it supreme control through absolute commitment of faith. There is no other way, and there is nothing else to be done.

If death cannot be conquered in a way to perpetuate the individual beyond the grave, this is the way to meet death in any case; for in this way alone can every power and possibility be released for making death yield whatever good it can. If creative transformation cannot carry the individual into a glory beyond this world, there is a glory to be wrought on this earth by death creatively met. This we know by the death of Jesus, if in no other way. Creative transformation can prevail against this destroyer in many ways, even though it cannot prevail in every way desired by man. Hence the only way to live and the only way to die are in the depth of the power and keeping of what generates all life, renews it from day to day, lifts it progressively to higher levels when conditions permit, transfigures the material world into significant events responsive to the human spirit with increase of meaning.

Death stands at the end of the trail of observable life and points with imperative gesture, commanding: Give yourself to the creative power. Give yourself in life and give yourself in death, completely and utterly, to serve it above all, to be transformed by it in any way it may demand, moving with it through every transition, through every disaster and fulfilment. Perhaps nothing delivers this command so implacably and finally as death.

WORSHIP

One cannot worship effectively unless he has been transformed by a fellowship of faith. Without such transformation and faith it is futile to "experiment" with worship. One cannot provide the conditions in one's own personality which are required for the experiment. But when these conditions are present in a personality and group, one can worship effectively without any intellectual understanding of what occurs in worship. Myths are quite sufficient, and some of the most profound and effective worship has been conducted under the guidance of myth alone. But conditions now prevailing call for an intellectual understanding. Otherwise, many will not practice worship at all by conscious intent, although it will always be practiced in some measure unconsciously and unintentionally by those who live under control of the creative event.

Worship is the practice of ritual which loosens the coercive grip of fears and desires obstructing the fourfold working of creative good. The use of such a ritual under proper circumstances and by one who has learned the art induces a reorganization of human personality which permits creative transformation to work more freely and potently in the life of that individual and in all connected with him. The reorganization is the removal of obstructive fears and desires. These last are of two kinds: First are the desires and fears which prevent the individual from relinquishing what must be relinquished if creative power is to produce the greater good. Worship induces the relinquishment of these and thus opens the way for the creative event to do its work of beneficence for the individual, for the group, and for others. Second are the fears and desires which prevent the individual from accepting the hardship involved in creative transformation.

The effectiveness of a ritual is not derived primarily from the meaning of the words but from previous usage, worshipful associations, and the influence of a group and a tradition.

We continuously practice nonreligious rituals as well as religious, often without knowing that we do. When we go away for a vacation we unconsciously practice a sort of ritual casting-off of the fears and anxieties, the driving compulsions and demands, of the work we are leaving. When we get in readiness to meet certain occasions, we practice a ritual (whether knowingly or not), gearing our personalities to the new undertaking.

Prayer is worship plus petition. Sometimes it degenerates into mere petition without worship. Then it is not genuine prayer at all. Petition added to worship serves to direct the sensitivity and responsiveness of the individual when undergoing the transformation accomplished by the creative event.

Prayer is answered when, in response to prayer, the creative event transforms the individual, his appreciable world, and his community in such a way as to bring forth what is sought in the prayer. The answer to prayer is the re-creation of the one who prays, of his appreciable world, and of his association with others, so that the prayerful request is fulfilled in the new creation.

The petition of the prayer gives one specific direction to the sensitivity, responsiveness, and outreach of the individual's personality. If this direction runs counter to the de-

[282]

mands of creative transformation, it will have to be modified. Perhaps it always is modified, but it need not be reversed or annulled, and it may be quite in line with some of the many different transformations open to creative power. How the creative event answers prayer may be seen by noting some of the different factors in the transformations accomplished in response to prayer.

Any one of many new meanings might emerge in the mind of the individual out of interaction with the physical world or in communication with others. This emerging of new meaning is the first stage in the creative event. If prayer has given to the personality a certain direction of interest and if worship has released the power of creativity to generate new meaning, that meaning is most likely to emerge which is relevant to the prayer. That this should occur is quite obvious to one who knows the selectivity of the human mind. The creative event brings forth the new meaning by way of interaction with the physical world or through intercommunication with others. But *which* new meaning it brings forth is in part determined by the prayer. In this way creative power answers prayer in the first of its four stages. The prayer does not answer itself. The answer is not the work of autosuggestion. The answer is the work of creative transformation, namely, the creation of a new meaning which opens the way to attainment of what the prayer sought.

The directed interest of the personality, which is prayer, plays the same role in the second of the four subevents composing creativity. This second step is the integration of new meanings with the old meanings in the mind of the individual, thus transforming his personality by giving it added scope and depth. This transformation might take any one of several directions. The prayer of the individual helps to determine which one of these many different forms the new organization of his personality will take as it is remade by

[283]

the fourfold event. As said before, if the direction of profound concern (the prayer) opposes any increase in depth and scope of meaning, it must itself undergo transformation. Some such change it probably always does undergo. Nevertheless, its presence in the personality when undergoing creative transformation will give to the newly re-created personality a character which may enable it to get what the prayer sought, even though this was entirely beyond his reach prior to this transformation.

A similar answering occurs at the third stage. As his appreciable world expands so that the individual sees, feels, and apprehends what did not exist for him before, many different things are disclosed by the widening horizon. What is disclosed from among the many possible disclosures is in part determined by the direction of interest and sensitivity determined by the prayer. If the prayer is concerned with how to improve health, or if it seeks how to redirect a wayward child or to restore a broken friendship or escape from some danger, the directed sensitivity of the organism will apprehend matters relevant to this concern in the expanding horizons of the world produced by creative power in answer to the prayer. The expanding of the appreciable world is what answers the prayer, and this is the work of creativity. Creative transformation works with greater freedom and power in response to worship for reasons already noted; and the directed interest of the worshiper (his prayer) helps to determine along what line the appreciable world is to be expanded by this augmented power of creativity released by the worship. So here again we see how energy in creative form answers prayer.

The fourth stage is the widening and deepening of community. Here also the prayer is answered and in much the same way. In response to worship as above explained, the creative event works with more power to widen and deepen community, to render associated individuals more respon-

RELIGION

sive and receptive to one another's needs, more effectively
co-operative, and more subject as a group to creative transformations which widen the scope of its operations and the
subtlety and potency of its action in changing the world.
The directed interest of one participant individual (his
prayer) becomes one of the directives determining what this
group shall accomplish. This does not require that any
other member of the group know what this one individual
is seeking by prayer. It is quite enough that his behavior
and all the subtle forms of conscious and unconscious interaction with other members of the group be given direction
by this unknown concern within him. Then, when creative
transformation magnifies the power of the group in response
to the individual's worship, and this magnified power is
given direction by the individual's prayer, we see how this
event may answer the prayer through widening and deepening community.

God transforms the world in answer to prayer if God is
the creative event heretofore described and if the prayer
seeks anything within the bounds of what can be created
under conditions then and there prevailing. When the
prayer is otherwise directed, it may be transformed by the
creative event and in that transformed state may find what
it seeks.

If prayer is a direction given to some ruling propensity of
the individual, how is it different from any other ruling
propensity, as, for example, lust, hunger, or hate, which
might have nothing to do with worship? We have put the
question in such a way as to carry its own answer. The difference between prayer and any other ruling propensity is
plain. The prayerful propensity is shaped and directed by
the creative event when its power is released through worship. Worship, as we have seen, is the practice of a ritual,
opening the way for a more profound and potent fulfilment
of the creative event. Worship renders the whole personal-

ity more subject to the transformation involved in new creation. Therefore, the ruling propensity of prayer differs from
every other in two respects. First, it offers itself to creative
power since it is formed in worship. This means, in theological language, that the prayer is directed to God as other
ruling propensities are not. It seeks fulfilment by way of the
creative event and not in any other way. This follows from
its origin in worship; and worship opens the way for more
potent creative transformation.

There is a second point of difference between the ruling
propensity of prayer and any other propensity. Not only
does it seek fulfilment in the creative event, but it is much
more readily transformed thereby. Since it is formed in worship and is a part of worship, it does not resist the transformation of new creation. Every other ruling propensity does.
Therefore, every other ruling propensity will either seek
and find fulfilment in ways obstructive to creative transformation and the increase of life's abundance or else will itself
be obstructed and frustrated. The conclusion to be drawn
from this is obvious: No fateful decision, no profound re-
solve, no reordering of life, should be undertaken except in
worship, because the ruling propensity established by decisive choice or deep desire will impoverish life if it does not
seek fulfilment by way of creative transformation and subject to that power. Worship helps to assure that it will seek
fulfilment in this way.

FINALITY OF CHRISTIAN FAITH

It is sometimes alleged by Christians that nowhere else in
the history of the world has God been redemptively revealed save in Christ. Whether or not this is true is an empirical fact to be discovered by inquiry. Nothing is more
difficult to establish than a negative statement asserting
that nowhere at no time did something or other exist. One
can only say that to date the inquirer has not discovered it.

[286]

When the thing sought has the intimacy and profundity of revelation and faith, one is not likely to detect its presence in a tradition alien to his own, even when it is manifest to those who have inherited the other tradition. If God revealed himself redemptively by way of despair and new creation in some other tradition, we might never be able to discover it. Therefore, it would seem to be unjustifiably dogmatic and arbitrary to say that only to Christianity is this redemption and salvation given. One can certainly say that for us, in our tradition, Christ alone is our salvation. Furthermore, this faith should be carried to others as far as possible. The Christian tradition has so merged with others and is so much a mixture of many traditions that this is quite possible. But to say that we alone have the saving faith of the world is not a warranted statement.

On the other hand, one can assert that the Christian religion is ultimate and final if it is true that creative good, as over against all created good, is the last stand and the ultimate deliverance of man, provided he apprehends it by faith and gives himself to its supreme control. In this sense our faith may be ultimate. But this does not exclude other traditions from also containing a strand of redemptive revelation, wherein the same final consummation of life is attained. Whether or not they do the present writer does not profess to know, and he cannot point to anyone who claims to know on grounds of reliable evidence. Christianity is final if through it man attains to the last freedom and the unconquerable hope through ultimate commitment to creative good. If other religions also open the way to this salvation, it should be cause for great rejoicing. We do not have any knowledge that they do.

SALVATION OF THE WORLD

When this religious faith joins with education and the two work together with government, industry, and technology to meet the required conditions, creative power can transform not only the life of the individual and society but also the material world. Creative intercommunication and transformation, sufficiently profound and comprehensive, can demarcate this cosmic lump of matter in its temporal passage so that it will be composed of events, each event a sign carrying the fullest load of meaning. The happenings of material existence then become a kind of language. This transfiguration is accomplished when men in faith undergo every remaking imposed by creative intercommunication and are equipped with the powers of civilization so administered as to make all happenings increasingly vocal with human meaning and responsive to human need. Material existence then becomes spiritual in the sense that material things become expressive of the human spirit, symbolic of its history, and prophetic of its future.

Perhaps this cannot occur without changing human nature drastically. The ordeal of this transformation might almost reach the limits of endurance for the most transformable and might destroy all others. This ordeal of transformation seems to be the theme of the Christian myth about the "last things," or "the end of the world." This "end of history" is always imminent, although we never know when it will come. History may periodically move up toward such a transformation, then swing back, then up again and back, in the great social crises. It swings back because man lacks the faith to undergo the transformations demanded of him.

It may be that in the great crises of historic transition man has come more than once very near to the gates that open into the Kingdom of God but could not pass through because he was unable to yield up what he desired in opposition to creative transformation, or was unable to endure what was demanded in the way of hardship. And so, refusing to go on, he had to fall back disastrously, in suffering and loss, to some lower level. Perhaps even now, in the present historic transition, we are moving up to such a time of trial and choice. Possibly the magnitude of power and momentum of movement in the social process today may carry us beyond our power to hold back, until we are driven, through a thousand or ten thousand years of transformation, across the great divide separating us from "the end of history" and that great good which will be produced when man is able to receive it and do his part.

Whatever may be the outcome, a few of the next steps seem to be clear. We must learn to recover our sense of the richness of quality in events as they pass, which has been taken from us by science, technology, and rapid industrialization. This sensitivity can be recovered and more amply attained than in the past, if we use technology in service of the source of human good. We must learn to communicate not only with linguistic symbols remote from intimate contact with material things but also in close association with earth and sky and hill and storm and sun. These give substance and deep organic response to what we say and do with one another.

We must have long-continued association with one another in smaller groups, wherein all are deeply involved in struggles vital to each and common to all, meeting the thrust of sorrow and loss and shame and hope, dealing with heavy material things as well as with symbols. Association and intercommunication in such a group transforms the material world into objects and events so rich with meaning that they seem to sing a song that grows deeper and sweeter with the years.

If all this is true, we must learn to live in smaller groups, closer to death and birth and growing things and one another, more continuously in one place. The local group must assume responsibility for its own affairs to the limit of its competence, for only so can we work together co-operatively and communicatively on matters sufficiently vital to generate the enrichment of life. We have already seen how industrial plants must be organized to this end. How rural communities must be stimulated, how cities must be spread and decentralized, how family and local neighborhood must be advised and directed by experts, all to the end of releasing the full power of creative transformation and making the world more rich with qualitative meaning and responsive to the human spirit, are problems which would require several books, had we the competence to deal with them.

The massive, powerful, and far-reaching co-ordinating agencies of government, industry, technology, and scientific research must serve the local community and all human life, to the end of increasing the richness and spread of meaning. These agencies must provide the locality and functional group with what they need when they cannot get it themselves. But these widespread and complex social mechanisms must not do anything for the local group which it can do for itself if by such doing it will be brought into closer co-operation and more creative communication. The wider social mechanisms should provide the local group with stimulus, resources, guidance, and opportunity for its own initiative and creative action but should not deprive the local group of responsibility and initiative.[1]

Localities and functional groups must be regulated relative to one another so that the good of each will sustain and enhance, rather than destroy or impoverish, the good of others. To this end the power of government must increase as social connections become more complex, spreading to planetary scale. But this increasing power must be used to serve the growth of meaning, not merely to give people

[1] For a vivid account of how this can be done and has been done, see the record of T.V.A. by David Lilienthal in his *Democracy on the March* (New York: Pocket Books, Inc., 1945).

what they want. Above all, it must foster and equip local initiative, not suppress it.

Education must accept the responsibility and be governed explicitly by the concern to equip men and women with the knowledge of those general principles, those matters of fact, and those skills which are required for living creatively with one another and with material things. From kindergarten to university, from philosophical meditation to scientific research, education must assume this task, cutting off excrescences, removing irresponsible teachers who cannot see what education should do or who refuse to serve the imperative demand laid upon the school in our time. The vagrancy and irresponsibility of teaching cannot continue. If academic freedom means doing what one likes, there is no more place for it in the school than there is at the throttle of a locomotive which carries the lives of people in its train.

The church and its leaders must learn from the originative events of the Christian faith that this faith is not merely a vague reference to the "vertical dimension" but lays upon us the stern demand to have a clear understanding of the way God works in the midst of human life. Only with this understanding can the man of faith in our time serve with intelligence, firmness, and conviction. The primary duty of the church is neither mystical devotion nor trailing after other agencies in promoting social improvement. It is to demand insistently and everywhere that those human relations be provided between man and man and between man and nature which release the creative power of God. In the industrial plant, in the school, in the rural community, in the family and neighborhood, in the city, in the government—everywhere the leaders of the church must demand that these relations be provided. Religious leaders cannot have the technical knowledge to solve all these problems. They will not ordinarily know the *specific* sort of thing that should be done to meet the demands of the creative event. But they must know how this creative power works, and they should know more about this way of God's working than others do. This should be their special field of competence. Since religious leaders know more than others about how creative energy operates in human life, they should understand the general sort of thing that God demands in the home, in the industrial plant, in the relations of races and of nations to one another, and in other human situations. Thus they should be able to provide wise counsel on these issues, even though they must also be ready and eager to receive wise counsel on matters that lie beyond their competence, particularly the more precise and technical problems and the more intimate concerns in these several different kinds of human situations.

The church is the only agency that is free and empowered and commissioned to strike in every quarter, to demand in every area, that the stern conditions of creative power be met. If the church in the form of its leaders does not know how creative energy works and what its demands may be for the life of man in our time and in all time, it must relinquish the name and office of church and give place to some other agency that will do this work. Such an agency, pointing directly to the source of human good and directly to the duty of man to meet its demands with assured promise of growing good when these demands are met, can lead the march of humanity in this time of danger.

Things that must be done to provide conditions releasing creative power in our midst, to realize the vast potentialities of human good resident in our present situation, and to evade the evils equally vast and imminent might be classified under three heads:

First, we must modify our basic institutional structure, economic, political, and educational, to establish that kind of relation between people and that access to resources

[292]

which they must have to participate in creative interchange with one another.[2]

Second, we must awaken the initiative and responsibility of people in each local situation to undertake the problems of the neighborhood, not only to solve those problems, but also and primarily to develop the culture and personalities of that locality with the consequent good of creative living.[3]

Third, we must propagate a religious faith, a self-giving, which will put the individual under the dominant control of the creative event, to be transformed by it and to serve it first, and all else second.[4]

Two primary conditions must be met to release creative power and open the way to material and spiritual abundance: The common good must be served above the private; human persons and social structures must be more transformable by way of creative interchange. The common good is the creative event, and a faith of the kind just mentioned would make it dominant over private good, at least in some of the major crises of decision. Also, persons and social structures become more readily transformable by way of creative interchange when we have the three things above noted, namely, institutions, neighborhood, and faith directed to this end.

We have the knowledge and power to meet these several demands except in one respect. We have lacked an operational understanding of the nature of human good and the creative source from which it springs. The present study is an attempt to correct this grave deficiency in our human equipment for dealing constructively with the problems of our time.

[2] *Democracy on the March*, by David Lilienthal, shows one way in which this is actually being done today.

[3] *Reveille for Radicals* (Chicago: University of Chicago Press, 1946), by Saul Alinsky, shows one way in which this is actually being done today.

[4] A forthcoming book by Regina Westcott Wieman shows how this is actually being done today.

Technical Postscript

Technical Postscript

CONTEXTUALISM, both as theory of value and as metaphysic, has been a recurrent theme throughout this writing. Yet it would be a mistake to identify either the interpretation of value or the metaphysic in this book with those of contextualism. These distinctions must be made clear.

Our own interpretation of value might be called "creative" to distinguish it from contextualism. The latter identifies value with qualitative meaning, which is to say, any demarcation and interrelation of events which awakens conscious awareness of vivifying contrasts of quality and meaningful connections between them. This interpretation of value we accept as true and have used it more than any other because we think it more useful. But we are equally ready to accept as true every other one of the six different ways in which value may be interpreted. On the other hand, no philosophy of value, not even contextualism, has interpreted the creative event as a fourfold process basic to all value. No philosophy of value has set forth the demands of this fourfold process as being the only reliable guide to greater good and the only trustworthy criterion for judging what is the better alternative and what is the worse in any situation.

This criterion for judging what is better among alternative possibilities comprehends all the different theories of value and can work with any of them because the creative event operates (when its demands are met) to increase value, whether value be called "satisfaction of human desire" or "fulfilment of the cosmic purpose" or an "indefinable quality" or an "eternal and changeless reality" or a

[297]

"relation between subject and object" or a "situational context of quality." It is true that eternal and changeless reality cannot be increased in respect to its transcendent being; but human devotion to it and appreciation of it can be increased, and to this end the creative event is indispensable. Consequently, the interpretation of value in this book cannot be uniquely identified with any one of the historically developed theories of value but can be united with each and all of them and has a place for every one. This is not to say that the creative event and its demands provide the last word in the theory of value. Quite the contrary is true. The source of human good, so meagerly and inadequately sketched in terms of the creative event, is vastly more complex and profound than this little delineation can suggest. Someday someone will interpret it with an adequacy and profundity that will cast into oblivion what we have said about it. Not what is here said, but the reality so imperfectly presented, is the important matter.

This brings us to the problem of metaphysics. Not only our theory of value must be distinguished from that of contextualism but also our metaphysics. In contextualism, change is ultimate. Nothing is immune to change; no structure, order, or form is permanent. Hence, also, there is no basic unity. Unities come and go, integrate and disintegrate, but nothing continues forever. In contrast to this view, the present writing asserts that there is something which retains its identity and its unity through all change in itself and through all change in other things. It is creativity. Creativity characterizes one kind of event. Every event is continuously changing, and so also is the kind of event characterized by creativity. But this kind of event has a certain identity and unity throughout all its manifestations, namely, the character of being creative of all the changing orders of the world so far as they are accessible to human life at all. To speak of anything as not accessible to human life in any way is to speak of nothing at all, so far as concerns human life. We who do all the speaking are in the predicament of being human life, whether we like it or not. Therefore, to speak of what is not accessible to human life in any way is to speak nonsense.

Creativity and the creative event are inseparable, but the two words carry an important distinction in meaning. Creativity is the character, the structure, or form which the event must have to be creative. Creativity is therefore an abstraction. The concrete reality is the creative event. Every event is inexhaustible to human inquiry. We can never learn all that enters into an event, but we can know some aspects of its character. In the case of the creative event, this knowable aspect is its creativity.

Every event is not only unique and changing but also multiple. It can be divided into subevents and can be a component of more inclusive events. This applies to the creative event as well as to every other. But the infinite multiplicity of creative events displays one single self-identical character or structure running throughout. It is the structure of creativity. Identity of structure is unity, and unity can be nothing else according to this metaphysics. Therefore, the creative event is not only multiple but also unitary.

The creative event is, therefore, changeless in respect to that structure whereby we call it "creative," even though the concrete wholeness of the event is always changing. It is unitary by reason of that self-identical structure, even though an infinite multiplicity of events displays this unifying character. Unity and multiplicity do not exclude each other. Unity, like changelessness, pertains to the abstract character of the event, while multiplicity and change pertain to the concreteness of it.

The creative event is always and absolutely good. It is always good in the sense of creating value. Yet it must often destroy value already created in order to achieve the best possible under the conditions prevailing. Furthermore, what it creates may be turned against itself and so become evil, as, for instance, if I give a man one hundred dollars he may use it to destroy me. If by "evil" one means the destruction necessarily involved in the creation and conservation of the best possible, or the perversion of what has been created, then in these senses the creative event is evil. But this assertion does not involve any contradiction of the affirmation that the creative event is absolutely good when the precise meaning of this affirmation is understood. Also we must remember that evil is in the world independently of the creative event.

The creative event is material if by "matter" is meant a form of energy which determines the very structure of time and space, together with all else that exists or is possible. The creative event is spirit if by "spirit" is meant (1) the continuous creator of ideals, aspiration, and value; (2) the supreme manifestation of freedom; and (3) the source and sustainer of human freedom.

Man is free to the measure that he is committed to the creative event, is continuously transformed by it, and strives to provide conditions releasing its power. In any sense in which freedom is good, men lose their freedom to the measure that their lives are lived in opposition to the creative event. Freedom, in any sense in which it is a high value, we understand to be (1) awareness of the alternatives which might be chosen in any situation, (2) the use of a reliable criterion of choice to distinguish the best practicable alternative, (3) the will to choose and seek the best, and (4) the power to achieve what is chosen. If any of these is lacking, freedom is lacking. Freedom is a matter of degree, since no one will know all the alternatives or have a criterion infallibly trustworthy on application or a will completely devoted to the best or power sufficient for every choice. Even if the criterion were absolutely trustworthy in itself, ignorance of factual detail would always make its application something less than perfect. But man, so long as he is human, always has more or less freedom, and whatever freedom he has is a gift to him by grace of the creative event, given on condition and to the measure that he accepts its absolute sovereignty over his life. Freedom is not the opposite of being under domination and control. Rather, it is the concomitant of being under domination and control of the creative event and thereby free from other dominations.

The metaphysics we are defending interprets freedom as a kind of determinism. Also this metaphysic is a materialism including what is spiritual. It is a spiritual metaphysics which is none the less material through and through. The creative event is changeless, a unity, absolutely good and eternal in respect to creativity. But every concrete instance of this event also displays change, multiplicity, and temporality. These affirmations are not contradictory when their true meaning is seen in relation to one another and to the nature of the creative event.

We must say of this metaphysics, as we said of our interpretation of value, that it is not the only true one. There are several metaphysics, all of which are true, because a metaphysics is true if it selects some element necessarily involved in all human existence and explains everything in terms of it. There are several such elements. The metaphysics of creativity herein developed is chosen in preference to any other because we believe it provides a better guide to action than any other. This is not the pragmatic test in respect to truth, because a metaphysic must first meet the tests of truth before it can become a candidate for choice on grounds of utility.

The place of quality in this metaphysics must be further clarified. Every event accessible to human experience is a quality or a complex of qualities; also every event is an instance of energy. Whenever energy is experienced by the human organism, it is a quality or a complex of qualities.

Therefore, relative to human experience, all energy is quality, and every event is quality. Quality, then, is the ultimate substance of the world out of which all else is made. Hard, soft, bright, red, odorous, painful, miserable, joyous, sorrowful—all are qualities experienced as events. The demarcations and interrelations of events are also the demarcations and interrelations of qualities, because qualities and events are identical when experienced by man. Quality is substantial, concrete, massive, inexhaustible in the fulness of its existential reality, which is the concrete event.

Diversity of kinds and nuances of change in the quality of events as they occur are infinite in their complexity, although we have names to discriminate only relatively few of them. "Structure" is the name we give to the demarcations and interrelations of events whereby we can apprehend them as different events and yet in meaningful relation to one another. One structure is better than another if it enables us to experience more of the qualities of the events by way of vivifying contrasts and meaningful relations. When qualities are complex, only a few may reach conscious awareness, but those at the subconscious level are still qualities in the sense that they add a massive undertone of qualitative experience and, at the crises and peaks of human existence, make possible the ultimate depth and richness which bring the life of man to its supreme fulfilment in pathos and glory. These peaks may be the promise and foretaste of a level of life as yet unattainable but possibly attainable through some revolutionary transformation.

Quality is always intrinsic to the total situation. It does not characterize merely one object in the situation, even though we do say: "The tree is green," "The person is joyous," "The wound is painful." Analysis reveals that the total situation, which is always a complex, total event, bears the quality and not merely the particular object which may seem to be the bearer of it. Our own sensitive organ-

[302]

isms, the apperceptive structure by which we distinguish happenings in one way rather than in another, the light, the vibrating air, the cultural milieu, what happened in the immediate past and what is anticipated, and much else are all required to yield the quality. Take any of these away, and the tree will not be green or the person joyous or the wound painful. The total situation, the concrete event, excludes everything which makes no difference to the qualities experienced. Whales spouting in the open sea make no difference to the taste of my dinner, and neither do the other changes throughout the universe, except a very few. Yet these few, including my own organism and the near environment plus a long reach of the past leading up to and producing this organism, this mind, this culture, and this physical situation, are very complex. They are, in fact, inexhaustible to analysis. This complex inexhaustible event is the bearer of the qualities; or, rather, we should say that this event *is* the quality.

The quality is not in the organism or in the mind or in the table or in the air or in any one of the several components necessary to yield the quality. The quality is *in,* the quality is *constitutive of,* the total complex of components which, by their togetherness in this structure of relatedness, yield the quality. They do not merely *yield* the quality—this complex, structured togetherness *is* the quality. The quality is these components in their total operative togetherness as one single inclusive event with its components immediately experienced; and beyond such experience we cannot go.

Quality, then, is objective fact. It is ultimate reality. It is the substance of which all is made. It can be structured into diverse forms; and, when it is so structured, we have all the different things to be found in this existing world. The world is essentially and substantively quality. It is energy, but energy is quality to human experience, and that means ultimately and absolutely for human living.

The claim that energy is quality rests upon the following evidence, derived from the analysis of human experience. All energy, when we are able to attain immediate experience of it, is some sort of quality; and every further analysis, penetration, discrimination, or comprehension of the components and reaches of energy reveals some further quality when it is in any way accessible to immediate experience. Hence we are led to say that all energy is quality because we cannot go beyond human experience. What we experience is ultimate reality. What we experience may be error, in the sense that we misinterpret what we experience; but it can be error only if there is a reality there different from our interpretation of it. That reality being experienced and underlying the error is ultimate. This we find to be quality apprehended by way of feeling.

In this metaphysic the goal of life (the conservation and increase of value) is to structure the world so that qualities will be more appreciable. The qualities of the world become more appreciable as they are connected with one another by way of meaning and are so related as to vivify one another by contrast. The fourfold process, the creative event, is that kind of change which renders the world more appreciable by connecting its qualities in the form of meanings and vivifying contrasts. The distinctive character of this creative change, the structure by which this kind of change is identifiable in every time and place and level of existence, we have tried to set forth throughout this book, but most especially in chapter iii.

The individual, society, and all history have the same goal in living, according to this metaphysic. It can be attained only by way of the creative event. For the individual it is to absorb all the influences from the physical and social world so far as (1) they can be integrated into the living of this individual and (2) the qualities of these influences can be vivified rather than canceled by one another and (3) their relations to one another can be rendered meaningful by representing one another. Only the individual can absorb influences in this way but he must do it by participating in an association of individuals so ordered that they help one another by doing it interactively. An association of individuals can do this to a high degree only when a sequence of generations has built up the forms of integration and the sensitivity and responsiveness required. Thus the goal of life for the individual is also the goal of life for society and history.

We have identified God with the creative event, but this requires some qualification. Any intellectual formulation about a concrete reality is never more than a meager, sketchy abstraction pertaining to it. The concrete event is infinitely complex and rich in quality. The intellectual formulation about it is not. Even this does not make plain the full disjunction between the true concept of a concrete reality and the concrete reality itself. In the chapter on truth we tried to show a true concept to be a form of possibility pertaining to concrete events, although never fully ingredient in those events. For example, the most accurate scientific description of a falling body is never a description of all those deviations and variations of the falling body due to currents and pressures of air, the proximity of other bodies, and the whole gravitational structure of the universe in its bearing upon that particular falling body. Truth is a form of apprehension (1) fitted to the capacities of the human mind and (2) fitted to guide the human being in dealing with other concrete events. The mind is not fitted to apprehend the concrete events which we immediately experience in feeling, but it is fitted to apprehend structures of possibility, which may approximate to various degrees the demarcations and interrelations of actual events. If such approximation is the best we can say for so simple an event as a falling body, the approximation must be more remote

[305]

and more meager for such a reality as the concrete source of all human good. In such a sense only, can we call creativity a true concept about God. If it is a better concept than others (as we believe it to be), it can be so only in the sense that it is better fitted to intellectual formulation by way of the tests of truth; is a concept which is not the structure of the actual events of God's reality as these are accessible to feeling but is a possibility which can be made to approximate one feature of this concrete reality, and, most important of all, is better fitted than other concepts to guide practical action in meeting the demands of the source of all human good.

These are very severe qualifications of the claim that the kind of event we have described is identical with God. In one sense it is not identical at all. But in whatsoever sense any concept of God can be identified with the reality of God, this concept can be. God, according to this interpretation, is immediately accessible to human living and human feeling in all the fulness of his concrete reality. He is not immediately accessible to the intellectual formulations of the human mind, but, for that matter, neither is any other concretely existing reality. Truth about concrete events, including truth about God, is not identical with the structure of those events, nor is it even one ingredient in that structure. The concrete events are qualities immediately apprehended by feeling. The truth about them is a structure of possibility which the human mind can formulate and use to guide those events called "human beings" in their meaningful relations with other events. Truth about God is a structure of possibility which the human mind can formulate and use to guide those events called "human beings" in their meaningful relations to that kind of event called "God."

The creative process makes qualities more appreciable by creating sensitive organisms; by making them progressively more sensitive; by generating signs with meanings and thus producing mind; by bringing forth communication of meanings and thus establishing society; and by sustaining the continuity of history and thus accumulating meanings through a sequence of generations.

When the continuity of history is added to all the other ways of increasing the appreciableness of the world, vivifying contrasts and systems of meaning may grow beyond any known limit.

History is the supreme achievement of the creative event. At this new level creative power rises above the narrow limits of the single generation. In history it can work with an indefinitely prolonged sequence of generations, developing a technology and a culture that need put no bounds to the growing power of the one or to the means of communication and appreciation provided by the other. Thus working through history with a growing technology and a growing culture, the creative event might conquer inertia, destruction, and oblivion beyond any known limit. Technology might magnify industrial production to the point at which it no longer depended upon purchasing-power but could be free to all to the measure of their need. In such a case the hierarchy of economic privilege would be overthrown, and the power exercised by a few over the many would no longer be economic. Doubtless, other kinds of hierarchies would arise, and other instruments of power would be used, but they would need to be more concerned with what we call the "ideal" or "spiritual" needs and interests of life. Their misuse would be more deadly, but their right use more vitalizing and enriching. With growing technology and culture, power gravitates into the hands of men more sensitive and appreciative of the interests and needs of their fellows, because no others are able to operate with these new instruments of control. The power of the Nazis could not continue on this account. With growth of technology and culture, evil becomes more subtle and complex, but the opportunity to foster the good of life increases.

As historical research extends its bounds and acquaintance with history grows, dead things come alive, and the far past tells the present of its wonderings, sorrows, and joys. Four thousand years ago an unknown poet wrote *Gilgamesh*, an epic of old Babylonia. For millenniums it was lost, but it was recently discovered and translated. Thus the deeps of the past rise up to tell us their story when history is our heritage. As history enables each generation to acquire a growing technology and a growing culture from the past, delivering them enriched to the future, the creative event is empowered to render more appreciable the deeps of quality in the existing universe and the reach of possibility beyond.

This conquest of time and space and matter by the creative event is not inevitable, but history makes it possible as it could not be within the bounds of any single generation. Linkage of the ages through history brings a hope which nothing else can provide. It is hazardous, but it magnifies enormously the good and evil that wait upon the outcome of the battle. History may teach despair—it should—but when despair issues in the commitment of man to a power not his own, a power creative as he cannot be, it opens a way into the progressive restructuring of the universe until vivifying contrasts of quality reach through all things. When history acquires Christ (the creative event become dominant in a continuing fellowship), creative power can save the world unto everlasting life.

Those who look to man for *self*-transcendence and creative power are driven to despair of history and hence look beyond it for salvation. They have not yet cast off that adolescent arrogance which swings between folly and hopelessness. In ages when things go ill, they appeal to super-history for deliverance; and when things go well they think they need no deliverance. Religious liberals gone Barthian or near-Barthian or otherwise transcendentalist are of this sort.

There is a creative power in history which is able to conquer and to save, but it is not any power of man, even though it works through man. In all times, both good and ill, man must live under its control if history is to be fruitful. In history and only in history can we find the perilous way through destruction of self-centered concern and self-centered confidence and on into the keeping of creative power. This is salvation. Whoever in despair appeals beyond history betrays the holy cause for which we fight, for here in time it must be lost or won.

Frail and brief must be the life of an organism sufficiently sensitive and responsive to bring the world to qualitative abundance. When man becomes sufficiently mature to apprehend the deeper meanings, he begins to die. The glow of life is always a sunset glow. Every supreme fulfilment is swiftly transitory in love, beauty, wisdom; and none is so swift in waning as the supreme union of these three. It cannot be otherwise. Resources of appreciative consciousness are not sufficient to withstand the onslaughts of change, the evil impulses of the heart, and the wearing-down of continued effort. This is the tragedy of man and of creative power; but history is the answer. History cannot lift this fate, but it can make the glow of swift decline cumulative through a succession of generations. History can give to all things mean and noble a voice to speak from out the past, bringing to the sensitive mind a love of earth and all things in it and the sky above. In this way it can endow the dying day of each generation with a splendor deepening through the ages. History is the field in which creative power wins this tragic victory over time and matter and the evil ways of men.

INDEX